Praise for Interactional Creation of Health

"I'm speechless - in a good way. In the book, Chris describes his "Health Ecosy
And wow, it's a complete model... and I mean COMPLETE. It's a holistic, unified model of lived experiences with health; a model that leaves no factor or root cause unexplored. The HEVD model captures every force affecting the lived experiences of people with health issues; providing a path and a hope for improving the lives of those who suffer. What nobler pursuit is there? Thanks, Chris for this amazing contribution." **Scott Burleson, Author of The Statue in the Stone: Decoding Customer Motivation with the 48 Laws of Jobs-to-be-Done Philosophy**

"Over the last 10 years or so I have watched Chris unfold his ecosystem ontology based on extensive readings of philosophy, journal research, practice and deep, deep reflection. I'm not surprised the five-star reviews he's receiving. Leaders in the health field should view some of his conference talks as a taster before reading his book on total health systems." **Simon Knox, Emeritus Professor at the Cranfield SOM and Honorary Professor at the UNSW Business School, Sydney**

"Chris does not allow us to be sloppy or lazy. If we let him, he will guide us on a better path forward. His book and models are cutting edge and essential to thinking differently and well about healthcare." **Peter Sorensen, Organization Design Consultant, Adjunct Professor at SMU Lyle School of Engineering, Board President STS Roundtable**

"A much-needed paradigm shift in co-creating transformational change toward an enhanced state of our wellbeing. An outstanding, remarkable and masterful job." **Professor Venkat Ramaswamy, Ross School of Business, Michigan University**

"Chris Lawer's re-conception of value provides the breakthrough thinking that health systems need to repurpose resources and transform delivery systems." **Professor Neal Halfon, UCLA Fielding School of Public Health, inventor of Life Course Health Development model**

"Chris Lawer's Health Ecosystem Value Design is an invaluable framework for understanding how to reimagine, redesign and transform our global health ecosystem. This book is an extraordinary next step in your leading edge thinking on the evolution of health and care systems. Kudos to you for providing a pathway towards a new paradigm of global health." **John Scully, retired US healthcare executive**

"Awesome! Brilliant! And super impactful! I admire and appreciate your work and your deep ecosystems approach. I can see how it would extend and enhance my work in terms of clinical reasoning for advanced practice in nursing. The Umio framework is comprehensive and just what we need to help deal with the complexities of health care as we learn to value differences and activate capacities. Chris Lawer is doing amazing work." **Daniel Pesut, PhD, RN, FAAN, Principal Consultant at Strategic Foresight Consulting and Coaching, Emeritus Professor of Nursing, University of Minnesota**

"Chris Lawer's model is way ahead of how medical service providers and pharma / device manufacturers think today. It gives them a way to categorize and simplify complexity and understand healthcare interactions at a much more actionable level." **Rob Schade, Chief Customer Officer, Strategyn**

Acknowledgments

I am delighted to present the full second version of my Health Ecosystem Value Design® framework, the product of three years intensive development, six years of continued evolution since I first began conceiving the idea, and a very focused low-risk lockdown experience in which I barely left the house. It is no exaggeration to say that the framework has consumed thousands of hours of my life since 2015 and there are a number of people who I would like to thank for their support, creation, inspiration and encouragement.

First, I would like to give very special thanks to Venkat Ramaswamy. I am extremely indebted for his deep words of Vedanta-inspired co-creation wisdom, sage advice and unstinting commitment to read and proof my work and ideas. Thank you to for your wonderful foreword. I look forward to many more stimulating conversations and the further enrichment of our collaboration as we progress our ideas and take them to the world together in publications and projects. I will get up-to-speed on that whole one consciousness unified ontology soon.

No book of this detail and effort can be produced without the help and conversation with many who have input and suggested improvements to my work and given me a platform to speak. I owe a debt to all who spent some time and energy with me to discuss, listen, affirm, critique and challenge the ideas in earlier frameworks that set me on the path to this book. My thanks to Julia Chamova, Dan Pesut, Paul Hobcraft, Bob Heath, Paul Barnett, Bernard Mohr, Mike Taylor, Bill McAllister-Lovatt, Tilly Briggs, and Gianluca Gambatesa. Special thanks to Neal Halfon and Peter Long for bringing me over to California to explore version one of the framework at Blue Shield Foundation.

I wish to pay special thanks to all my former Strategyn UK and ZinC colleagues, Nicki Sutton, Gillian Brydon, Javier Romero, Jerry Hutchinson, Lance Bettencourt, Sandra Bates, Eamonn Murray, John Scott, Petr Salz and Bruno Levy who undertook a number of brilliant health and other innovation research projects with me all around the world and who so ably helped laid the foundations of my enthusiasm for innovating in health. Thanks to Rob Schade and Tony Ulwick at Strategyn who saw my OMC work and brought me into the Strategyn fold.

I have been inspired by several thoughtful clients, particularly Paolo di Vincenzo at S&N, Peter Kragh of Coloplast, Calum Mayland, Patricia Seigle-Vatte and Omar Hoek of Ahlstrom and John Boyer at Mundipharma.

Thanks also to my long-term health care system partners, Andres Melik, Joan Escudero and Frank Weber with all of whom I have spent many enjoyable days roaming the EU hunting down research grants. I hope that despite Brexit we can continue to work together to tear down the walls of EU Horizon projects and challenge their technology-first thinking.

Special thanks to my PhD supervisors at Cranfield, Prof. Simon Knox and Prof. Stan Maklan, for knocking my writing into shape in the early days and for your commitment and patience during my ups and downs with health problems and work. I suppose this is the PhD I never completed. I just need to add the references....

I could not have written this without the unwavering support of Mum and Dad. Thanks too to Emilia and Tom for their patience and tolerance. Thank you for all your love, help and encouragement.

Finally, I would like to give a very special thanks to Seonad for her incredible love, support and sacrifice throughout the development of this work. The capacity to immerse myself in a prolonged real duration of creation (as Henri Bergson would say) would not have been possible without her.

I sincerely hope this book inspires you to widen and elevate your perspective to that of experience ecosystems, and to see the power and potential of an interactional creation mode of health in all our lived experiences.

Chris Lawer, Buckingham UK, January 2021

The layout, text and all the visual content (figures, charts, framework representations) in this book were conceived, designed, produced and edited by the author

Interactional Creation of Health

Experience Ecosystem Ontology, Task and Method

Published by Umio limited 2021

Oxford Centre for Innovation, New Road, Oxford. UNITED KINGDOM. OX1 1BY.

ISBN: 9798511219950

Table of contents

Foreword
by Venkat Ramaswamy

Foreword by Venkat Ramaswamy

The late C. K. Prahalad and I began exploring the implications of the Fourth Industrial Revolution (or "Industry 4.0") with the advent of Internetworked enterprises at the turn of the new millennium. We co-authored a book, The Future of Competition (2004), in which we put forth the idea of "co-creation", one based on the experiences of individuals in an interconnected world of de-centered and democratized value creation through event-based networked flows of interactions. A few years later, Francis Gouillart and I co-founded the Experience Co-Creation Partnership and wrote a book together on The Power Co-Creation (2010) based on our consultative engagements with over forty organizations across twenty sectors of the modern economy. By then it had become evident that industry 4.0 was about harnessing the power of interactive intelligence in the daily lives of people to design and augment value in ways not possible before.

The first industrial revolution was powered by water and steam in the wake of mechanization, then electric power in the second, and computer power in the third. Industry 4.0 not only entails cloud computing and smart, connected devices from mobile phones to the Internet of Things, but also social media and community engagement with the Internet of People who are connected and active in their own ways. It calls for an "Internet of Experience" with a value design process that is open, participatory, inclusive, collaborative, and ultimately co-creative, with the opportunity and challenge for enterprises to engage in designing platforms of offerings, engagements, and organizations, together with stakeholders in "all-win more" fashion.

Fast forward to today, and as I write this, we are in the midst of a global COVID-19 pandemic crisis. While the pandemic disrupted lives and livelihoods in unprecedented ways, it simultaneously accelerated the adoption of digital technologies, increasing the digitalization of interactions by several years. Consider, for instance, Microsoft's Cloud for Healthcare offering, rolled out amidst the crisis, offering service capabilities to address challenges faced by healthcare organizations in engaging with patients. It enables individualized experiences of healthcare, empowering employee experiences, and improving care provider and clinical operations experiences, while amplifying systemic capacities through an enhanced network of partners. Its Healthcare Bot Service enabled healthcare organizations to build and deploy AI-powered virtual health assistants and chatbots during the crisis, augmenting care provision and patient self-service. In about two months, more than 1500 instances of COVID-19 service bots had gone live, impacting more than 30 million people in over 20 countries, and ultimately reducing the strain on emergency hotlines and hospital visits.

The above example points to how harnessing the interactive intelligence of connected offerings and enterprises can help in navigating our way through a health crisis. But, going beyond the crisis itself, it points to the importance of organizations connecting beyond mere "delivery" of care with the lives and lived experiences of individuals, underscoring a "declaration of interdependence" as it were. It emphasizes the need to go beyond the "B2B2C" (business-to-business-to-consumer) industrial system of goods and services toward "I2N2I" (individual-to-network-to-individual) ecosystems of experiences that enable interactional flows and valuable experienced outcomes of impacts as a result. This entails a transformative shift, not only in becoming more resilient and adaptive to individual experiences but anticipating a better future by co-creating them. Organizations must engage with all stakeholders in their respective ecosystems of experiences by conceiving environments as "assemblages" that engender valuable impacts of economic, social and ecological well-being, which are developmentally sustainable. This includes "Mother Nature" and in the case of a pandemic, the virus itself. As Laura Spinney, a science journalist writing in The Guardian noted, "The key thing to understand is that we are not passive bystanders; we form the virus just as it forms us."

Conceptualizing co-creation of value as a joint enactment of interactional creation via (increasingly digitalized) ecosystems of experiences, and entailing all actors, human and nonhuman, has occupied much of my research over the past decade. Around 2010, Kerimcan Ozcan (whose dissertation I had chaired in 2004), introduced me to the work of Gilles Deleuze, and others including Felix Gauttari, Manuel DeLanda, Bruno Latour, and

Michel Callon, to name a few. I resonated with it all, given my earlier exposure to the lofty Advaita ("nondual") philosophy of the Vedanta, elaborated in the Upanishads, in the Indian spiritual metaphysical tradition (via the exposition of Swami Krishnananda). In our quest for a more unifying ontology of co-creation, we began a deep scholarly, but equally practice oriented, dive into synthesizing various strands of metaphysics and philosophy of experiences, phenomenology, psychology and cognitive neurosciences, morality and ethics, economics and social sciences, information, design, complexity sciences, natural sciences, policy, and organizational and business studies, which contributed to a more progressive, pluralistic, and constructive foundation of an "interactional creation" paradigm of value co-creation in contemporary enterprises, markets, economies, and societies.

In 2014, we published The Co-Creation Paradigm that articulated a foundation of joint creation and evolution of value, intensified and enacted through platforms of engagements, virtualized and emergent from social, business, civic, and natural ecosystems of capabilities, and actualised and embodied in domains of experiences, expanding wealth-welfare-wellbeing. Then, in a series of papers, we expanded upon this foundation by theorizing experience ecosystems as assemblages having affective agency and perceptive experiences, whose capacities engendered valuable developmental impacts from platformized resourced capabilities, via enactment of interactional flows. This "interactional creation" foundation of co-creation went beyond the integration of resources in exchange of service, as in the "Service-Dominant Logic" (SDL) work of Robert Lusch and Stephen Vargo, to theorize the very act of creation through interactional flows involving matter, energy, communication, data, capital, images, meanings, and narratives. It also put the spotlight on the lived experiences of individuals. The enactment of interactional creation of lived experience value was central to what we have come to call as a Co-Creation Paradigm (CCP).

Following the CCP, the unit of inquiry is not only the "patient" seen as an assemblage of agency but also as an "experiencer" acting as a system-environment hybrid together with its "environment", with the latter also being an assemblage. In other words, health is conceived in terms of "experience ecosystems" of assemblages having particular affective capacities and engendering qualities of experienced outcomes. Health becomes an emergent adaptive process of experience and capacity formation formed from relational interactions of forces, affects, and events over lived time. Suboptimal health and care and inappropriate use of treatments can lead to delayed healing, and increased infection and pain, all of which impact a patient's quality of "life". Assemblages of health can suffer from ineffective orchestration of ethological means from a patient's perspective of "lived" experiences. At the same time, as Cameron Duff has argued from a Deleuzian perspective of Spinoza's ethics of joy, there is a need for a "more positive and substantive account of health capable of yielding diverse ethical principles for the restoration, maintenance and/or promotion of health in an assemblage of human and nonhuman forces."

This brings me to Chris Lawer's outstanding framework and book on "Health Ecosystem Value Design". Chris Lawer is no stranger to rethinking, redesigning, and actualizing greater health and wellbeing having immersed himself in a parallel journey over the past decade, by diving deep into the lived experiences of individuals, following his large-scale studies of health in Europe (and Ireland in particular) and the US, and thinking long and hard about the deep systemic challenges that persist in our health and wellbeing today. What naturally drew me to Health Ecosystem Value Design (HEVD) was the shift made in this updated version, beyond the earlier SDL based perspectives, toward a whole and unified view of lived experience with health, and the very visual and dynamic way in which interactional flows of creative differentiation, and the production of experience in assemblages was communicated and articulated, from the perspective of both assemblages as "affectors" and "affectees". What was even more remarkable was how it laid a systematic and unified ontological and epistemological foundation for health ecosystem value design and bringing about transformational change by both arresting negative lines of flight of health deterioration, while emphasizing positive lines of flight in achieving joyful wellbeing. Its blueprint and templates for seeing, enabling, and catalyzing the emergence of better health experience ecosystems, put to work through a process of "reverse parabolic transformation" provides a much-needed paradigm shift in co-creating transformational change toward an enhanced state of our wellbeing. If anything, the COVID-19 pandemic crisis only amplified the need for such a shift if we as a human species are to thrive amidst "de-territorializing" tendencies. It calls for reimagining a more immanent ethics situated in a body's power of acting upon interactional flows, and being affected by them, and how the forces of life that course through lives and livelihoods can be folded in and "re-territorialized" in everyday practices of health and wellbeing. This is the promise that is passionately and eloquently placed before us with the HEVD framework and templates.

The first part of the book does a masterful job of laying out a sequence of seven foundations that build on each other. Foundation One identifies four distinct domains of interactions (social-cultural, material-spatial, bodily-motor, and perceptual-cognitive) that provide a unifying dynamic model of whole lived experience with health, wherein health, dis-ease, and illness are expressions of the occurrence, nature, and patterning of interactions in these domains. Foundation Two puts forth (positive and negative) affects as pre-individual intensities or forces, affording (augmented and diminished) capacities, or powers of acting, in forming differentiated experiences and transitioning from one state of embodied experience to another. Taken together, they imply a movement or becoming in a plane or continuum of real duration (i.e., a continuous multiplicity of affects), sensed by experiencers in psychological time over lived journeys, with their interpretive reflections and discursive feelings (i.e., as emotions).

Affects forming lived experiences with health are actualized via virtual interactional flows modulated by tendential forces, the basis of Foundation Three, which may be fast-occurring high-intensity events over a limited duration or sedimentations or more hardened obdurations with an enduring pervasiveness. Various types of flows across domains of interactions are intensified in processes of creative differentiation (in the virtual) engendering affects in the whole unified model of lived experience (in the actual). Entities not only affect other entities (as affectors) but are affected by them (as affectees). The linguistically detached use of affectors and affectees avoids falling into a trap of fixed roles of actors in health systems (whether patient, nurse, doctor, pharmaceutical company, etc.).

Foundation Three not only expands upon the concept of flows to explain differences in lived experiences but explicates the virtual, actual, and empirical registers of creative differentiation in the production of lived experience. Using an accessible example of the flow of a river in which bodies are caught up, including that of a social body that might become entangled with it, one can feel the intensification of differences from the virtual (real that is not actual yet) to the actualization of events that we empirically recognize. Chris reminds us that it is the intensive not extensive generalizable differences that define our world. The discussion of flows of a natural body followed by that of a social body nicely sets up the concept of social desire as the basis of his new unified ontology model of virtual (natural with social) body, intensive, actual, and empirical. This allows Chris to unify nature with society, while exposing the roots of ill-health in alienation of social bodies from nature and disconnected metabolism motivated by capital and labor tendential forces. Co-creation of wellbeing together with experiencers can indeed help escape deteriorating lines of flight, while accentuating positive movements. But I'm jumping ahead, for we need to purposefully take stock of reality from actualized events of flows. Foundation Four, thus, introduces the notion of quality into lived experience, via poles of positive and negative affect quality and affective capacity. The tracing of affect drivers and their visual representation in affecting the quality of experiences in negative and positive movements (itself best experienced online) provides a means for better understanding of current states of experiences. Taken together, Foundations Three and Four put forth interactional flows and events as producing affects as experienced by affectors and affectees.

This leads to Foundation Five of how lines of flight give rise to states of experience, from deterioration to recovery, between the two poles of negatively and positively valued affects (i.e., at risk, worsening, and chaotic states versus emerging, building, and stable states), for any given experience context. Foundation Six then conceptualizes the unit of enquiry as an assemblage that goes beyond the individual person (such as the typically objectified or categorized "patient"). Taken together, Foundations Five and Six lead to an affective assemblage-based view of whole unified lived experience, i.e., a lived experience ecosystem.

Foundation Seven distinguishes cut-outs of focal experience ecosystem environments (or FEEEs) that afford a dynamic view and ongoing unit of discovery and enquiry, constituted by interactional flows of affectees and affectors, having a certain force, capacity, tendency, identity, quality, and impact. FEEEs, as noted by Chris Lawer, are foundational to HEVD, helping to overcome disciplinary fragmentation in modern health sciences and the "transformative limitations of biomedical reductionism and its "boxing in" and management of lived experience into abstract disease identities, categories, conditions and outcome measures."

Of major significance is how the HEVD framework reframes our conception of value in health and care systems in terms of positive health and wellbeing and developmental impact of experience ecosystem environments from the discovery, co-design, and transformational change of surplus potential affect qualities and capacities. This leads to the "parabolic" HEVD process of transformational change that forms Part Two of the book, with major implications for organizational practice, while also exposing the limitations and flaws of rather dominant social-determinant and structure-based views that prevent us from seeing, let alone addressing, the "dynamic confluences of affects that course inside lived experience with varying intensities", as Chris puts it.

Part Two provides a well delineated and wonderfully detailed twelve-steps framework that covers two primary activities of organizational virtual exploration and ongoing co-creation, entailing six linked phases of Frame, See, Assemble, Reflect, Design and Emerge. Each step contains a detailed template for enquiry and action. These are tremendously useful for practitioners in affecting capacities of health and care systems toward achieving valuable developmental impacts. The detailed guidance on use of templates and practical tips is nothing short of remarkable. It is bound to evoke creative lines of flight among practitioners, as they capture and reflect on their own learning from their appreciative deep-dive enquiry of focal experience ecosystems of interest to them. In turn, the activity is fascinating. It not only supports creative collaboration using an experience ecosystem view but also facilitates ideation and co-design of value propositions. In particular, the delineation of co-designing affectee value propositions and affector value propositions, and linking the two, is quite novel, in that it fosters a more co-creative approach to value creation across organizational boundaries.

In an age of increasingly digitalized platformization, where it is all too easy to fall into a technology-based view of value creation, the HEVD framework promotes lived experience value co-creation toward becoming what I call a "co-creational living enterprise" – an experience ecosystem enterprise entity that purposefully learns and adapts through interactional creation with all stakeholders, to transform platformized impact ecosystem engagement experiences, in the lived journey of interactional value creation of developmental wellbeing. Consider again Microsoft's Cloud for Healthcare offering, during the COVID-19 public health crisis. It helped integrate medical content from trusted sources, understand the intentionality of individuals with medical terminology built-in, handle human error, topic changes, and interruptions, and allow photos by patients to be attached as part of the conversation, while connecting with secure telemetry of health data in instances where providers had already moved toward telehealth service provision models (with compliant insurers).The net result was that it delivered credible symptom checking and triaging, with intelligent dialogic healthcare experiences at scale, escalating those instances that needed telehealth interventions to nurse practitioners, and scheduling them with patients based on nurse schedules. The telehealth interactions helped in visual triaging and conversing with physicians to determine if acute care was needed, which in turn, triggered collaborative workflows of health teams, empowering employee engagement and decision making around human experience value creation.

As humanity, we have come a long way in the fourth industrial revolution from mechanization, mass production, and digitalization, to now AI-powered experiences enabled by the Internet of Things (IoT), which has blurred the physical, digital, and biological spaces. This book is a clarion call to re-imagine health and care centered on a developmental ethology of valuable co-creative experience ecosystems of wellbeing. A key premise of co-creation is that by sharing experiences, all the actors involved will acquire a deeper understanding of what is happening on the other side of an interaction, enabling them to devise a new and better experience for both sides. Organizational linkages must enable employee/internal co-creation, customer/community co-creation, and partner/network co-creation across experience ecosystem environments. This calls for co-creative design thinking in executing affectee and affector value propositions. The key is to view the innovation process as a co-creative process of engagements, together with stakeholders, and using the power of experience ecosystem visualization to generate new insights about what aspects of offerings and experiences are of value. The deep-dive phases of the "parabolic" transformation process facilitates organizing actors in visualizing current states of lived experience ecosystems to engage in dialogic interactions for best courses of action on their part moving forward. Organizational enterprises are themselves "capacitative sense-making" assemblages that entail engagement in continuous cycles of enactment and strategy formation. They are emergent from decisioned actions and act as system-environment hybrids in interactional flows with other assemblages as lived experience ecosystems, both in terms of what creates them and what they create. It reminds me of a question posed by ecologist Stephan Harding, "What kind of economy is consistent with living inside a living being?", which inspired Marjorie Kelly in understanding that: "You start with life, with human life and the life of the planet, and ask, how do we generate the conditions for life's flourishing?"

What makes Chris Lawer's work unique is that it moves us in this direction in health systems by pulling together, and capturing very visually, a detailed what and how framework of embracing a dynamic creational and interactional view of health ecosystem value design based on whole unified lived experiences. It provides a valuable guide to navigating co-creative experience ecosystem environments in practices that combine generating and understanding deep insights, co-designing value propositions, and the engagement of organizations in bringing about transformational change, by ultimately co-creating developmental wellbeing in lived experience ecosystems together with stakeholding individuals as agencial experiencial co-creators.

Best wishes to all in nurturing the mindset and practices that this book inspires in co-creating a better ethologically developmental world of life, living, and lived experiences.

Prof. Venkat Ramaswamy

www.venkatramaswamy.com

Introduction

"The attempt to live according to the notion that the fragments are really separate is, in essence, what has led to the growing series of extremely urgent crises that is confronting us today. Thus, as is now well known, this way of life has brought about pollution, destruction of the balance of nature, over-population, world-wide economic and political disorder, and the creation of an overall environment that is neither physically nor mentally healthy for most of the people who have to live in it."

David Bohm, Wholeness and the Implicate Order, 1980

Introduction

As we survey the tragic loss and unexpected crash of Covid-19 into all our lives, we can be forgiven for asking how did we get here? We may also justifiably ask, what can we learn and what can we do differently to reduce its ongoing impact and prevent similar crises from happening again? To answer these questions, I suggest we must first study the pattern of Covid impacts more closely. Then we must determine the prevailing logic of perception, method and action found in the health and related social sciences in order to assess how it has guided government policy, defined professional responses and shaped even our own personal actions.

It is not only Covid-19 impacts and responses that we must have in our collective questioning sights. We must also reflect deeply upon the prior-to-Covid (and now worsening) situation of rising chronic disease, mental illness and health inequality in Western societies, as well as fast emerging countries. When we consider such structural ill-health together with Covid, we may learn why they have both arisen and variously persisted, despite our many best efforts to prevent and eliminate them.

Having reflected deeply myself, my explanation of these complex human phenomena begins with a single statement describing a prevailing tendency in our health-and disease-related thinking, organization and action. I suggest that our current predicament is the consequence of the continued elevation of *homo economicus* over *homo ecosystemus* in our conception of the human. By homo economicus I mean the now rather tired idea of human beings as free-choosing, intentionally motivated, goal-setting, rationally reasoning, material resource-seeking individual agents, each acting episodically in pursuit of desired outcomes to improve their life experiences. In reality, homo economicus does not exist and has never done. Whilst some of us do have a greater capacity to objectively assess a situation, calculate our interests and acquire what we need to achieve our goals, we all need a supporting environment and enabling connections to facilitate our projects. We are all pervaded by complex emotions, virtues and morals given to us from our numerous social, cultural, material and natural relations, encounters and movements.

In contrast, homo ecosystemus, a new term, defines humans not only as interactional social beings but also as just one of many agencial entities - both living and non-living - interacting in open experience ecosystems consisting of fluid social, spatial, natural, material and semiotic arrangements, with each entity embodying a particular modality of action and degree of agency. In this beyond-social conception of the human (as it incorporates nature), agency is not located in individual homo economicus humans and enacted via rational action but rather is distributed and de-centred in agencial assemblages[1] consisting of many "homo ecosystemus" interacting with non-human entities and with each other. As embedded interactional entities, homo ecosystemus is enriched and imbued with social-cultural, material-spatial, bodily-motor and perceptual-cognitive sensations, feeling states and impressions (collectively termed affects) arising from intensive interactions in flows of human and non-human entities bearing pre-individual affects and tendencies; interactions and transitions that not only create and shape our actual lived experiences but also influence and moderate our differential capacities for self-agency of our own health and the agency of others.

Through the lens of homo ecosystemus distributed within agencial assemblages, we can discover and define a new interactional and creational perspective of health in actual lived experience. I shall now introduce this in context to the lived realities of structural chronic disease and health inequality, and first Covid-19.

Covid-19 and homo ecosystemus

Many have remarked how Covid-19 has raised appreciation of the collective nature of all our health situated within a common sense of humanity, where one infected or sick individual, group or species can have impact on the health of many other living species. Many others have commented too on how in the early days of the

[1] This term coined by Venkat Ramaswamy and Kerimcan Ozcan (2016)

pandemic especially, we saw the emergence of hidden societal reserves of strength, resilience, cooperation and solidarity in both organized and individual responses. In the UK for example, more than 750,000 people volunteered to work for the NHS. Across the country, hundreds of local community action hubs were set-up to offer assistance to vulnerable shielding persons by fetching groceries and medications and by providing a lifeline of emotional support for the hidden unwanted lonely. Whilst we all now have a greater sense of "we are all in it together" whether in relation to our shared health or the rise of the new forms of social support we may offer to one another, and whilst we may hope that our lived experience of Covid-19 serves to counteract pre-Covid-19 forces of rampant hyper-individualism in the long-term, less well-known is how the virus has surfaced the interactional and creational mechanisms shaping all our health.

To reveal this interactional picture of creation, we do not need to look far to see how the burden of Covid-19 has fallen on those with either the least interactional capacity to affect, avoid and mitigate and sometimes even understand the risk of the disease in their lives[2]. Persons with underlying health conditions, elderly residents at home and in exposed care homes, those with learning difficulties, disabled persons and their full-time carers, vulnerable children being abused in new family arrangements, schoolteachers in crowded classrooms, multiple generations of families in overcrowded homes, prisoners in shared cells, those needing to use public transport and their drivers, workers pressured by their employers to come to work or those on zero hour contracts needing to work to have any income, and key workers interacting with others in high density of interaction enclosed spaces, all have been the most exposed to the virus due to their lower interactional agencial capacity (or what I term affective capacity) to mitigate its risk. When we add the forces of capital needing labour to sustain a semblance of an economy and the state seeking to control and regulate population behaviour and compliance in its blunt one-size-fits-all biopolitical rules and laws, both defined and enacted from a homo economicus view, we see how the burden of Covid-19 has fallen hardest on those at the frontline of the virus. Not just the brilliant medical teams but also the highly regulated and controlled workers, the carers, the poorest, the disabled and the ethnic minorities that the virus finds easiest to penetrate, wreak havoc and tragically, cause death.

When we adopt a homo ecosystemus view of the human to study this diverse picture of disproportionate risk exposure, burden and injustice, we can discern a moving pattern and distribution of agencial assemblages in experience ecosystems for the focal context of Covid-19, each with varying agency and affective capacity to affect and be affected by the virus. As I explain in the book, an agencial assemblage is an emergent open body consisting of an ensemble of heterogenous, self-subsistent and variously stabilized human and non-human entities whose arrangements of interaction create, differenciate, repeat and/or recover a state of lived experience (with health). Characterised not by any representation of the types of persons (or personas) within them but by their content and expression of affect capacity, quality, stability, duration and impact in lived experiences, an agencial assemblage interacts with interactional flows of pre-individual affects and forces of tendency that course over the social and natural body, When doing so it creates, differentiates and variously stabilizes and reproduces diverse lived experiences in the lived journeys of individual and groups of homo ecosystemus affectees, those whose lived experience is affected in the interactions.

Altogether, I identify six contingent assemblages forming a whole body of interactional agencial capacities in relation to the focal experience ecosystem context of Covid-19 as depicted in Figure 1. These flow around two poles of affective capacities, the most positive pole of strong affective capacity and the most negative pole of limited affective capacity. Connecting each is a line of deterioration from the strong to the weak pole and a line of recovery from the weak to the strong pole. Between the poles are six assemblages, each having a distinct quality and degree of interactional affective capacity to avoid, mitigate, prevent, manage and recover lived experiences in interactions with Covid-19, itself a non-human entity having agencial force. Within each

[2]In England, the death rate for people aged 18 to 34 with learning disabilities was 30 times higher than the rate in the same age group without disabilities. https://www.gov.uk/government/news/people-with-learning-disabilities-had-higher-death-rate-from-covid-19 (Accessed Jan 2021)

assemblage, we find hidden contexts and presences of homo ecosystemus of similar agencial capacities shaped from the occurrence, force, content and patterning of their interactions in material-spatial, social-cultural, bodily-motor and perceptual-cognitive flows of affects and tendencies.

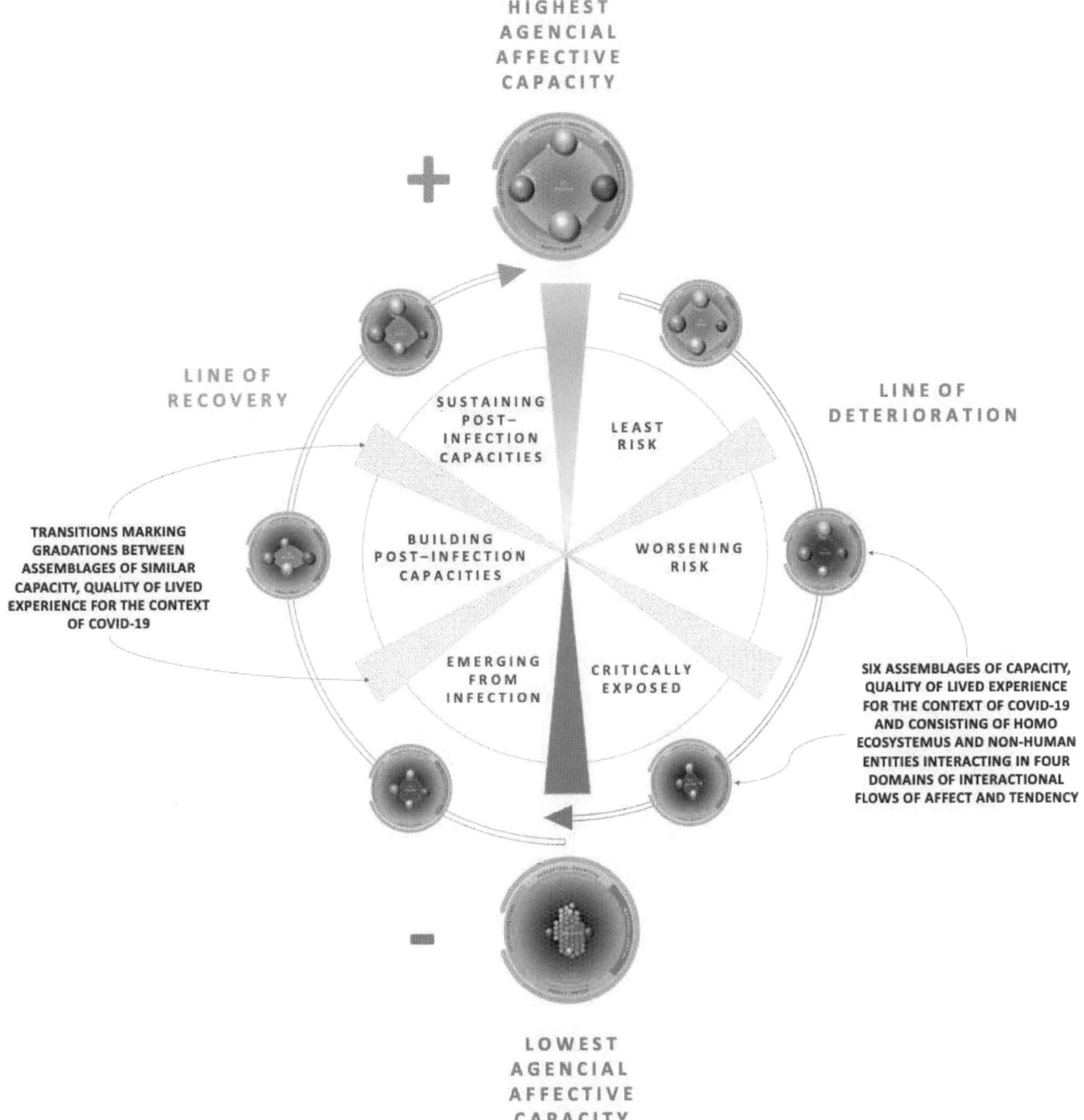

Figure One – The body of agencial assemblages of affective capacity for the focal context of Covid-19 lived experience

In the top-right assemblage of the model, we have an assemblage of highest affective capacity. Here we are likely to find "homo ecosystemus PLUS", the most equipped, capable and lowest risk human in the whole body of assemblages. They interact in interactional flows bearing entities of least risk and most positive affect in the Covid-19 experience ecosystem. This assemblage supports high agencial capacity by enabling the homo ecosystemus here to avoid interactions or follow compliance. In contrast, moving down the line of deterioration to the bottom-right of the model, we find an assemblage of least affective capacity. Here we are likely to find "homo ecosystemus MINUS", the least equipped, least capable and highest exposed human in the body of assemblages, such as those I described in the paragraph above. This assemblage consists of flows bearing high-potential transmission risk of the virus infection. On the left-hand side of the model are assemblages on the path to recovery after a Covid-19 infection, for those lucky to have survived. Here we may find Homo Ecosystemus that may no longer be infected yet still bear long-term symptoms of effects of their illness that we do not yet know about. Important to note is that any homo ecosystemus may transition between assemblages on either side at different frequencies and occurrences depending on their movements into and out of different arrangements and the particular confluence of interactional flows and tendencies of potential affect and tendency driving more or less risk of virus transmission. Persons who have just been vaccinated will likely move back up the line of deterioration though we do not yet know to what degree their risk has been mitigated.

Deploying this interactional assemblage view of distributed agency, as well as seeing different bodies and movements of various agencial capacities, we are able to reveal *differences beyond representation*. By difference beyond representation, I mean that Covid-19 has exposed hitherto concealed variations in health-related agency and capacity that transcend a priori standard socio-demographic, economic and disease categorizations and identities drawn from empirical observation of populations, bodily and mental symptom states. By revealing differences beyond and also within representation, we discover new dimensions of the health problems we are trying to address. We see differences in kind that transcend accepted identities and challenge our judgments and decisions when using static representations.

Whilst Covid-19 presents a stark interactional picture of differences in agencial capacity variation through the lens of homo ecosystemus, the picture is similarly pervasive in all chronic disease whether mental or physical. Also, this picture explains the hidden mechanisms at work in producing widening health inequalities.

Chronic disease, health inequalities and homo ecosystemus

As I mentioned above, prior to being dislodged by Covid-19, chronic disease and mental health issues were at the forefront of the health concerns of most Western societies and emerging economies. Consider obesity in the US. After thirty years and billions of dollars spent on public health research, prevention and treatment, obesity levels continue to rise. It is estimated that 42% of US adults were obese between 2017 and 2018[3]. If the trend continues, it is predicted that more than 57% of today's US youth will be living with obesity at age 35, a burden concentrated mostly in non-white ethnic groups and in poorer communities[4].

Until now, we have sought to explain the emergence and persistence of high levels of obesity using objective representations of obesity such as BMI and by studying their correlation with individual human behaviour, lifestyles and motivation (homo economicus tendency personified). Yet given the obvious collective failure to stem the continued rise of obesity through expensive health promotions and messages targeting individual behavioural change, weight loss and rational prescribed action, it is clear that these methods are simply not working. Much less appreciated and understood are the ways in which obesity is intertwined at a systemic level with social, cultural, economic, environmental and psychological flows, with its negative perception and stigmatization in society and with forces contained in everyday agencial interactions and experiences; all of which negatively impact the life trajectories of individuals that become obese and then have to live with it.

Consider also chronic pain (which with obesity is the disease context I reference most throughout the book). In most Western nations, around 40% of the adult population are suffering from chronic or persistent pain (defined as pain lasting for longer than three months). Whilst the pharmaceutical industry makes billions of dollars in pain-alleviating drugs, introducing increasingly stronger and more addictive varieties (with many negative social

---

[3] Hales CM, Carroll MD, Fryar CD, Ogden CL. Prevalence of obesity and severe obesity among adults: United States, 2017–2018. NCHS Data Brief, no 360. Hyattsville, MD: National Center for Health Statistics. 2020

[4] Ward, Z. J., Belich, S. N., Cradock, A. L., Barrett, J. L., Giles, C. M., Flax, C., Long, M. W., Gortmaker, S. L. (2019). Projected U.S. state-level prevalence of adult obesity and severe obesity. New England Journal of Medicine, 381:2440–2450

consequences), we still cannot explain the factors producing adult pain, many of which are beyond the body and fall outside biomedical explanations alone. Asking again why obesity, chronic pain and many other chronic diseases continue to originate and persist and finding our answers once more in a narrow and frankly self-defeating conception of the human as homo economicus, we discover two linked tendencies governing perception, method and action in the health and related social sciences.

First, we tend to be more concerned with understanding and acting within accepted representations of existing *being states* or phenotypes of abstracted body and separated mind-based disease and illnesses along with their prevention, diagnosis and treatment. Though the systems biology omics are pursuing process pathologies of certain chronic diseases[5], we have struggled to elevate an appropriate frame, practical set of methods and tools for the study of the origination, emergence and differencing of actual lived experiences with disease or illness. In short, we do not know how to see let alone explain the becoming, difference and recurrence of actual lived experiences with health, disease and illness.

Second, and elevating the first explanation, we typically place more emphasis on understanding and motivating individual human behaviour (through the lens of homo economicus) in relation to the risk of future and management of present disease states at the expense of understanding and intervening in the social body of health or more widely experience ecosystems of health. This is because we struggle to see how social, cultural, material, natural (especially) and other flows, forces and tendencies originate, emerge and diverge and variously stabilize the lived experiences of health, illness and disease in each and every one of us, in our families, in social groups, in communities and in places. Not as upstream linear social determinants that get lost in a morass of overlapping contexts (when context is everything and everywhere, we lose all power to explain their origination) but as forces of tendency that become folded within us, that intersect with our individual and collective perceptions and cognitions to produce our subjectivities and then variously enable or limit our individual, group and community capacities to avoid and manage disease or create health. Furthermore, we fail to see how varying capacities in lived experience differentially *act back* on the social body or experience ecosystems of health as an inside-out force of agency, action and creation itself. Although the unit of ecosystems (typically seen as networks of actors and technologies) has gained popularity in recent years, we still lack perception and understanding of such a holistic interactional, outside-inside-outside frame to explain the emergence and recurrence of different lived experiences with health, disease and illness.

Altogether, I identify eight limiting characteristics of epistemological tendencies in the health and related social sciences. These are:

- An overly narrow and reductive biomedical, bodily and individual person (patient) with behavioural focus
- A transactional, exchange-based model of value as outcomes over cost (yet outcomes do not exist in ongoing real emergent actual experience)
- A bias to fit solutions into established categories, concepts and discourses of disease
- Freezing and framing of problems using badly analysed usually quantitatively differentiated composites of homo ecosystemus experience (meaning that true problems are never fully or correctly identified nor stated)
- An emphasis on science-based discovery and intelligence that tends to exclude insight and perspective from more social disciplines

[5] Such as the work of the Arthritis Therapy Acceleration Programme at the Kennedy Institute of Rheumatology, University of Oxford. https://www.kennedy.ox.ac.uk/about/translational-research/atap

- A concern with matter or material forms of health phenomena (the genetic, physicochemical and biological) and their growing abstracted representation and measurement in data rather than social and spatial experiential dimensions of health
- A view and definition of health as an independent, standalone functional object of research rather than one imbricated with all other domains of human experience (e.g., nature, the built environment, politics, education, transport, food, housing, etc.)
- A lack of emphasis on "origination and recurrence stories and explanations" of disease

When adopting these views, I argue that prevailing design thinking, co-creation and innovation practices can make only superficial connection with people's actual lived experiences using overly functionalist, utilitarian and analytical approaches that deploy a limiting language of emotions and which substitute quantities for quality in their segmentation, measurement and monitoring methods.

Combined, the health sciences tend to either circumvent life without ever getting sufficiently close to actual experiences, or they bury themselves deep within molecular, cellular and genetic mechanisms to try and discover the pathology of disease and detect potential treatments and corrections. They seek an ordering of our physical-chemical-biological material states through empirical realist scientific method. Unquestionably, this has been hugely successful especially in acute diseases. Undoubtedly though, it is less successful when applied to lived experiences of chronic disease and mental illness and massively societally shifting pandemics; contexts where homo ecosystemus lives and interacts in a rich, complex tapestry of flows and forces of diverse agencial entities.

An interactional creation perspective

Combining my assessment of tendencies of perception, method and action in Covid-19 and chronic disease as I suggested, we can at least begin to adjust our perspective to learn why our efforts to learn, organise and act to prevent and address both are not working too well. Though the simplistic answer is often to see and act more holistically and now eco-systemically, there is still a large hole when we frame our models and peer into the holistic. This is because we do not know what to look for, what to study or how to look. To fill this gap in our capability to look into the whole, we must study more closely prevailing tendencies and logics in our approaches to understanding, managing and responding to health and disease in its actual lived experience. The most important of which is the dominant logic of agency itself and its relation to structure, the traditional point of debate in all the social sciences. I shall attempt to resolve it.

In an interactional creation ontology and perspective, agency is not distinct from structures. Individual human agents do not act independently in contexts of underlying structures or upstream social determinants. Rather agency is distributed, de-centred and variously democratized in the actions of all entities. In a distributed model of agency, the lived experiences with health of homo ecosystemus are not viewed as separate from outside socio-environmental contexts, from social determinants of health or from underlying social structures (as is typically the case). Rather, these forces are seen as present in potential pre-individual affects in interactional flows and are actualised in our lived experience depending on the force of capacities to affect them or be affected. This view of *agency being conjugated with structure* redefined as immanent tendencies in flows moves us away from a limiting context-is-everything view of disease and illness causation and also from a separating upstream force and downstream outcome model.

Furthermore, our understanding of action in this view of distributed agency is not limited to human action but is widened to that of assemblages of all entities, whether human or non-human. Shifting far from a model of deliberative rational action, action is now seen as arising in the intensive transitions or movements of assemblages that produce and variously repeat events in lived experience. Not only is action distributed in assemblages but also in cognition too. The cognitive calculations, learnings and decision-making capacities of homo ecosystemus and increasingly of non-human artificial machines are all fed by signs, symbols, codes, algorithms, brands, procedures and guidelines that are created by others and presented to us and with which we interact in our daily movements through life and increasingly on our personal devices.

In a distributed sense of agency and action in which homo ecosystemus is just one entity of agency, our perspective in health shifts from a focus on humans, their mostly standardised bodies and the baseline norms of its functioning to a focus on lived experience in all its differences. With an interactional creation model provided by the Health Ecosystem Value Design framework, we now have the concepts and tools to see how lived experiences with health, disease and illness originate, differentiate and variously persist in the social and natural body. We have the means to study the mechanisms of force and tendency in interactions that immanently transition and actualize differences in lived experience. In this framework therefore, lived experience and not human bodies or even human beings becomes the focus of our interest and unit of enquiry. And surrounding them, experience ecosystems of bodies of interactional agencial assemblages become the wider focal context for locating and understanding the intensive mechanisms and patterns of their creation, differentiation and reproduction.

In Health Ecosystem Value Design, our perception and frame of health and also of agency and action is enlarged to that of a focal experience ecosystem environment, and our view of affective capacity expands to the capacity of all affectors (human and non-human) and affectees to co-create surplus potential and/or novel affects shaping actual lived experience. With this perspectival expansion, we now explore and address differences in health affective capacity within affectees at all levels (individuals, families, communities, social groups, places and populations) and we focus our learning efforts on understanding where potential affective capacity exists, where it is being generated or enacted, where it is stuck and where it is absent in different agencial assemblages acting upon interactional flows and tendential forces coursing over the virtual social and natural body. We work with a *philosophy of difference* to question the structures of representation that mask difference. We reveal hidden variations in lived experiences that exist but are buried from our view due to their immanent properties of tendencies and capacities that transition lived experiences via homo ecosystemus interactions in interactional flows. When we uncover difference, we begin to see the true nature of actual lived experience along with the real conditions and possibilities - or lack of them - that enable or limit our desires for a better life. In short, we have turned over the stone to reveal the hidden differences of striving, scurrying and variously succeeding lived experiences with health, disease and illness.

Marking a distinction between matter and life, between stability and vitality, between function and creation, between standards and flexibility and even between need and freedom, an ontology of interactional creation is concerned with understanding the conditions of real experiences with health, disease and illness and not just the mastery of matter forming our bodies and their disease. Interactional creation is a philosophy of the force and flows of creation of difference in life itself, of origination, of the becoming of difference and of persistence.

When we harness the tools of this philosophy, we elevate, expand and extend our intellectual and intuitional faculties to see the widest context and mechanisms of health and disease. We enter into the domain of the real conditions and possibilities of lived experiences and we discover how to unlock, design and mobilize immanent creational capacities in individuals and communities to produce and reproduce the real lived experiences they desire.

In summary, we shift our perception from representation to difference, essence to tendency, being to becoming, capacity building to capacity creation, disease to health, norms to novelty, resources to interactions, collaboration to creation and management to enablement.

Health Ecosystem Value Design®

This second version of the Health Ecosystem Value Design® (HEVD) framework has been designed to rise to the challenge of the "no return to normal" that Covid-19 offers us whilst addressing the shortcomings of the prevailing health and related social sciences and associated innovation/design and co-creation practices.

To prevent, address and recover negative experiences with health, we must break with unquestioned habits of how we see, intervene or affect and manage experiences with health, disease and illness. We must acquire knowledge of the emergence and differentiation of human experiences with health/disease over time. We must reveal and explain our varying capacities to create, prevent, recover and adapt our and others' experience. We must gather deeper understanding of the pattern, processes and mechanisms of differentiation, divergence, inequality and capability in experiences with health/disease.

HEVD informs how we can better see, enable and emerge more positive experiences with health at multiple levels: whole experience ecosystems, places and spaces, communities, social groups and families as well as individual persons. To do so, it deploys a philosophy of ecosystem, emergent, relational and affective design thinking to advance the health and social (care) sciences. It goes beyond the dominant biomedical, reductionist and individual person-centric view of health as normal baseline functioning, end-state absence of disease, risk mitigation and a resource for living. Rather, HEVD adopts a wider socio-ecological view of health as individual, family, neighbor, community and social group powers of acting and creation in the pursuit of valued affective capacities that form positive real lived experiences with life or what I call social desire. Affective capacity epitomizes a new view of value beyond the transactional exchange and economic outcomes model. It addresses the over-objectified and abstracted limitations of the dominant symbolic medical/clinical order and method of individualist-centred (patient) health behaviour thinking.

HEVD does not search for absolute truth and predictions (nor claim they exist) but rather pursues "thick explanations" of health, disease, illness and related phenomena and especially their differences, movements, likelihoods, tendencies and probabilities. Only by being concerned with understanding the becoming of difference within experience ecosystems will we see hidden possibilities, co-design and emerge novel propositions and enable the interactional creation of health in the hopefully soon, post-Covid-19 era.

Who has Health Ecosystem Value Design® been created for?

The following is a brief summary of who HEVD has been created for.

- **Care providers, trusts, bodies and institutions** ... wishing to improve and adapt care practices, pathways and models in order to address complex disease and illness areas, improve the care experience and accelerate outcomes
- **National, regional, local governments** ... looking to create health and wellbeing, build greater collaboration and convergence around real lived experience, co-ordinate efforts, build more resilient communities and reduce the costs and burdens of disease and illness
- **Social, patient and community organizations** ... wishing to design and execute impactful community and patient programmes, support disadvantaged populations, widen access-to-health, address social determinants and build local and social cultures of health co-creation
- **Pharmaceutical, medical device, medical technology companies** ... seeking to avoid the "race-to-the-bottom", widen their market offer, escape the trap of outcome incrementalism, transform their growth profile, discover new sources of value, develop/validate new technologies and make compelling, differentiating ecosystem-level market access and payer cases
- **Academic and research institutions** ... wanting to develop new trans-disciplinary silo-busting health and design educational content and programmes, deploy a systemic health research framework, develop and secure grant applications and undertake outreach programmes into local communities as part of applied student and professional learning
- **Investors, insurers, payers, commissioners** ... wanting to assess new technologies, more certainty when making complex investment, risk, policy and purchase decisions and trade-offs

Structure of the book

The book is structured in two parts.

Part One contains two chapters. Chapter one describes the foundations of an interactional creation ontology of health in experience ecosystems that underpin the HEVD framework. Chapter two explains how this ontology help us to rethink real lived experiences with health, disease and illness, the nature of value and the task and flow/method of their interactional creation.

Part Two contains the twelve templates that make up the task, flow and method of Health Ecosystem Value Design. It contains examples of each template used in an Umio study of chronic pain that I conducted in winter 2020 just before Covid-19 lockdown.

Part One
Experience ecosystem ontology, task and method of interactional creation of health

Chapter One

Foundations of an ontology of interactional creation of health in experience ecosystems

"Seen as the product of its natural history, the mind is a machine for solving problems. To solve problems, however, it must be more than a machine. Its formulaic and modular aspect must coexist with its plastic, surprising, and transcending aspect. These two aspects meet in the need to survey a situation as a whole and to relate its parts to one another. A capacity to grasp structures and relations is the crucial precondition of our problem-solving capacity. To enjoy this capacity, we cannot simply think according to established formulas, as if we were machines. We have to be able to think more than any preexisting formula will countenance, and then we have to establish the formulas that make sense of our insights after we have first made our formula-breaking discoveries. We must be able to construct new ways of understanding, of explaining, of seeing what stands before us, in the scene of imminent or imagined action, as an ordered whole or as a set of relations."

Roberto Mangabeira Unger, The Self Awakened (2007, 98)

Chapter One | Foundations of an ontology of interactional creation of health in experience ecosystems

Introduction

Diverse beliefs about the reality of health and disease phenomena, their properties, observability and knowability, variously influence how we explore, know and respond to a believed reality. Like any philosophical endeavour, the pursuit to understand health is characterised by distinct perspectives, each defined by certain assumptions concerning the reality of health and its experience and an attendant epistemology that shapes the questions asked, the scope, content and forms of knowledge sought, and the justifiability of the truth, validity and usefulness of the insight produced. Over time, prevailing beliefs evolve into dominant ideas and institutions of health and disease. Deeply embedded in these are conceptions of value or what we deem to be moral, ethical, equitable, practical and worthwhile health-related endeavours, interactions, beings and doings. In turn, ideas become represented in the categories we use and the routines we create and reproduce to improve, create or modify our and others' health. Such representations consist of standards, guidelines, artefacts and performances that are enacted repeatedly and routinely in health systems for health and disease contexts of a certain identity, content and expression and by persons and patients of a certain role, discipline, relation and mode of action.

In this chapter, I introduce seven foundations that together constitute a novel ontology of the interactional creation of health in experience ecosystems, foundations that underpin the Health Ecosystem Value Design (HEVD) framework, task and method. I do so in a logical sequence where each successive foundation builds upon earlier ones.

The ontological parameters and the related questions addressed by the seven foundations are as follows:

1. **Perception**: How can we see the holistic and interactional nature of lived experiences with health[6]?
2. **Phenomena**: What is the generative material constituting lived experiences with health?
3. **Creation**: How do lived experiences with health originate, become different and variously persist?
4. **Difference**: How can we see differences in actual lived experience *within the same context* of lived experience with health?
5. **Transition**: How can we see different states and their transition *within the same context* of lived experience with health?
6. **Process**: How do different states of actual lived experience with health within the same context originate, differenciate and persist?
7. **Collective**: How do we see and define experience ecosystems of interactional creation of health?

I begin with the first ontological foundation, a whole unified and interactional view and model of lived experience with health, disease and illness.

[6] When stating lived experience with health, I also infer disease and illness, whether chronic or acute, mental or physical (albeit this distinction fades as will become clear in the foundations).

Foundation One | How can we see the holistic and interactional nature of lived experiences with health?

Given that the word health is derived from the Old English words *hal* or *hale* meaning wholeness or whole, I suggest that the first important task for any health creation framework is to develop a model of whole as well as unified lived experience with health. To be whole, such a model must include all the different entities and mechanisms forming individual lived experiences with health. To be unified, it must support us to explore how these elements interact and function to originate, emerge, diverge and variously repeat lived experiences over time, both individually and collectively.

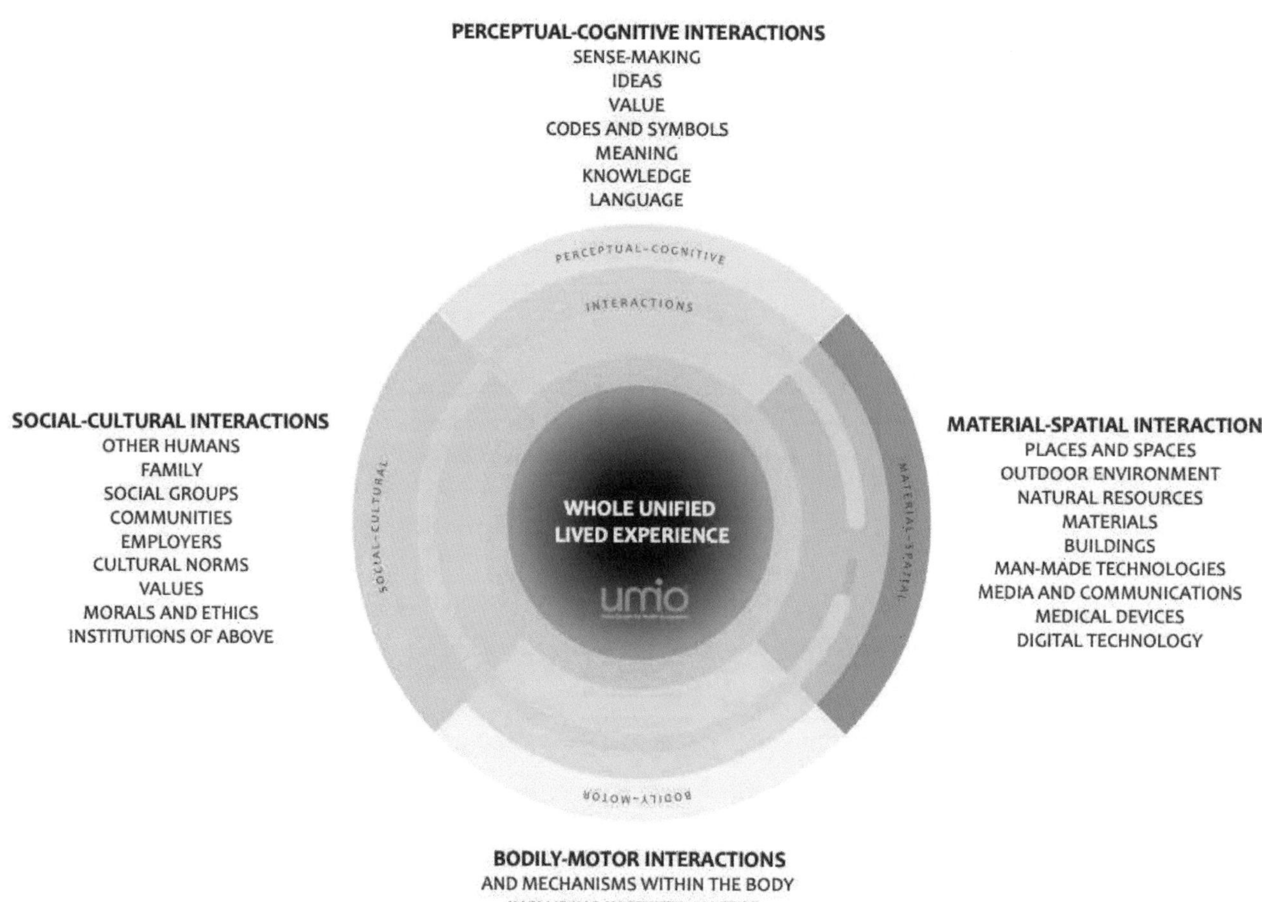

Figure 1.1: Base model of whole and unified experience with health arising from interactions with bodies of entities in four interactional domains

In Figure 1.1, I depict my base model of whole unified lived experience formation consisting of four interactional domains. Each domain is comprised of distinct types or bodies of social, material, semiotic, bodily, cognitive and other entities whose interaction (between and within the domains) forms actual lived experience. In the dynamic moving version of the model available in Umio videos online, the light blue "INTERACTIONS" ring rotates around the centre to indicate ongoing experience formation via interactions within and between the variety of bodies of entities in all four domains.

Over the seven foundations, I shall build up and elaborate the model into a complete ontology of lived experience formation. First, I briefly introduce each of the four interactional domains in the model.

Social-cultural interactional domain

The social-cultural domain consists of interactions with other people, in our families and with friends, in our communities and social groups as well as with human actors or agents within organizations of all types. They include interactions with professional health agents in physical or virtual clinical and care practices. Social interactions tend to follow certain standards, habits, routines and activities shaped by cultural norms, brands, signs and symbols, ethics and morals, roles, identities, values and institutional arrangements and rituals (e.g., marriage, the couple, the nuclear family).

Material-spatial interactional domain

The material-spatial domain consists of embodied human interactions with external natural matter and man-made objects such as consumer products, buildings, vehicles, tools, furniture, information, communications and media technologies (analogue and digital), devices and data, as well as our interactions within and movements through real and virtual (online) spaces and places, whether natural or built environments. Interactions with non-human species and with nature and the outdoor environment itself are included in this domain too.

Bodily-motor interactional domain

The bodily-motor domain consists of organismic interior interactions and mechanisms of molecular, cellular, tissue, organ and musculoskeletal functions and matter within the body, including those arising from motor functioning and movement of the body, its situation and posture. Also included in this domain are interactions of the body's *interior consumption*, use and conversion of external natural matter and energy such as food, water, air, light and heat and also of drugs (located in this domain as they are administered into the body).

Perceptual-cognitive interactional domain

Finally, the perceptual-cognitive domain consists of our immediate and reflective consciousness as well as our cognition, representation and interpretation of interactions in the other domains. Perception is seen from the point of view of action and of potential affordances or possibilities for interaction with bodily and motor, social and cultural, and material and spatial entities in the other three domains. Cognitive interactions include semiotic and discursive encounters with brands, information, signs and symbols, concepts and ideas. They invoke the language we use to express our experiences, interpret and explain their meaning and justify our choices and behaviours. They also determine how we value and perform valuations of the different entities we interact with in terms of the events, outcomes and impacts in our experience they produce. They shape how we distinguish, assess and determine the extrinsic or intrinsic worth of interactions in the other three domains.

Imbrication of nature and the intersectional and external perspectival shifts

Note how in the model the domains of *social-cultural* and *material-spatial interactions* sit opposite one another on the same horizontal axis indicating there is no separation of the social-cultural from the natural domain of interactions. This is important as until only recently, the Western tradition has been to leave nature, ecology, climate and the environment in the background when framing and explaining our modern predicaments with health, disease and illness, and even the status of humanity in general[7]. Now, by bringing them together into the same whole unified interactional model of lived experience, we return nature and ecology onto an equal footing in our ontology of health and in our subsequent explorations. We consider the health of the environment, climate and of non-human living species as fundamental imbricated factors shaping all lived experiences with health. Being on the same horizontal plane of human interactions and our interactions with material entities such as products, technology and the built environment, we now fold all of nature into our lived experience and we become more sensitive to its nurturing and protection. If we can see more the impacts of our damage

[7] We have tended to stop at the body or the skin as the boundary limit of our investigation into health, disease and illness

to ecologies of the natural environment in our own lived experience with health, we are more likely to do something about our damaging actions. We can develop research methods that incorporate and study our impacts on nature and the environment as well its impacts on lived experience in humans. By elevating all social, natural and material entities onto the same horizontal plane, we find a singular unifying perspective to discover our mutual interactional dependency in relation to the production and differentiation of lived experiences with health.

Interacting on the vertical axis in the model, *bodily-motor* and *perceptual-cognitive* interactions are interior interactions within a mind-body or sensorimotor dynamic. They define the relation between perception of external entities, their bodily manifestation or sensations and their cognitive representation and interpretation. Also, we can see the link between cognitive defects, dysfunctions or burdens and their bodily-motor expression, such as the relation between stress from cognitive overload and fatigue or pain in the body arising from work-related burnout. Being inside us, perceptual-cognitive with bodily-motor interactions on the vertical axis are harder to observe yet we can understand them more by studying their interactions with entities in the two domains on the horizontal axis.

Using the four interactional domains and two axes, this whole interactional mind-body-social-cultural-nature view of lived experience and its formation supports two perspectival adjustments in our ontology of health. These are intersectional interior and interactional external.

- **Intersectional interior perspective:** We are drawn to the immanent centre of the model as the point where the four domains interact to variously produce, differentiate and reproduce states, qualities and tendencies of action in the lived experience of individual persons and also groups. Here we see lived experiences with health as the product of the interior interaction of the four domains.
- **Interactional external perspective:** We are drawn to the exterior domain of social-cultural and material-spatial with nature entities and the forces and tendencies they bear that shape our lived experiences with health. Here we see lived experience with health, disease and illness as the product of forces of the outside as well as their interior intersection. We become interested in external entities and bodies that humans interact with to originate different lived experiences.

In making these two perspective shifts, we see how experiences actually *become different* from forces and tendencies in the interplay of interior and external interactions. The model helps to see and understand the processes involved in the subjectification of humans, as opposed to merely affording a means for the subjective expression of a personal lived experience, usually stated in terms of emotions. This a priori mode of seeing experience in its *becomingness* arising from forces and tendencies in interactions and as detached and independent from individual human subjects has important implications for how we perceive health. We start with the widest outside-in, beyond-the-body and beyond-the-person (and certainly beyond the patient) perspective. Now lived experience itself becomes the primary phenomena of interest in our ontology, not individual human beings and their personal subjectivities. In chapter two, I explore this perspectival shift in further detail and offer a new definition of health to use it practically.

Homo Ecosystemus

The whole unified model of lived experience described above suggests a new interpretation of the human, an interpretation I call homo ecosystemus. Homo ecosystemus defines humans as agencial entities interacting in open experience ecosystems consisting of fluid social, spatial, natural, material and semiotic entities. As embedded interactional entities, the lived experience of homo ecosystemus is formed, enriched and imbued with social-cultural, material-spatial, bodily-motor and perceptual-cognitive sensations, feeling states and impressions, passions and values arising from their intensive interactions in the four domains. The next foundation defines these generative materials of lived experience with health.

Summary

In summary, supporting all subsequent foundations and forming a base model for the entire experience ecosystem ontology and Health Ecosystem Value Design framework, the first foundation provides a dynamic, interactional, unified model of lived experience. It states that whole lived experiences with health, illness and disease are embodiments of the occurrence, force, content and patterning of human interactions in four intersecting domains: social-cultural, material-spatial, bodily-motor and perceptual-cognitive.

Foundation One
Whole lived experiences with health, illness and disease are embodiments of the occurrence, force, content and patterning of human interactions in four intersecting domains, social-cultural, material-spatial, bodily-motor and perceptual-cognitive

Foundation Two | What is the generative material constituting lived experiences with health?

The second foundation identifies the generative material that form, organize and differenciate[8] whole lived experiences with health arising from embodied human (or homo ecosystemus) interactions within and between the four domains. These materials are termed *affects*. They have two related dimensions and roles in the formation and differenciation of lived experiences: sensations and capacities.

- **Affects as sensations**: Affects are sensations, feeling states and impressions that mark transitions within and between lived experience states. Actualized via interactions in what I term four affective domains, affects themselves interact, combine and can fuse together to qualitatively differenciate and variously stabilise and reproduce lived experiences with health.
- **Affects as capacities**: Affects also determine what a person can be and do, or their potential capacity to affect or be affected by other persons and non-human entities in interactions within the four affective domains. As an *affective capacity*, affects are a *power for creating and acting* in and upon lived experience, whether to be affected or to affect – positively or negatively - when entering into relations and interacting with persons or entities (or collectively, other bodies) in the four domains.

In Table 1.1, I show examples of affects as sensations and affects as affective capacities. Both are drawn from a recent (2020) Umio study of lived experiences with chronic pain that I conducted in Northern Ireland. I shall use this study throughout the book to exemplify the framework and also the templates in Part Two of the book. In Figure 1.2, I add affects and affective capacities into the centre of the whole unified model of lived experience. Both are actualized from movements in the "AFFECT" ring (the newly added darker grey ring in the centre) via interactions with and within the (light blue) interaction ring moving across the four affective domains. Note that all elements in the model are in motion at different rates. A slow rate of movement indicates a more stable or stuck lived experience (with affects concentrated in the centre of the model due to a dominant centripetal force of capacities in experience). A fast rate of movement indicates a more changing and diverse lived experience with health (the affects move to the edge of the centre of the model with capacities acting as a centrifugal force).

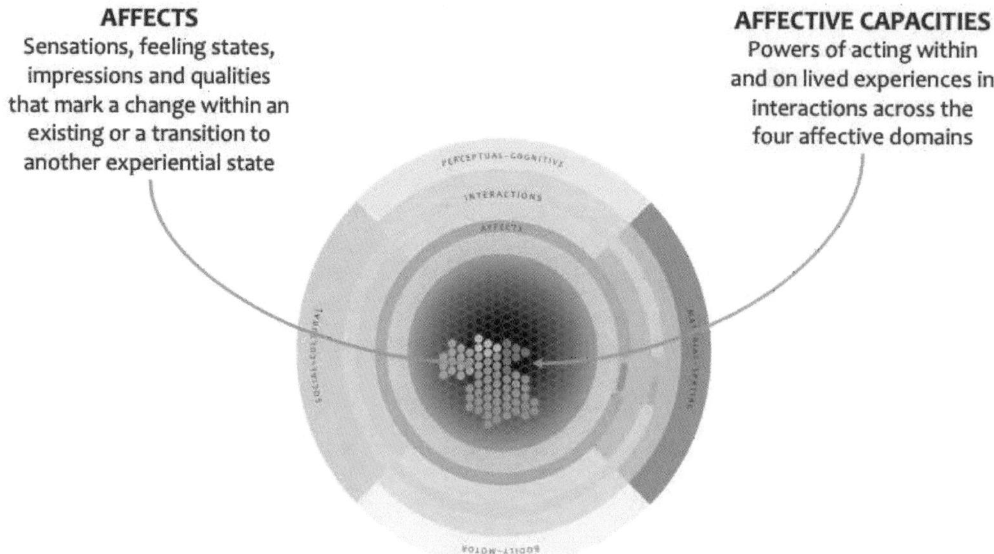

Figure 1.2: Affects and affect capacities in the model of lived experience

---

[8] I use the term "differenciate "with a "c" to denote the process of beComing different and actualized in lived experience. This is distinct from differentiate with a "t" meaning to distinguish differences in ideas, things or entities before they are actual or when they are actualized.

Table 1.1: Example affects and affective capacities from Umio chronic pain study organised by the four affective domains

AFFECTIVE DOMAIN	AFFECT	AFFECTIVE CAPACITIES
SOCIAL-CULTURAL	• Sense of being blamed by others • Sense of not belonging to a social group • Sense of rejection • Sense of unwanted loneliness (itself a social construct) • Sense of being a burden or of dependency on others • Sense of loss of intimacy with a partner • Sense of grief at loss of partner • Sense of isolation or withdrawal from social life	• Capacity to work regular hours / to a routine • Capacity to socialise with others • Capacity of dependents (and their dependents) to be socially mobile • Capacity to obtain useful help with pain when needed • Capacity to find and choose suitable employment when living with pain
MATERIAL-SPATIAL	• Sense of unwanted dependency on a digital technology • Sense of being quantified or objectified by data • Sense of anxiety when outdoors in the local neighbourhood • Sense of insecurity in my own home • Sense of losing control of medication use • Sense of material deprivation • Sense of having limited movement	• Capacity to avoid a dependency on technology to intermediate social connections • Capacity to use digital pain self-management tools • Capacity to choose suitable places and spaces to visit or navigate in built environment • Capacity and desire to leave the house • Capacity to be comfortable in the home
BODILY-MOTOR	• Sense of pain arising from a persistent load on a part of the body • Sense of pain arising from a primary pain syndrome, e.g., fibromyalgia • Sense of pain arising from trauma, whether injury or surgery-related • Sense of pain linked to specific activity/motor movement • Sense of low or no physical energy • Sense of loss of bodily strength • Sense of fatigue	• Capacity to take compensatory actions to reduce pain that work consistently • Capacity to appropriately question / challenge GPs advice • Capacity to communicate pain experience and affects to GP/clinicians • Capacity to access / obtain pain care and support when needed • Capacity to understand relationship between intensity of activity and a pain response
PERCEPTUAL-COGNITIVE	• Sense of lost personal identity • Sense of always waiting for something to happen • Sense of loss of personal autonomy • Sense of living day-by-day or only in the present • Sense of a loss of power • Sense of diminished free will or freedom • Sense of a lack of progress • Sense of diminished hope	• Capacity to develop a useful "pain memory" • Capacity to see pain and its causes as "beyond the body" • Capacity to identify and recall personal physical/motor factors forming an experience of pain • Capacity to understand how personal outlook / mindset affects pain experience • Capacity to achieve effective pain self-management negated by non-pain affects

Affectees and affectors

At this point, I introduce two important new terms, affectee and affector. An **affectee** can be an individual person, a family, neighbour(s), a community or a social group of any kind (ethnic, gender, age, political or religious affiliation, patient group) or even a place or space that is experiencing affects and has a degree of affective capacity. An **affector** can be another individual person, family, neighbour, community, social group or organization that is directly or indirectly responsible for generating or influencing affects and affect capacities being experienced by the affectee. An affector is also an "experiencer" but in HEVD, I distinguish them from affectees to discern important relational cause-affects (not effects) that provide better explanations of the production, differenciation and persistence of lived experiences with health, disease and illness. Also, an affector may be a non-human natural, material or semiotic entity, such as polluted air, a drug, device, a digital technology or an objective universal representation of a type or state of an illness such as a symptom description or a score.

I use the new terms affectee and affector to escape the straitjacket of anthropo- and actor-centric thinking that dominates the study, design, management and innovation of health and social systems, organizations and practices. Ongoing use of terms such as patient, informal caregiver, doctor and pharmacist tend to objectify, harden and even narrow perspectives of roles, agency and practices in health. By introducing new language, I have more freedom to explore the widest possible set of human and non-human agents involved (actively and passively) in creating, modifying or limiting affects and affective capacities forming lived experiences with health. Most importantly, a linguistic detachment and renewal facilitates my search for more holistic, novel and deeper understanding and explanation of the origin, emergence, persistence and decline of any *focal lived experience with health context* such as chronic pain. Making another linguistic shift, I now define what I mean by this term.

Focal lived experience with health context

Any experience with health, disease or illness originates, differenciates and variously endures from either a single intensive affect or more commonly from a multiplicity of individual affects and affective capacities that move, combine and fuse together like several notes forming a chord or a melody in a song. An affect lens can be applied to any *focal lived experience with health context*, a term I use to select and frame enquiries into qualitatively distinct and recurring lived experiences defined by a *particular type, relation and quality of affects and affective capacities*. A focal lived experience with health context (NB I will shorten the term to *focal experience context* on occasion forthwith) can be one or combination of the following:

- A physical disease or illness such as type 2 diabetes, chronic pain, cardiovascular or respiratory disease (defined primarily by bodily-motor affects in combination with certain affective capacities in the four affective domains)
- Mental illnesses such as depression and schizophrenia (defined by mainly perceptual-cognitive affects also in combination with certain affective capacities in the four affective domains)
- Behavioural problems such as drug addiction and eating disorders (expressed in material-spatial affects)
- Chronic multi-disease states such as obesity (defined by affects and affective capacities in all four domains)
- Feeling states such as insecurity, unwanted loneliness and hopelessness (perceptual-cognitive and social-cultural affects)
- Wider-than-health yet ill-health inducing social problems such as racism, inequality, bullying, violent crime and domestic abuse. Through an affect lens, HEVD can be used to support systemic-level insights and interventions into these lived experiences also.

Real duration of lived experience

It is important to understand how affects differenciating lived experience are sensed in individual psychological rather than spatial, representative or objective time (i.e., hours, minutes or seconds). This personal sense of time – or real duration[9] – serves as the plane of composition upon which affective capacities provide powers to discover, construct and reconstruct affects forming lived experience on a continuous basis. Real duration can be an important diagnostic differentiator in certain lived experiences with disease and illness characterised by a distortion of real duration as well as space. For example, persons with major depression can experience a sense of time *slowing down* whereas persons with schizophrenia suffer from an *abnormal time experience* (or what's known as ATE) in which they become detached from a sense of time[10]. The fields of phenomenological psychiatry and psychopathology study such temporal distortions in mental illnesses, distortions that tend to be marginalised by more readily observable behavioural descriptors. They pursue systematic accounts of subtle and hidden changes in people's actual lived experience with mental problems and seek to reconstruct the interactional affective framework in which they arise. In chapter two, I explore the limitations of the dominant tendency in the empirical health sciences to abstract and quantify the inner real duration of lived experience of all diseases and illnesses, not just mental disorders.

Figure 1.3 depicts affects and affective capacities (in the centre of the model of whole unified experience) as the generative material that move and transition a lived experience upon a plane of composition over a real duration of sensed psychological time.

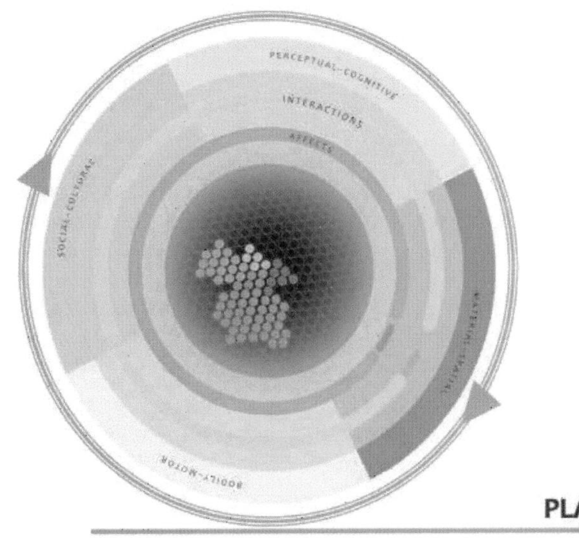

Figure 1.3: Movement of lived experience on a plane of composition over real duration or sensed time

Summary

In summary, foundation two states that lived experiences with health, disease and illness are formed from single and multiplicities of affects defined as sensations, feeling states and impressions that mark a transition in experience, as well as affective capacity, the power to affect, act and to create affects and to be affected in interactions in the four affective domains. Affects and capacities are the generative materials forming the process of subjectification of individual experience; they emerge, interact, fuse and dissipate in various degrees to define

[9] See Henri Bergson's Matter and Memory (1896) for a description of real duration and of differences in kinds of experience arising in a continuous multiplicity of affects. Bergson emphasized the subjective quality of experienced time as opposed to the objective, spatial externalized character of dated time counted in hours, minutes and seconds.

[10] For a seminal psychopathological study of lived time in disease experience, see Eugene Minkowski's Lived Time (1933)

certain qualities and intensities of actual experience that dynamically move and unfold in a real duration of sensed time on a plane of composition.

Foundation Two
Actual experiences with health, disease and illness are formed from individual and multiplicities of affects - defined as sensations, feeling states and impressions having real duration (sensed in psychological time over lived journeys) that mark a transition in an experiential state, as well as affective capacities defined as the capacity or power to act and to create affects and to be affected in interactions in four affective or interactional domains

Affects and emotions

Before moving onto foundation three, it is important to make a clear distinction between affects and emotions. The simplest means to do so is to state (as I have described) that affects (as sensations, feeling states and impressions and affective capacities) are the generative differenciating material of individual experiences whereas emotions are interpretive *reflections of our discursive feelings*. Whilst we can only ever rely on language to describe our affects and enquire into those of others, distinguishing them as the dynamic formative constituents of lived experience allows us to ask questions of how, why and where different lived experiences with health, disease and illness originate, diverge, change and persist.

Next, in foundation three, I describe the actual mechanisms of the *origination, production and differenciation of lived experience from affects* via homo ecosystemus interactions in the four interactional domains.

Foundation Three | How do lived experiences with health originate, become different and variously persist?

Foundation three identifies that affects (sensations and capacities) forming lived experiences with health are actualized in experience from human and non-human interactions with *virtual interactional flows modulated by tendential forces*. By virtual, I mean that in the world there exists real flows and forces consisting of different natural, material, social, semiotic and other entities whose properties contain distinct qualities, gradients and intensities of capacity, tendency and potential affect[11]. When human and non-human (technologies, non-human species, natural phenomena) agents interact with these flows and forces, the capacities, tendencies and affects they contain are unlocked and mobilized to originate, differenciate and variously repeat actual lived experiences. Put another way, the world consists of a *virtual-real* domain or register of flows and forces bearing pre-individual or pre-experience affects, capacities and tendencies and an *actual-real* domain or register of actual experiences that are produced and differenciated from mechanisms of interaction with these flows and forces in the virtual-real domain. Once actualized, the affects, capacities and tendencies return to the virtual-real register shaping ongoing interactions and further differenciation of lived experience. In Figure 1.4, I update the whole unified model of lived experience once more to include two further dynamic "rings": a ring of interactional FLOWS (on the outside of the interactions ring) and a ring of tendential FORCES (between the interactions and the affects ring). I also show the virtual-real domain or register of flows and forces that are external to lived experience (and the whole unified model).

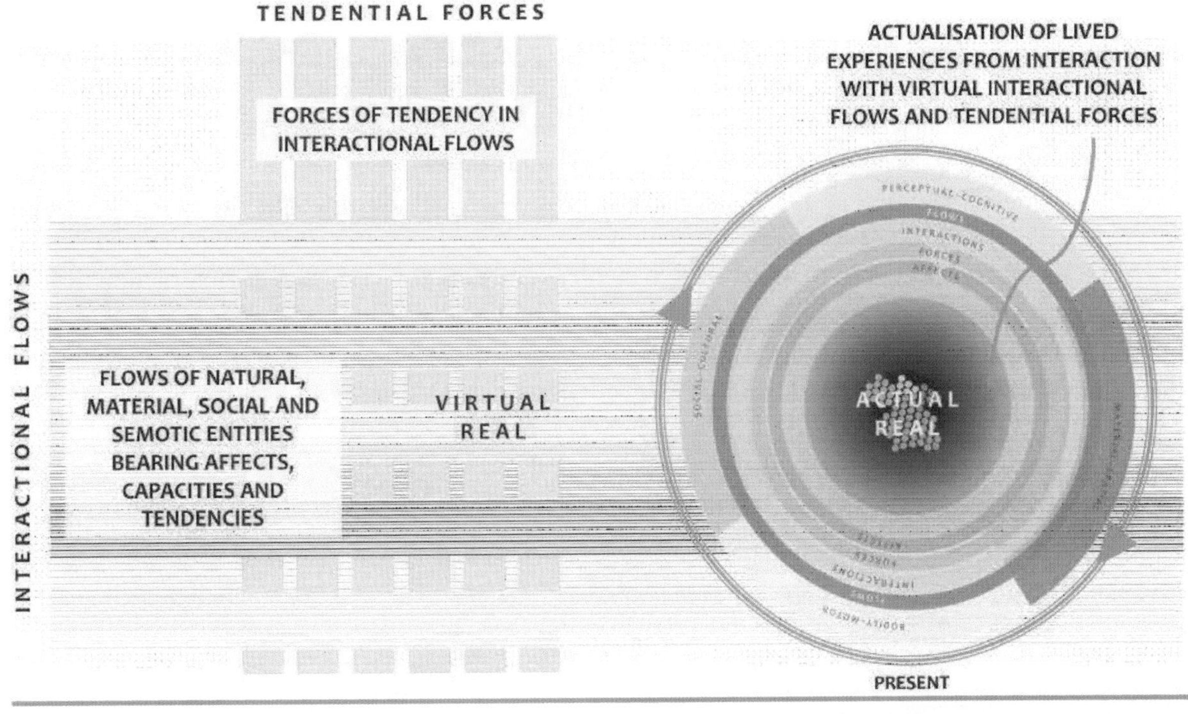

Figure 1.4: The virtual-real (dotted background) and actual-real domains or registers of lived experience

Next, I shall explain virtual interactional flows in further detail.

[11] I do not mean virtual in the sense of a technological domain or mode of virtual reality.

Virtual interactional flows

A virtual interactional flow is a dynamic moving body of natural, material, social, semiotic and other entities bearing *virtual* affects, capacities and tendencies (tendencies are added by tendential forces – more on those later.) When an interactional flow is interacted with, the *pre-experience* affects, capacities and tendencies it contains are actualized in a process of creative enactment producing a state of a certain expression, content, quality, intensity and stability of lived experience. This process of actualization of a lived experience state is an *event*. They may be a micro-event such as a passing flush of happiness or sadness, an intensive event of concentrated affects such as an event of hyperglycaemia, repeated events over a real duration such as recurring episodes of domestic abuse or discrimination at work, or continuous events experienced over a lifetime such as variable waves of intensities of chronic pain.

River analogy

To help with understanding of virtual interactional flows and their production and differenciation of transitions in lived experience via human interaction with pre-individual affects, tendencies and capacities, imagine you are standing bare-footed in the middle of a turbulent fast-flowing river. In the centre of the river where it flows at its fastest and with greatest force, the water comes above your knees. The cold rapid current pushes against the palms of your hands as you cup them under the surface in an effort to hold yourself stable. After a while, you struggle to stand upright on the smooth slippery bare rock underfoot and you feel the strong force of the river pushing heavier against the back of your legs as they gradually weaken. Now, you sense the river is about to overwhelm your (affective) capacity to resist its force (marking the first transition in your experience). Suddenly your feet slip, you fall into the river and you sink up to your neck as it drags you downstream. You are now in a fast-moving flow engendering strong sensation affects of fear and a loss of control albeit mixed with exhilaration and possibility. As you are pulled along, your capacity to affect the flow has diminished and both sensation and capacity transitions have shifted your actual experience again (the second transition). Approaching a large rock protruding above the surface, you reach out and manage to grab onto it on the downstream side. Securing yourself, you pull yourself upright to stand. Here, stood in the circular swirling eddy behind the rock, the water flow almost stops, the force of the river dissipates, and you feel the soft mud sediment beneath your feet as you sink into the riverbed. Now, your experience state transitions to a sense of safety and relief (the third affect transition). That is, until you realise you are stuck where you are and cannot get out of the river without re-entering the faster flow again (a further sense of a loss of capacity and hopelessness marking the fourth and final affect transition).

Using this nominal concept[12] of virtual interactional flows containing heterogenous entities with properties of pre-individual affect, capacity and tendency and which via their interaction originate, differenciate and variously stabilise and repeat lived experience states, we can envisage numerous virtual interactional flows moving continuously and also merging over the surface of a *virtual social body* (just as tributaries join together to form a larger river flowing over the earth's surface). Like the affects, capacities and tendencies in interactional flows, this whole one social body is *virtual* in that the possibilities of experience (affect transitions) it contains are real yet not yet actualized. In other words, the creation, movement and transition of actual experience from pre-experience affects, capacities and tendencies held in the *virtual interactional flows* is not yet actualized via our interaction with them. Using the river metaphor, we can say that the *possibility of affects* in different interactional flows exists, yet it is only when we stand in (interact with) the river (interacting in the flow) and get swept away and then stuck do they actually materialise and become real in our lived experience.

---

[12] Concepts like interactional flows are tools to help us to better explain differences in lived experiences. Even though we cannot "see" and measure an interactional flow of experience empirically, we can use the concept to understand the processes of differenciation of experiences with health, disease and illness as well as the tendencies for some persons, social groups, places and communities to suffer disease and ill-health more than others.

Before elaborating the social body and the differenciation of lived experiences with health via interactions with interactional flows bearing different entities and properties of capacity, tendency and affects, first I wish to explain further the interactional flows of capacity and tendency that occur in the natural material world or what I shall call the natural body. I do so because similar principles apply to the interactional flows that we interact with in the social world. Also, we can then see how our lived experiences are products of joint interactions with the natural with social body. By understanding them, we can study nature and human society as a single unity and source of differenciation of lived experience as I explained when introducing the whole unified model in foundation one.

Virtual interactional flows of the natural body

Using the river as an example of an interactional flow once more, we can first say with confidence that every river is different from other rivers and also that every part of one river is different from other parts of the same river (as Heraclitus would affirm[13]). Second we can say that each actual river and every part of a river is a distinctive actualization of heterogeneous matter, energy and forces of tendency combinations; *matter* in the form of the chemical, physical and biological particles in the water and constituting the plant and animal species living in the river; *energy* in the form of matter-altering intensities of light, heat, speed and sound occurring at different depths and points of the river, and *tendency* in the form of the gravitational, traversal and internal *forces* acting upon, across and within the river. Third, if we step back to the time before the river or any part of it came into being, we see that all the matter and energy presently constituting the river existed in a virtual or whole unified one body[14].

Over time, the river became "cut-out" from this whole one unified body[15] by flows of matter and energy that have a certain ongoing tendency of force to differentiate the body from *within itself* (as there can be no external force acting upon a whole unified body of matter and energy). Finally, as the river is always becoming a different river, the actual flow of the river (which we jumped into and maybe survived) is itself formed from ongoing differenciation arising from the tendencies of the same forces adding new and acting upon existing matter and energy within the river.

Before applying the river example of natural flows of force and tendency to the social body, I draw out six important lessons from the above paragraph.

Forces of differenciation exist in the virtual whole

First, life itself is an ongoing vital force that differenciates a virtual natural body of pure differentiated matter and energy into living bodies that are different in kind from the same and other living bodies (one river is different from another river, one part of one river is different from other parts of the same river. A river is different from a mountain).

Flows have potential tendencies

Second, this continuous vital force is the creative evolutionary and differenciating process of nature itself. It is formed of interactional flows of matter and energy that have different potential tendencies to actualize living bodies in time and space and that differ in kind from the same and other living bodies.

---

[13] To update Heraclitus' famous river quote we should say, "No homo ecosystemus ever steps in the same river twice, for it's not the same river and he's not the same homo ecosystemus."

[14] This perspective on the virtual body and the vital force or *élan vital* is drawn from Henri Bergson's Creative Evolution (1911) and Deleuze's Bergsonism (1966, translated into English in 1988) in which he used Bergson's concepts of real duration, intuition, differences in kind and continuous multiplicities to form an ontology of the virtual and the creation of the actual.

[15] Note that the use of the body here is not referring to the human body but the body of flows of matter and energy from which emanates the vital force of life that produces and differenciates other living bodies, whether plant and animal species including humans and non-living yet dynamic bodies in environments (such as a river, a mountain, a habitat and an ecosystem).

Continuous becoming of difference

Third, living bodies continue to differenciate or "become different" arising from the tendencies of the same forces acting within them as well as from interactions with tendencies of forces in other bodies (e.g., a bend of the river having a certain internal tendency of force interacting with the soil and bedrock in a riverbank having a different internal tendency of force of density of matter. Note that the soil and bedrock is as much a living flowing body as the river, we just cannot easily see its flow of becoming different in objective representative human time).

Possibilities of creative differenciation exist in the virtual and in flows

Fourth, such internal tendencies can be viewed as *possibilities* in the sense that any living body (soil, river etc.) *already* contains *potential* future differentiations *of itself*. In other words, future possibilities exist in the tendencies of a living body to differenciate itself in certain directions and forms; the tendency embodies a creative differenciation of possibility that has not yet been actualized yet does already exist. In this sense, possibility does not only occur after the actualization of a body or thing, but already exists in the virtual flow and force of tendencies within the body. For example, a river has a tendency of force to cut off one of its own meanders to form an ox-bow lake, a body of water isolated from the main river.

Events of actual differentiation

Next, when a tendency of force acting upon a flow of matter and energy intensifies and then actualizes a difference in a living body, then this actualization can be described as an event. An event marks an intense transition in a living body in the flow; it is an actualized becoming of difference. When the river finally cuts off its meander, the transition of the meander to an ox-bow lake is an actualized event.

Intensive not extensive generalisable differences define our world

Finally, we can now describe the world not by differences in how things appear to us (a representation of their essential, external properties) but rather by differences in their tendencies to creatively differenciate themselves (their internal or intensive forces or creative processes). For example, we can describe a river according to its force of tendency and likelihood to form ox-bow lakes and by the rate, intensity and difference of those tendencies compared with other rivers, not by the shape of its meanders, its length, depth or its appearance. Doing so provides better understanding of individual rivers and their processes of differenciation in relation to other rivers. It affords a new virtual science based on interactional flows and tendential forces of difference rather than of their representative similarity or generalized identity.

In Figure 1.5, I draw together the six lessons above into a model of the creative force of tendencies, capacities and possibilities of differenciation of living beings or bodies in flows coursing over the natural body. The model now distinguishes three domains, this time forming the whole reality of the natural body. These are the *virtual-real* and the *actual-real* as before, and also the *intensive-real* domain. The virtual-real is an open domain consisting of interactional flows of various intensities and qualities, tendencies and capacities of different entities (matter and energy) coursing over the virtual whole one natural body. The actual-real is the actualization of these intensities, qualities, capacities and tendencies via intensive ongoing interactional creative processes of differenciation in the intensive-real domain that produce actual living bodies, events and also states of living bodies (in both living species such as humans and non-living beings such as rivers, mountains and plants). What emerges in the actual from the intensive and the virtual domain is something new; it does not and cannot resemble what pre-existed it in the virtual.

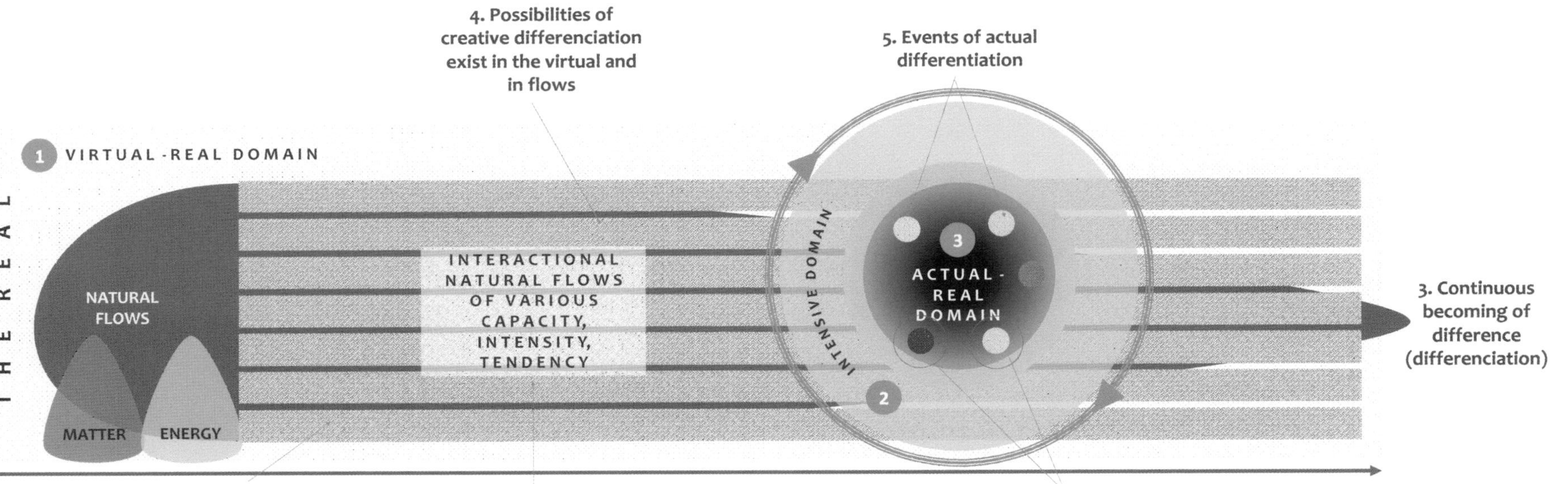

Figure 1.5: Base model of creative differenciation of the virtual natural body and of living bodies actualizing from internal tendencies and capacities in interactional flows of matter and energy. Note that in each of the five different coloured circles in the actual-real domain (3), a micro-version of the whole model exists too. Here, the actualized living bodies continue to interact with the same matter and energy flows having force of internal tendency and capacity to creatively differenciate and actualize the living body into new forms.

Having defined three domains of a virtual-real of heterogenous interactional flows of entities, capacities and tendencies, an intensive-real domain that differenciates and transitions matter and energy into an actual-real domain of actualized living bodies, I now apply the same concepts to the social body to explain how human lived experiences including those with health are similarly produced, differenciated and variously recur.

Desire in the social body

To begin to understand the production, differenciation, various stabilization and recurrence of lived experiences with health, disease and illness, we can now make three ontological leaps from the above analysis of natural flows, tendencies and capacities (now getting out of the flowing river so to speak.) First, we can identify that humans are both product and producer of ongoing creative differenciation by nature in virtual interactional flows of matter, energy, affect, capacity and tendency. Second, we can identify that the social body is part of the same virtual whole one body of being from which interactions with nature's *material (matter and energy) flows* of capacity and tendency creatively differenciate and actualize the natural realm of *living bodies* (including human species) and from which interactions with social flows of social, cultural, material and semiotic entities, capacity, tendency and affect creatively differenciate the social realm of *lived experience*. In this way, both nature and the social are inseparable. Nature is not external to our experience; it is in us. Our interactions with both natural and social (human) interactional flows that course and coalesce over a virtual one whole body differenciate (produce differences in) our actual lived experiences (including those with health). Third and finally, we can see also how flows that produce and differenciate lived experiences in the social body are generated from one original social force which itself interacts with original matter and energy flows of tendency and capacity in nature. After Deleuze and Guatarri (1972) (who label it just "desire"), I call this flow-generating original source in the social body, *social desire* and now describe it.

Social desire as the original source of flows of affect

Social desire defines the innate inclination, purpose and content of the virtual social body. It contains the idea of a positive, normative striving of human (homo ecosystemus) existence and experience that acts as a force of individual and collective being and becoming[16]. Like the pure originating spring of a river, social desire is the primary source of interactional flows bearing different entities, tendencies, capacities and affects that course over the social body. Modulated by tendencies of material forces of matter and energy in the natural body (and other tendential forces that I describe below), social desire defines the universal values, impulse and want of (most) humans to strive to be healthy, to continuously explore, to experiment and create their life, and to connect and interact with one another. As an intrinsic productive and positive power of human existence, thought and action, including health and wellbeing, social desire differs from the more typical meaning (and the rational liberal homo economicus conception) of desire as the "lack" of something (or somebody) and the desire to obtain it (or them); a calculated want, passion, pleasure or need for personal utility and material accumulation. In the language of affectees and affectors, social desire is a predominant non-human affector that flows through all lived experiences. Also, it is a circulating energy of force that binds affectees to affectors in cause-affect relations, not all of which are positive.

Used normatively and as a tool, the concept of social desire helps to distinguish and then trace different types of interactional flows forming lived experiences with health in individuals, societies, cultures, social groups, communities and places both historically and in the present. It provides a novel frame to reveal and explain how, where and why negative affects forming lived experiences with health arise and persist, positive affects are unequally distributed and where surplus affects of potential positive experience may be found and/or created. In foundation four, I identify the constituent elements of social desire and use them to define a model

[16] The concept of social desire is derived from the philosophical term *conatus* meaning "effort; endeavor; impulse, inclination, tendency; undertaking; striving" in Latin. Conatus was elaborated by Spinoza and Descartes in the Seventeenth century to denote the innate inclination of a thing to continue to exist and enhance itself.

of the most positive and negative qualities of affects differenciating lived experiences with health. I also define the production of social desire using a model of the immanent drivers of affective capacity. First, I distinguish the interactional flows that course over the social body and that via their interaction variously generate and differenciate social desire in actual lived experience.

Interactional flows in the social body

Altogether, I identify nine interactional flows that course over the "virtual social (desire) with natural body". Each interactional flow can be distinguished by the particular material, social, spatial and semiotic entities they contain, and the potential affects (sensations and capacities) they bear, all of which are moderated by forces of tendency. When interacted with, each may or may not generate affects and events to transition lived experience. The nine interactional flows are as follows.

Bodily interactional flows

Interactional flows of capacity, tendency and affect arising from biological and physicochemical interactions within and with entities of human bodies at molecular, cellular, genetic, organ, tissue or musculoskeletal levels including ingestion, digestion and (waste) outflow interactions of the body with natural and prepared foods, water and other liquids, drugs, alcohol and other substances. Bodily interactional flows also include genetic DNA flows that occur between humans and families arising from reproductive activities over generations. These flows are the primary subject of the clinical, medical and life sciences and the new "omics" technologies of systems biology and related disciplines.

Motor interactional flows

Interactional flows of capacity, tendency and affect arising from musculoskeletal movements and motor functions, situations, postures and relations of whole and parts of human bodies. These flows cover bodily movements, coping and functions such as sitting, crawling, balancing, standing, walking and running that tend to occur automatically and independently of any conscious awareness of the bodily movement, or of objects that are present within the movement and in the immediate environment (such as furniture, floor, terrain, obstacles and openings such as doors). Motor interactional flows also cover interactions with worn items of clothing and footwear in which the interaction is automatic and ideally unconscious unless there are problems. Despite their non-awareness, capacities and tendencies in motor interactional flows bear important affects that can produce and differenciate negative lived experiences with health, such as long-term back pain problems arising from prolonged sitting at work.

Material (artefactual) interactional flows

Interactional flows having capacity, tendency and affect arising from external-to-body cognitively aware and non-automatic human interactions with man-made objects and technologies such as consumer products, buildings and vehicles and increasingly with digital technologies and devices. I include data and algorithms in this material artefactual flow along with the platforms bearing them and the interfaces that mediate our digital experiences. Increasingly, digital interactions and data capture are hidden in both bodily and motor interactional flows, becoming automatic non-conscious interactions within lived experience such as the monitoring and tracking of vital signs, of our movements in places, and the recording of motor activities such as steps and standing frequencies.

Material (natural) interactional flows

Interactional flows bearing potential affects and capacities arising from human interactions with natural matter and energy having tendency and force to originate and differenciate lived experiences with health, and especially to produce environmental-linked affects forming disease and illness. These include interactional flows bearing different qualities, quantities and intensities in matter and energy of air, light, heat, water and radiation, along with their combination and fluctuation in local environments, habitats and places. This includes climate and its forces of differenciation of lived experience. These flows also include interactions with non-human living species and their ecologies in local ecosystems, whose balance and adaptive capacity are affected by and affect human capacities.

Social interactional flows

Interactional flows having differential capacity, tendency and affect arising from physical or virtual (online) interactions between individual persons, within and between groups, with, within and between organizations and within other social bodies such as social networks at different levels. These interactions include those with professional health and care affectors and also non-professional health affectors having often significant yet indirect impact on lived experiences with health and especially disease. Social interactional flows also include conscious bodily and motor interactions with other human beings such as during sexual activity, group activities and sports games. They include interactions with living animal species in leisure pursuits such as horse riding or when interacting with pets too. Social interactional flows often contain an established power relation and role dynamic that can condition tendencies in the creation and types of affects in an affectee by an affector.

Cultural interactional flows

Cultural interactional flows contain capacities, tendencies and affects forming lived experiences arising from individual and group norms and expectations, values, habits and routines of interaction with institutions and norms of gender, race, class, family, work, money and consumption, and in a health context, of the norms of a healthy lifestyle or the management of a disease. This is not to say that these norms are fixed structures; they too are dynamic, emerging and evolving in cultural interactional flows coursing over the virtual social (desire) with natural body. Whilst cultural interactional flows are complex, vast and certainly hard to frame and study, we can determine their influence and impact on affects forming and differenciating lived experiences for any focal lived experience with health context. For example, chronic pain has a varied cultural history of metaphors and meanings that have translated into different ideas, powers, priorities and practices of pain care over time. In its modern medicalized representation, chronic pain is usually expressed as an abstract object and bodily "thing" that is given a quantity based on its described intensity and also labelled with its locational origin. Today, there is little cultural conception and determination of chronic pain as whole embodied, interactional events of intensive transitions of affects mediated by affective capacity in interactional flows.

Spatial interactional flows

Spatial interactional flows contain capacities, tendencies and affects with the potential to produce and differenciate lived experiences arising from individual human and group presence and movements within particular physical and virtual spaces and also between spaces. They determine how physical spaces can generate positive or negative affects such as a sense of awe when looking up at the Empire State Building for the first time or a sense of fear or insecurity when walking along an empty, badly lit street in a known urban crime area. When looking at a place through the concept of spatial interactional flows bearing pre-individual affects, it is possible to obtain a sense of what that place is really like in its actual experience. Typically, representational devices such as videos, photos, tourist brands and texts mediate our sense of a place when we are not present in a place, such as when thinking about where to visit. But geographers and others are looking for other ways to understand place beyond such empiricist representational devices[17]. They argue this helps to acquire a deeper understanding of place and its actual experience, not just the current experience of a place,

[17] There is a field of non-representative geography that is concerned with the sense of place or space through the lens of affect theory. See Nigel Thrift (2007). Non-representational theory: Space, Politics, Affect (Routledge, London)

but how experiences originate, develop and persist, and sometimes deteriorate over time such as in disadvantaged communities or declining cities.

In their spatial sense, affects exist across and between people, objects and spaces and not within humans. They are pre-individual and exist outside of ourselves, just like the affects we encountered and actualized when jumping into the river. In the map of the Algarve region in Figure 1.6, produced for some post-Covid health experience work I undertook with local Portuguese research and tourist bodies, I depict a number of distinct, primary affects that may exist and may be experienced from interactions with spatial interactional flows in different parts of the region, varying from the wild, rugged Atlantic-facing beaches in the far west to the modern, built-up tourist destinations to the east of the region.

Places of spatial interactional flows may be wild, recreational, rural or urban environments, with the latter defined at different levels, whether neighbourhoods, public spaces, towns and cities. They may also be indoor places such as healthcare settings, homes, workplaces, places of worship, public buildings, shops and indoor entertainment facilities. Transcending artefactual and spatial interactional flows are online communities and networks that people increasingly interact with (especially during Covid-19 lockdown in advanced economies).

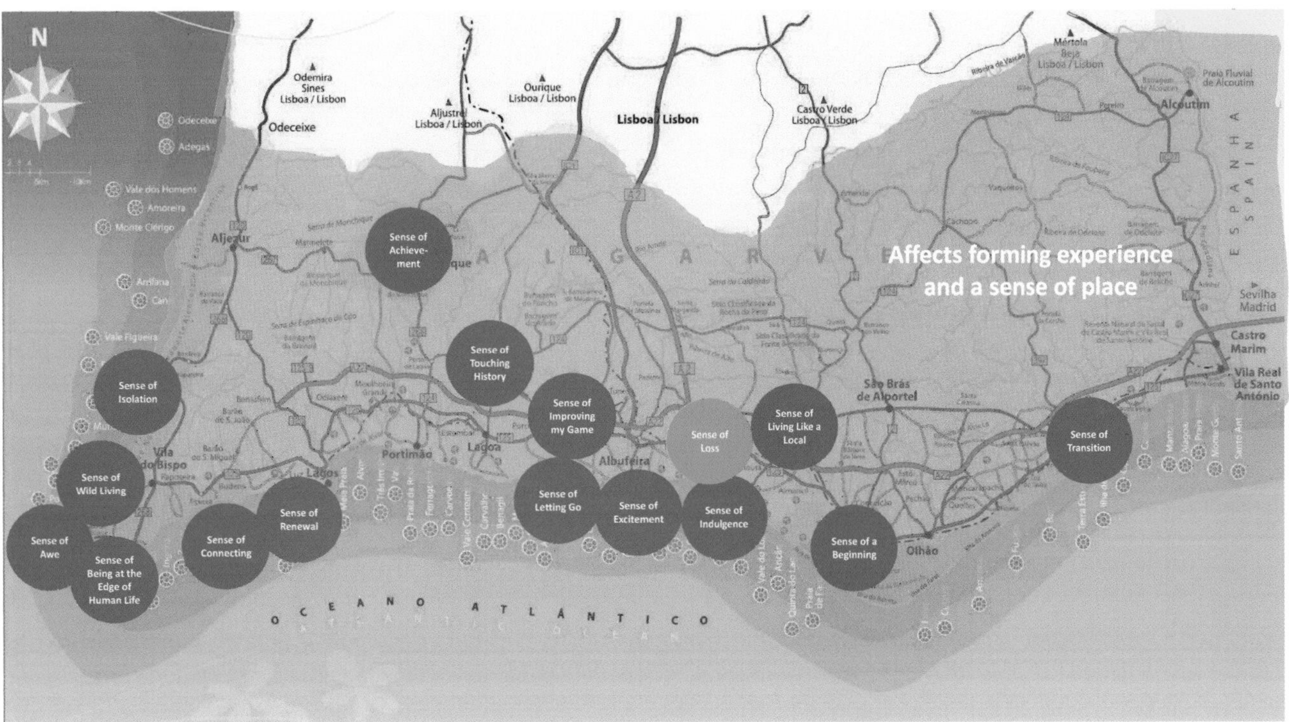

Figure 1.6: Simplified view of primary affects to be potentially found in spatial interactional flows in different parts of the Algarve tourist region (to represent the idea of potential affects being already present in the virtual social body and that are actualized from interaction in the flows)

Perceptual interactional flows

Perception in HEVD is defined as an intensive present encounter with an outside entity or entities in virtual interactional flows in relation to potential action. When we perceive entities in the different interactional flows, our cognitive memory of their value comes to us in the present moment. We create and perform an intrinsic valuation of an entity, a valuation that contains a tendency to inform a potential and type of action to undertake in the present. In this regard, perception is linked to embodied action itself within real duration, the lived experience of time of affectees. The past we hold is a realm of representation informed by cognition that comes to us in the present at the moment of encounter with an entity in an interactional flow.

Cognitive interactional flows

Finally, cognitive interactional flows contain capacities and tendencies producing lived experience arising from intuition, knowing and heuristic (e)valuation of interactions in all the other flows. Whilst prevailing models of cognition are based on a rational, individualist, behaviourist, intention-predetermines-action and information processing model (I discuss this *individual agency* view at length in chapter two), my model of whole lived experience (arising in the above interactional flows) emphasises intrinsic affects and their transitions as the generative creational mechanisms of lived experience and their differences. Here, active cognition as conscious reflective rationalistic knowledge-based option processing plays less of a role in human decision-making and behaviour than heuristics, intuition and perception-valuation-action in the immediate present enacted via homo ecosystemus in interactional flows. This view of the outside affective interactional nature of formation of lived experience contrasts with the prevailing view of the cognitivist neurosciences. Using an interior machine-based information processing model of the brain, cognitivism views the mind as detached from both the body and the environment in which it is situated, and therefore from a view of the dynamic interactions of all three in forming lived experiences. In my whole unified lived experience model formed of affects (sensations and capacities) located virtually in pre-interactional flows, I offer a framework for putting the three back together again, the absence of which has arguably stalled the reach and influence of the *enactive or embodied* cognitive sciences.

As well as interactional flows of affect, capacity and tendency which via homo ecosystemus interactions produce and differentiate lived experiences, I identify what I call *tendential forces*. They generate and also intersect with interactional flows to populate or (like the river) sediment them with their tendencies. Tendencies influence affectee encounters in interactional flows in everyday experiences. Also, they shape the habits, routines and actions of affectors that observe and act upon lived experiences (like the tendencies of cognitive scientists to use a computer metaphor for the brain or pain care professionals to use quantitative intensity scores as a discursive tool). I now introduce tendential forces.

Tendential forces in the social body

Producing tendencies of force, affect and affective capacity in the above interactional flows as well as their differenciation into events of lived experiences are *tendential forces*. They are also flows in the sense they have fluid properties of ongoing creation and emergence of tendency (as opposed to affect) yet are distinguished from interactional flows by their power to originate, attract, moderate, regulate, promote or otherwise influence the interactional flows in the social (desire) body. A dominant tendency can take hold of and direct the original force of social desire to generate and reproduce powerful interests in society, especially within political and economic systems (globalization and capitalism for example) as well as systems of knowledge creation such as the scientific method. In this regard, tendential forces constitute a complex machine acting upon and within the social body. They not only drive the fragmentation, access, inclusivity and differenciation of social desire in lived experience with health in different societies, groups and places but also condition and set the how and the "agreed-upon-rules" of the actions we *tend* to take to prevent, recover or modify those experiences whether personally or collectively, hence their tendential nature. Next, I explain each of the six tendential forces.[18]

---

18 The study of the influence and relation of each of these tendential forces on the production and differenciation of lived experiences with health would entail another book defining a unified ontology of health, society, markets and the state in relation to the social body of social desire, and that develops the framework of the flows and forces within it. Whilst I am able to offer generalized explanations of, for example, the role of capital with labour in appropriating our social desires for its own reproductive ends, I believe that these and many other influences of tendential forces are best examined in context to a focal lived experience with health context for a given place or geography. Doing so allows us to look practically at their differential influence in order to design positive interactional creational interventions, policies and programmes to modify the tendential forces and their influence in lived experience. Of course, this is what Health Ecosystem Value Design does. Template 4.0 in the framework helps to explore the influence of tendential forces within a focal lived experience with health context.

Ontological tendential forces

Ontology is a way of seeing reality. A particular ontology is a systematic school of thought or set of beliefs concerning the origins, observability, relations and knowability of the reality of the world in which we live and the kinds of phenomena it contains. To be understandable, useful and impactful, an ontology must be both internally coherent and consistent with our actual experience of the world. It must orient us toward a certain way of thinking about the phenomena we are studying and away from others. In this, any held ontology influences how we may or may not separate domains of reality such as society, nature, culture and the human body.

In Western countries, positivist or empirical realist ontology is the most influential philosophy in the health sciences and in related economic-based assessment of value in health. It continues to fundamentally shape how we perceive the reality of others' and also our own health and disease, and its (our) experience. It has important ramifications for the next tendential force concerning theory of knowledge, truth and belief and method, or epistemology. In chapter two, I contrast empirical realist with the interactional creation ontology of HEVD.

Epistemological tendential forces

Prevailing ontological tendencies evolve into epistemological tendencies concerning the truth, validity and types of knowledge created, distributed and used when interacting with interactional flows. Epistemological tendencies profoundly inform how we gather, share, assimilate and act upon knowledge. They influence how we research and learn, develop and deploy methods, and create and communicate information and measures. They also determine how we conceive of value and how we then organise and act to create it.

Key epistemological questions asked by HEVD for a focal lived experience with health context ("focal experience context") are:

- How is a focal experience context defined and what are its constituent elements? What are the different perspectives of affectees and affectors when defining the context and a related purpose? Then, how does that definition organise knowledge and learning for the context?
- Where is the boundary of the focal experience context set as the object of learning? Does the boundary stop at the individual human body or does it extend to the whole social body? Then for that boundary, what knowledge of health, disease and illness and its experience is deemed truthful and valuable to guide action? Who is trusted to produce this truthful knowledge? Who owns this knowledge and what power might it afford them?
- How do people living with a focal experience context (e.g., obesity, pain) acquire and apply knowledge about their own experience? How useful is this knowledge? In what circumstances might it not be useful and why?

Epistemological tendential forces influence our approach to and priorities for design and innovation in a focal experience context. These are the next tendential force.

Innovation tendential forces

Innovation tendential forces consist of current paradigms, powers, priorities and practices for making progress within a focal experience context. Influenced by norms and goals of improvement for a context (defined in the biopolitical tendential force see below), innovation tendencies determine the content and expression of design and development activity and the focus, form and function of new technologies and services, organizations, systems and models of care, public and personal health. They also influence who works on problems and the extent that different affectors and affectees collaborate to co-ordinate their innovation activity. Innovation tendential forces can undo, unblock and renew tendential forces in other tendential forces and within interactional flows, especially when they become stuck or sedimented, a status I describe below.

Capital with labour (and organizational) tendential forces

Capital with labour tendential forces are fundamental drivers of capacities and affects within interactional flows in both positive and negative directions. Flows of positive or negative tendential force arise from the acquisition and appropriation of subjective human labour by capital (forming capitalism) and its tendencies to produce and concentrate affects (of social desire) in lived working and consumption experience in individuals and groups, places and spaces in society, including those that are health-related. Akin to the virtual flows of forces that combine matter and energy with tendencies to differenciate and actualize organisms and living bodies in the natural body, *capital with labour* is made of two interacting tendencies that differenciate and actualize lived experiences with health. These are:

- Tendencies of pure, unallocated, undifferentiated *labour* in the form of the social desires of humans to work or to need to work in order to acquire positive social desires (in terms of social connection, progress, a sense of belonging, etc.)
- Tendencies of pure, unallocated, undifferentiated *capital* in the form of money or debt to acquire or purchase a portion of the social desires (creativity, attention, effort and energy) of humans in the form of their labour

By studying historical and present interactions and combinations of pure capital with labour tendencies, we can see how capitalism takes hold of and adapts the originating source of ideal social desire for its own ends. We can study how it (re)produces, reinforces and extends its reach into the following, for example:

- Work types, roles, routines and performances in the workplace
- Markets and modes of organising and relating including networks
- Practices and technologies of material (natural resources, products), intangible (data, knowledge, information, services) and financial (money, debt, credit and wealth) resource extraction, production, trade, distribution and use
- Habits and patterns of consumption of products, technologies and services
- Consumer- and market-based incentives (involving money) to motivate desired human behaviour for example those defined by culturally constructed ideas of good health and body image
- Hierarchies of roles and relations in society and the practices of habits and routines within them
- Economic and especially neoclassical marginal utility and exchange-based perspectives on value

We can then study the production and differenciation of affects forming lived experiences with health arising from strong capital-with-labour tendencies in interactional flows, such as the negative affects arising from metabolic disruption driven by work, from excess consumption, from ideas of "the health consumer", from injustice and inequality, from status envy, labour exploitation, natural resource depletion and pollution, work stress and presenteeism.

Biopolitical tendential forces

Biopolitical tendential forces contains tendencies of thought, ideas, belief and influence concerning the role of the state, public sector bodies, industry and increasingly digitally networked technologies in promoting, intervening, quantifying, monitoring and regulating lives and health for political, governance, economic, market and other related purposes. For a focal lived experience with health context, HEVD asks the following questions pertaining to biopolitical tendential forces[19]:

---

19 These questions cover the main current themes of biopolitics. For a short yet useful history of biopolitics see Thomas Lemke (2011) *Biopolitics*. NYU Press.

- To what extent does the focal experience context attract attention from politics, science and industry in relation to other contexts and why does this attention differ? How does this degree of attention translate into funding, priorities and practices and profit-seeking potential? Is the attention driven by a certain ideology, by funding availability and/or by certain models of value and if so, how? How does a conception of value inform attention, perception, investment and policies for the focal experience context?
- What is the current political and policy debate, if any, for the focal experience context? How might the nature of the debate change?
- Who has current authority and motivates awareness, learning and action for the focal experience context? Does this lie with science and scientists, with politicians, with industry, with charity groups, with sufferers or in some cultures and contexts with religious or spiritual leaders? How is this authority changing?
- What is the emphasis on individual versus state responsibility for the focal experience context and how is this emphasis changing in relation to a) changes in political ideologies and state motives (e.g., a more liberal government promoting policies of individual responsibility for health and a greater role for private enterprise), b) changes in science and innovation (e.g., scientific breakthroughs, use of personal digital technologies) and c) ethics of self-management?
- Which groups are perceived and maybe treated differently to other groups within the current ideology, value conception and emphasis in policy and practice for the focal experience context? What categories of persons tend to be excluded, denied access or are the subject of bias within the current policy frame and why?
- What is the influence of an information processing model of the body (driven by cognitivist science) and new forms of bodily surveillance and related data on the role and responsibility of individual persons in managing their experience? How do people use digital technologies to work differently on their health, illness or disease, who is influencing these emergent practices and with what legitimacy and ethical permissions?
- Finally, relevant to some focal lived experience with health contexts, what is the reach, status and likely impact of reproductive, genetic and other bodily manipulative and corrective technologies and the ethics of their use in relation to their value to the individual, the private sector and the state?

Regulatory tendential forces

Finally, regulatory tendential forces have two types of influence on interactional flows for any focal lived experience with health context. These are:

1) Direct regulation of human interactions in interactional flows in the form of statutory laws, safety, ethics and other standards of professional health organizations and individual practices, whether public or private and ranging from scientific research through to front-line care and also including self-management
2) Indirect regulatory coding of norms of a focal experience context via language, measures, signs and other inscriptions that tacitly orchestrate, structure and shape collective and even universal ideas, representation, standards, understanding and action for the focal experience context

Next, I describe the effects of tendencies in interactional flows.

The rheological properties of interactional flows

In any interactional flow of entities, capacities and affects in lived experiences modulated by tendential forces, some flows may offer little capacity to create new affects; they are akin to a non-interactive encountering with an immoveable stuck force. Other flows may afford greater capacity and therefore, higher interactional creative potential. Like mass natural flows of solids and liquids (e.g., a mud slide, lava), interactional flows have *rheological properties* meaning their potential for creational capacity of potential and surplus affects is determined by the relative mix of their solid and fluid properties of tendency. Over time, interactional flows coursing over the social body become more sedimented by rigid tendencies and therefore can limit capacities for creation of novel affects in lived experience (I conceptualise this in Figure 1.7).

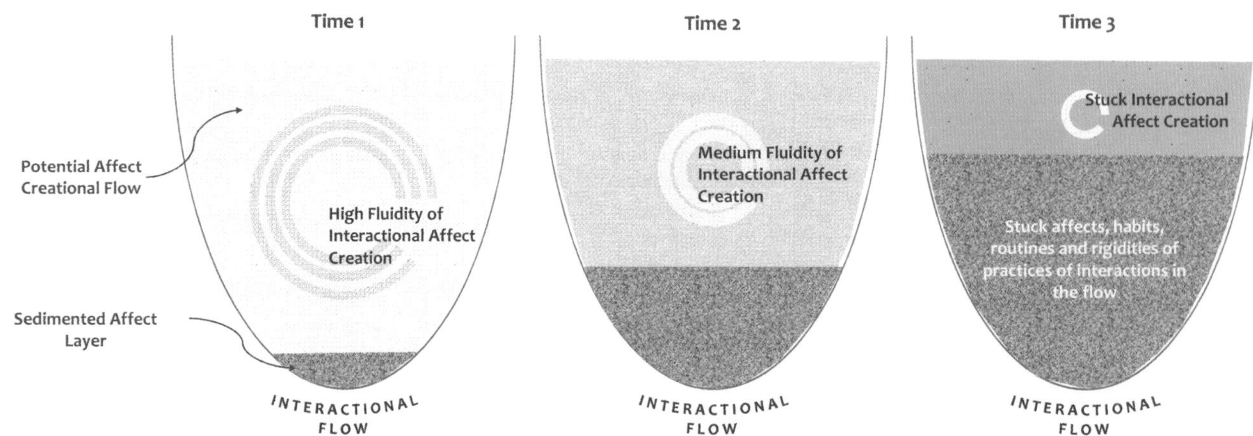

Figure 1.7: The sedimentation of interactional flows by tendential forces over time

When flows become sedimented in this way, they are characterized by stuck practices, limiting habits and routines, irrelevant or incorrect ideas, outmoded institutions and redundant or harmful technologies. They slow down and limit capacities for creation of novel affects. Then, potential positive affects become fewer, less diverse, more negative and stuck and affective capacities become restricted. This hardening of interactional flows and the accompanying limitation of capacities for creation of potential surplus positive affect explains how health inequalities and inequities can concentrate in distinct social groups (e.g., ethnic minority groups such as Native American or First Nation communities) as well as places (e.g., poor inner-city neighbourhoods); there is a social as well as spatial patterning of stuck sedimented interactional flows due to persistent pervasive forces of the same tendencies.

The sequence of interactional flows and tendential forces

Figure 1.8 depicts the nine interactional flows along with the six tendential forces that intersect with them. Note how the sequence of the tendential forces in Figure 1.7 follows a logic of cascading tendential influences across each tendential force category. This sequence is described in the caption below the figure. Similarly, the sequence of interactional flows also follows a certain logic and is described in the caption too.

In Table 1.2, I provide examples of interactional flows and categories of tendential forces from the 2020 chronic pain study. Also, I allocate the interactional flows to the four affective domains in the whole unified model of lived experience elaborated in Figure 1.4.

Next, I complete foundation three by stating the six principles of interactional flows and tendential forces differenciating lived experiences with health in the social body.

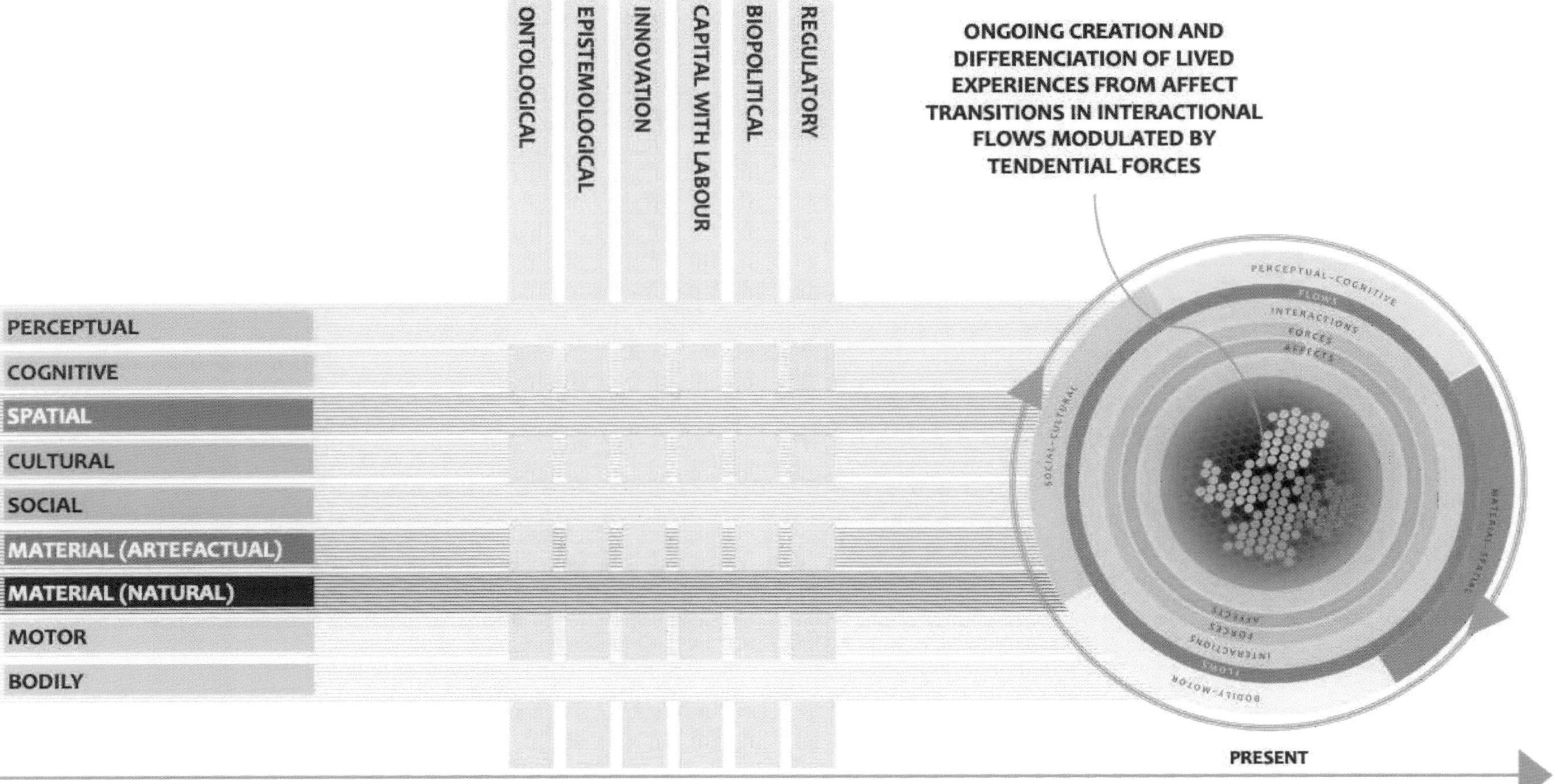

Figure 1.8: Model of six tendential forces intersecting with the nine interactional flows in the production and differenciation of lived experiences in the whole unified model on the plane of composition in lived journeys of experiencers. The nine interactional flows are ordered in sequence to their relative intensification and actualization in lived experience. The bodily flows are closest to the "base" plane of the virtual natural with social body, perceptual flows interact with the eight flows beneath them. In the tendential forces, ontological tendential forces influence epistemological tendencies that in turn influence innovation tendencies. Innovation tendencies influence how capital appropriates labour (or discards it in favour of technology) which influences a certain biopolitical orientation towards and intervention in health, life and the body by the state, industry, science and technology, which in turn is overseen by direct or indirect regulatory tendential forces. Tendencies in all six forces produce certain affectee and affector ideologies, powers, priorities and practices for a focal context in question. Step 4.0 of the framework supports exploration and reflection of the tendencies in the six tendential forces for a focal experience context.

Table 1.2 – Table of interactional flows and tendential forces used in the chronic pain study and with interactional flows allocated to the four affective domains

INTERACTIONAL FLOWS TENDENTIAL FORCES	AFFECTIVE DOMAIN FORMING WHOLE LIVED EXPERIENCE WITH HEALTH			
	BODILY-MOTOR	**PERCEPTUAL-COGNITIVE**	**MATERIAL-SPATIAL**	**SOCIAL-CULTURAL**
BODILY	Origins of chronic pain; Mechanisms of pain	Self-assessment; Self-treatment; Self-monitoring		
MOTOR	Bodily movement with pain		Pain when travelling	
SOCIAL (HUMAN)	Pain assessment and diagnosis; Pain treatment; Pain monitoring			1:1, family, neighbour, friend, peer, social group, professional interactions;
CULTURAL	Sex and pain; Diet and pain	Cultural meaning of pain		Gender roles and pain; family roles and pain; work and pain
MATERIAL (MATTER AND ENERGY)	Genetics and pain. Weather and pain		Natural environments and pain	
ARTEFACTUAL	Consumer products; Digital technologies; Pain medication			
SPATIAL	Pain in space, e.g., risk, level, terrain, obstacles, distance,		Pain when out and about; Pain in the home; Pain in public spaces	
PERCEPTUAL	Perception of a body with pain Perception of motor capacity	Self-perception of pain Intuition and pain	Perception of medication use	Perception of others with / without pain
COGNITIVE	Knowing the body and its pain(s)	Pain knowledge types and intelligence	Managing pain medications Managing consumption	
ONTOLOGICAL	Modes of perceiving individual pain and its lived experience (affectors); perceiving the pain experience ecosystem (affectors)			
EPISTEMOLOGICAL	Knowing pain and its experience (affectors); pain research (clinical, academic), social determinants of pain and use			
INNOVATION	Pain innovation (science, technology, practice) and priorities; digital pain technologies			
CAPITAL WITH LABOUR	Economic policies for persons with pain disabilities; employers, work and working persons with pain. consumption and pain; organization of pain care and practices in relation to other conditions			
BIOPOLITICAL	Value of chronic pain intervention (cost and impact); value of a life with pain (priorities); healthcare policy; social care policy; transport market and policy; housing market and policy			
REGULATORY	Pain language, scales, symbols and norms; Ethics of pain intervention; standards and guidelines of pain care practice; pain causation and law (e.g., workplace pain, employer responsibility)			

The six principles of interactional flows and tendential forces producing and differenciating lived experiences in the social body

Just as I defined for the natural body on page 39, the same six principles of flows, tendencies and capacities are present, and "at work" in the social (desire) body. In the descriptions below, I adapt the wording of the six principles I used for the natural body.

Forces of differenciation exist in the virtual whole social body

First, like the vital force of matter and energy in the natural body, social desire is a creational force that originates interactional flows of pre-individual affect and capacity and generates tendential forces that course and coalesce over the social body.

Flows have affects, capacities modulated by tendencies

Second, potential affects and capacities within interactional flows of diverse entities modulated by tendential forces continuously differenciate lived experiences with health that are different in kind from other lived experiences with health. Affects and affective capacities are the generative material that determines these differences in kind over a real duration of lived experience of homo ecosystemus. A focal lived experience with health context is different in kind from other lived experiences.

Continuous becoming of difference

Third, individual lived experiences with health continue to diverge and differenciate or "become different" from interactions with social, semiotic, bodily, material and other entities and mechanisms in interactional flows bearing pre-individual affects, capacities and tendential forces, all of which are influenced by the ongoing impulse or "machine" of social desire.

Possibilities of creative differenciation already exist in in interactional flows in the virtual realm

Fourth, such immanent tendencies, capacities and affects can be viewed as *possibilities* in the sense that any interactional flow *already* contains tendencies of future differenciations *of lived experience and of itself*. In other words, future possibilities of lived experience pre-exist in the tendencies of an interactional flow (like a river forming a meander) to differenciate itself in certain directions; the entities bearing affects, capacities and tendencies contained in the flow hold a possibility of further creative differenciation that has not yet been actualized yet does already exist. In this sense, possibilities for creating better health do not only occur in the actualization of lived experience, but already exist in the tendencies and capacities of an interactional flow to produce difference. This view of possibility as already existing in interactional flows affords a more optimistic view of the potential for novel creation of any lived experience.

Events of actual differentiation

When a difference in a lived experience (transition in one or more affects) comes about from interaction with an interactional flow by a human person (homo ecosystemus), then this becoming of an experience state can be described as an event. An event is an intensive transition in a lived experience; it marks the actualization of the creation of a difference.

Intensive not extensive generalisable differences define our world

Finally, we can describe lived experiences with health, disease and illness not by differences in how they appear to us (a universally held representation of their external identity of properties) but by the nature and tendencies of entities, potential affects and affective capacities that compose, originate, create and differenciate them. For example, we can deepen our understanding of the lived experience of chronic pain (usually limited to understanding of affects in the bodily-motor and perceptual-cognitive affective domains) with reference to affectee interactional flows in the other affective domains (social-cultural, material-spatial) and the six tendential forces that act on and within them all – ontological, epistemological, innovation, capital with labour, biopolitical and regulatory. Using these concepts, we can examine different lived experiences with pain on the basis of the different intensive tendencies, potential affects and capacities in these flows, such as the degree they trap people in a certain experience state or afford possibilities to change their experience. Doing so provides a more whole and unified understanding of individual and also collective lived experiences of a focal lived experience with health context.

In Figure 1.9, I update Figure 1.5 to include the concepts of social desire, interactional flows and tendential forces coursing over and coalescing in the social (desire) body and with the natural body. Note that the model now distinguishes four (numbered) domains or registers of reality. As well as the virtual-real, actual-real and intensive-real domains, I add an empirical-real domain. Briefly, I describe and distinguish each.

Virtual-real domain: The pre-individual, pre-experience virtual-yet-real domain of interactional flows of different entities and tendential forces bearing affects, capacities and tendencies.

Intensive-real domain: The domain of enactment, transition and creation of affects forming experience via interaction with interactional flows of force, tendency and affect located in the virtual domain and which emanate from primary flows of matter, energy and social desire in the whole unified virtual body. The movements and transitions of affects in the intensive domain are events.

Actual-real domain: The domain of actual lived experiences that exist, arise and occur from creational interactions within interactional flows and tendential forces in the social body and the natural body and which move or transition over a plane of composition in real duration of lived experiences of affectees.

Empirical-real domain: The domain of experiences that are sensed, observed and inscribed empirically and objectively by humans. In the health, life and social sciences, the empirical domain is made up of our experienced knowledge of health and disease experience states, observed events, (inter)actions and conjunctions. It is empirical in that the phenomena of interest have been or are capable of being observed, coded, understood and explained. Often, they have been quantified, coded, categorized and organized into (e.g., disease) representative taxonomies and sub-level bodies of knowledge to guide learning and action.

Summary

To recap, foundation three states that affects forming lived experiences with health are actualized from affectee and affector capacities for affecting and being affected in interactions with individual and combinations of interactional flows and tendential forces that course over a virtual social with natural body and which bear various capacities, degrees, intensities, forces and rates of creative affect realization.

Foundation Three
Affects forming experience are actualized from affectee and affector capacities for affecting and being affected in interactions with individual and combinations of interactional flows and tendential forces that course over a virtual social with natural body and which bear capacities, degrees, intensities and rates of creative affect realization

So far, I have defined the foundations of an interactional model of whole lived experience with health (foundation one), identified the generative elements of affects and affective capacities forming experience (two) and introduced the concepts of interactional flows and tendential forces that when interacted with, intensify and differenciate actual lived experience (three). Next, I introduce the differencing parameters of *quality* into lived experiences with health through further explanation of the normative concept of social desire and by exposing the immanent mechanisms defining and driving affective capacity itself.

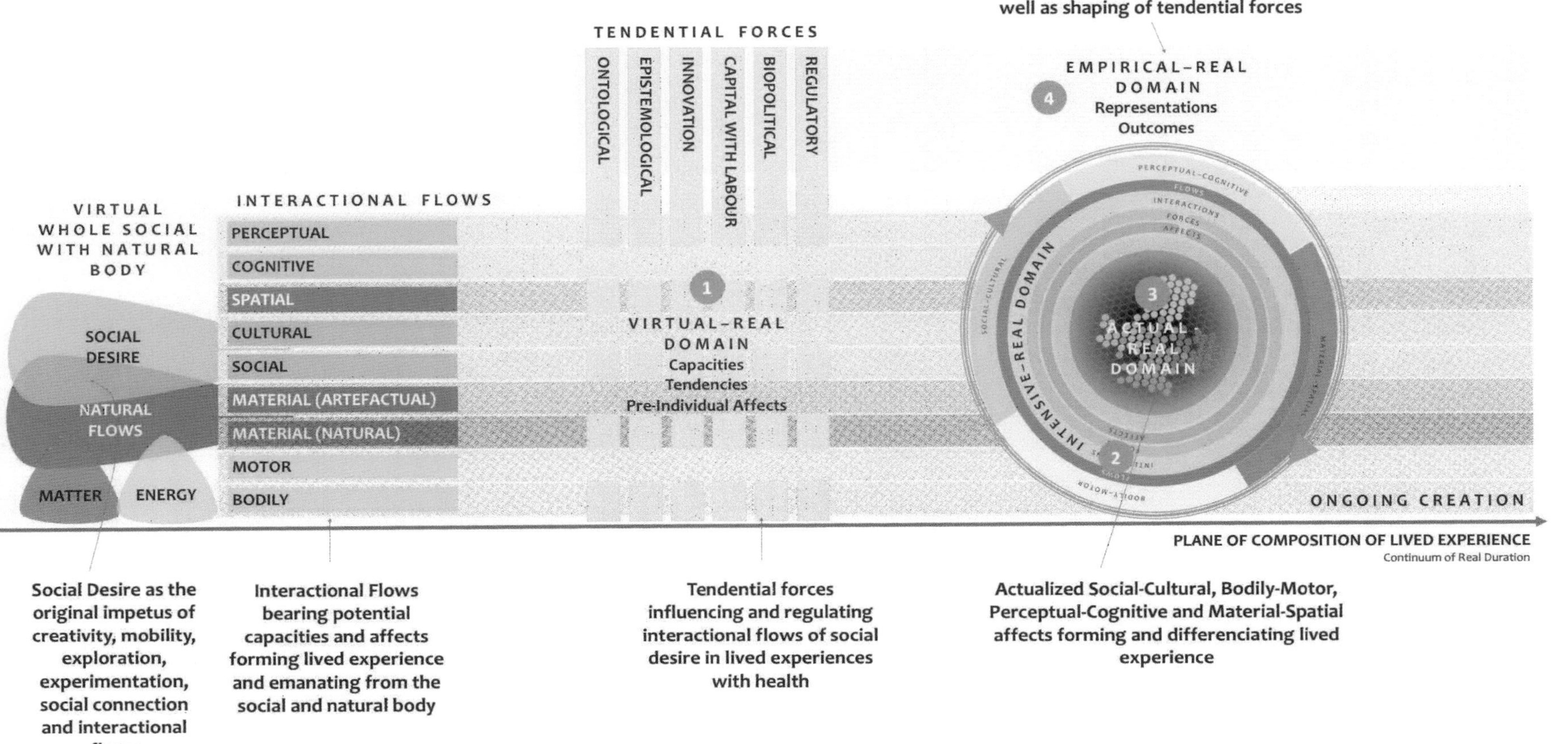

Figure 1.9: Model of creative differenciation and actualization of lived experiences with health in the natural and social body from interactional flows and tendential forces and showing four domains or registers of reality (virtual-real, intensive-real, actual-real, empirical-real) and their four-step sequence of movement from the virtual to the empirical-real. Note the model is open-ended; there is ongoing creative differenciation of the virtual. Actual events and experiences return to the virtual-real register (blue circled 1) either directly from their sensing or from the ontological and epistemological tendencies arising from their empirical representation and translation.

Foundation Four | How can we see differences in actual lived experience within the same context of lived experience with health?

To deploy social desire as a conceptual tool to understand lived experiences with health, their production and differenciation, first we must know the most ideal or positive qualities that constitute this vital original force in the social body. To do so, I restate *as social desires* Martha Nussbaum's ten Central Capabilities[20] that together define the most positive, dignified and flourishing state of human living, being or existence. Briefly, these are as follows:

- **Desire for a full life duration** – the desire for physical survival and to live to the end of a normal human life, not dying prematurely or to have one's quality of life reduced to the extent that life is not worth living
- **Desire for bodily vitality** – the desire to have and enjoy good health including reproductive health, to be adequately nourished with access to a variety of healthy foods and to have adequate, safe and secure shelter
- **Desire for bodily integrity** – the desire to be able to move freely from place to place, to be secure against physical or sexual violence or abuse, to have opportunities for sexual freedom and satisfaction and to have ethical and moral choice in matters of reproduction
- **Desire for experiencing, creativity and learning** – the desire to imagine, explore, think and reason in a human (not machine-like) way that is informed and cultivated by an adequate education and that allows a desire to experience, create and produce ideas, thoughts, works and events of one's own choice and interest, and that are guaranteed by political, religious, spiritual and artistic freedom of expression and exercise of mind, and without non-beneficial pain
- **Desire for emotional attachment** – the desire to form and have attachments to things, places, spaces and persons outside ourselves; to love those who love and care for us, to grieve, to experience longing, gratitude and justified anger and to develop emotions free of fear and anxiety in relationships with others
- **Desire for practical reason** – the desire to conceive of the good, to engage in critical reflection of one's experiences and to plan and conceive of purpose and to change one's own lived experiences in the future
- **Desire for social connection and engagement** – the desire to live for, with and towards others, to recognise and show concern and empathy for others, to form social connections and interactions and to be treated by others with dignity, respect and without discrimination or prejudice.
- **Desire for connection and engagement with nature** – the desire to live and act with concern for nature and to form a mutually beneficial connection with non-human species and the natural environment
- **Desire for play and fun**– the desire to laugh, have fun and enjoy recreational, sports and leisure activities
- **Desire for equal recognized participation and free rights (freedom)** – the desire to have freedom over one's environment, including political freedom and freedom of expression of political ideas and self, to hold property and rights to material goods on an equal basis, and to access and have work on an equal basis and recognition with other workers without exploitation, discrimination, bias or injustice.

In foundation two, I introduced the concept of affective capacity as the power of acting and creation in lived experience. Adding the concepts of social desire, interactional flows and tendencies, we see that affective

---

[20] Martha Nussbaum (2000) Creating Capabilities: The Human Capability Development Approach. Belknap Harvard University Press

capacity defines the human potential to strive towards, realise and preserve one, many or ideally all of the ten elements of social desire from interactions in interactional flows and tendential forces within the virtual natural with social body. Applying the concept, we can see that people, families, social groups, communities and places or geographies (which are all the possible types and levels of affectees that can be chosen for the study of any focal lived experience with health context) have varying affective capacities affording different potentials to realise social desire; some affectees have more potential affective capacity and therefore greater powers of interactional creation of positive qualities of social desire, whereas others have little. A lack of or suppressed affective capacity can lead to the development and recurrence of disease and illness amongst affectees due to diminished powers of acting on illness- and disease-generating or -bearing entities in interactional flows, such as pain affects in motor interactional flows, stress or abuse affects in social flows, inequality, bias and discrimination affects in cultural flows and respiratory bodily affects in material (natural) flows of polluted air. These affects serve to disable affective capacities and reinforce existing disease experience states by suppressing levels of creative energy and potential action.

The immanent capacities of affective capacity

We can look deeper into affective capacity to identify three immanent types of capacities that combine and interact to form an overall affectee capacity for creation and realization of social desire. These are interactional, creational and valuational capacities. Figure 1.10 depicts them rotating around and interacting with the ten elements forming social desire and below, I briefly define them.

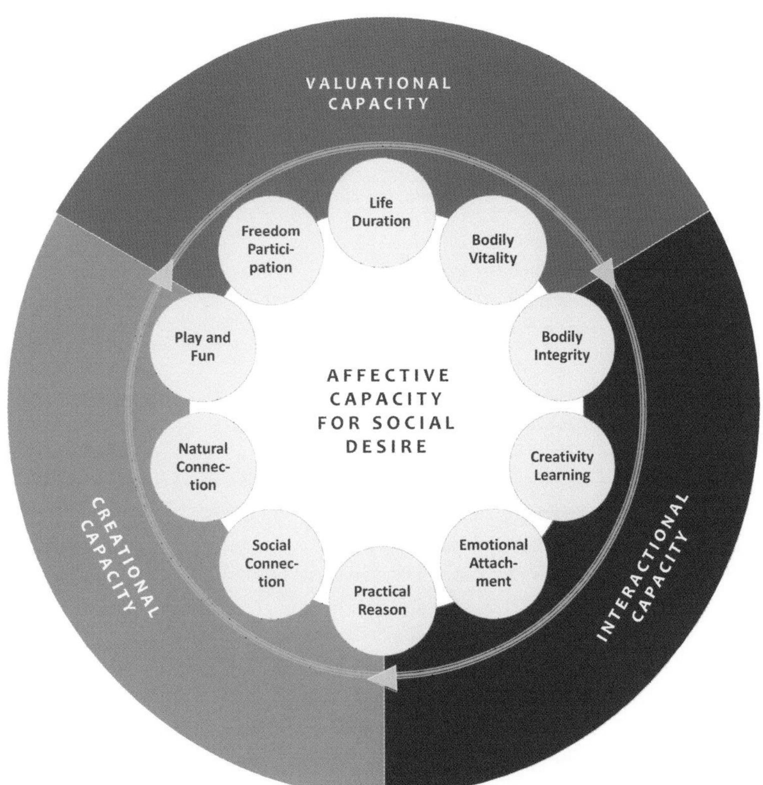

Figure 1.10 - The immanent capacities of affective capacity of social desire

Interactional capacity

Interactional capacity is the potential capacity of affectees to access, enter into, engage in and sustain interactions and relations in interactional flows with affectors (both humans and non-human entities) and other affectees in order to generate positive affects forming a potential of social desire. It is also the potential capacity to avoid or leave an undesirable or no longer useful interactional flow.

Creational capacity

Creational capacity is the sensing, thinking and knowing capacity of affectees to see, envision, imagine, discover, ideate, invent, experiment and create novel affects in interactional flows with the potential to realise elements of social desire. It determines the capacities and motive of affectees to pursue and realise change, growth, development and novelty in their lived experience by bringing pressure to bear against tendencies. For sick and/or oppressed affectees, as well as the creative power to act on and in interactional flows, creational capacity is the power to perceive and question representations by others of their experience, surface tendencies of affector powers in flows, escape tendencies of action or non-action and then challenge those powers via acquiring new powers of acting in affective capacities. Creational capacities for many disadvantaged affectees (whether individuals, communities or ethnic, gender, sexuality and other social groups) can often be structurally inhibited by negative stuck affects such as a diminished sense of belief, purpose, hope and possibility that may be multiplied by tendential forces such as bias, exclusion and injustice.

Valuational capacity

Valuational capacity is the capacity of affectees to identify, assess, value, reflect, store and recall valued and unvalued affects in interactional flows in their lived experience. It is the potential perceptual affective capacity to deploy a valuational intuition and instinct of situations and tendencies, and to discern and anticipate potential affects (including those having risk to health) in interactional flows. It is also a cognitive capacity to express and represent actual events of experiencing and experienced affects to others. In Table 1.3, I list specific capacities with some examples within each of the three immanent capacities of affective capacity.

Table 1.3 – Individual capacities in each immanent capacity of affective capacity

Interactional capacity to ...	Creational capacity to ...	Valuational capacity to ...
• Access an interactional flow e.g., access care • Enter an interactional flow • Interact in an interactional flow • Sustain an interactional flow • Leave an interactional flow, e.g., domestic abuse • Avoid interactional flows e.g., with Covid-19 • Share affects within interactional flows • Share creations within interactional flows • Share events within interactional flows • Share valuations within interactional flows • Share experience within interactional flows	• Discover desired interactional flows of affect • Create desired interactional flows of affect • Experiment in interactional flows • Combine interactional flows • Have incongruous perceptions • Have ideas and freedom to express them • Be able to be different from others • Express different opinions without risk, embarrassment or exclusion • Prevent, modify and remove unwanted affects • Create, repeat desired affects • Cope with negative affects • Modify and repel tendencies • Control, direct and retain belief • Release creative energies • Retain creational capacity	• Have intuition of a current situation • Assess tendencies in interactional flows • Self-reflect on actions and thoughts • Determine the worth of an action • Relate interactional and creational capacities • Sense and anticipate potential events • Assess past and present events of experience • Assess potential and actual impact of interaction • Make ethical judgments • Make moral judgments • Make comparative judgments • Value risk and risk-based judgments • Be aware of options • Value entities and affects • Value interactions • Use valuation entities and practices • Retain sense and memory of value

Affective capacities for the creation of one or more of the ten dimensions of social desire can be linked to particular interactional flows. For example, in the material (natural) interactional flow, affective capacity supports creation of affects of social desire related to connection with nature. In social interactional flows, affective capacity supports creation of social connection and engagement. In Table 1.4. I identify 41 sources of affective capacity within the nine interactional flows in the virtual-real domain. In the table, each flow is mapped to the ten elements of social desire. Each contains a certain type of potential affects forming social desire.

Poles of qualities of lived experience and social desire

With the immanent creational, interactional and valuational mechanisms of affective capacities revealed, we can now see how and why actual lived experiences with health divert from ideal social desire and to what extent. With an understanding of divergence from the ideal of positive social desire revealed, we can then distinguish which interactional flows and tendential forces are - via their interaction - producing negative affects and capacities in actual lived experience within a normative framing of ideal social desire.

Furthermore, for any focal lived experience with health context, disease or illness, we can identify extremes of positive and negative qualities and affective capacities of social desire for that context. I define these extremes as poles, as follows:

- **An ill-health experience pole** that defines the worst affect quality and affective capacity. Here, there is a stuck flow and low capacity to act arising from disagreement in relations and interactions with other entities and bodies in interactional flows, an experience of dis-ease and "stuckness" that diminishes the power or capacity of acting and creating in lived experience.
- **A desired (valued) experience pole** that contains the most desired affects and affective capacity. Here there is an intensity of affect creation arising from agreement and fluidity in relations and interactions with other persons, entities ("other bodies"), an intensity of lived experience that generates and augments a power or capacity of acting, interacting and creating.

In Figure 1.11, I depict the two poles together with brief descriptions of the opposing qualities of affects and affective capacities characterising each.

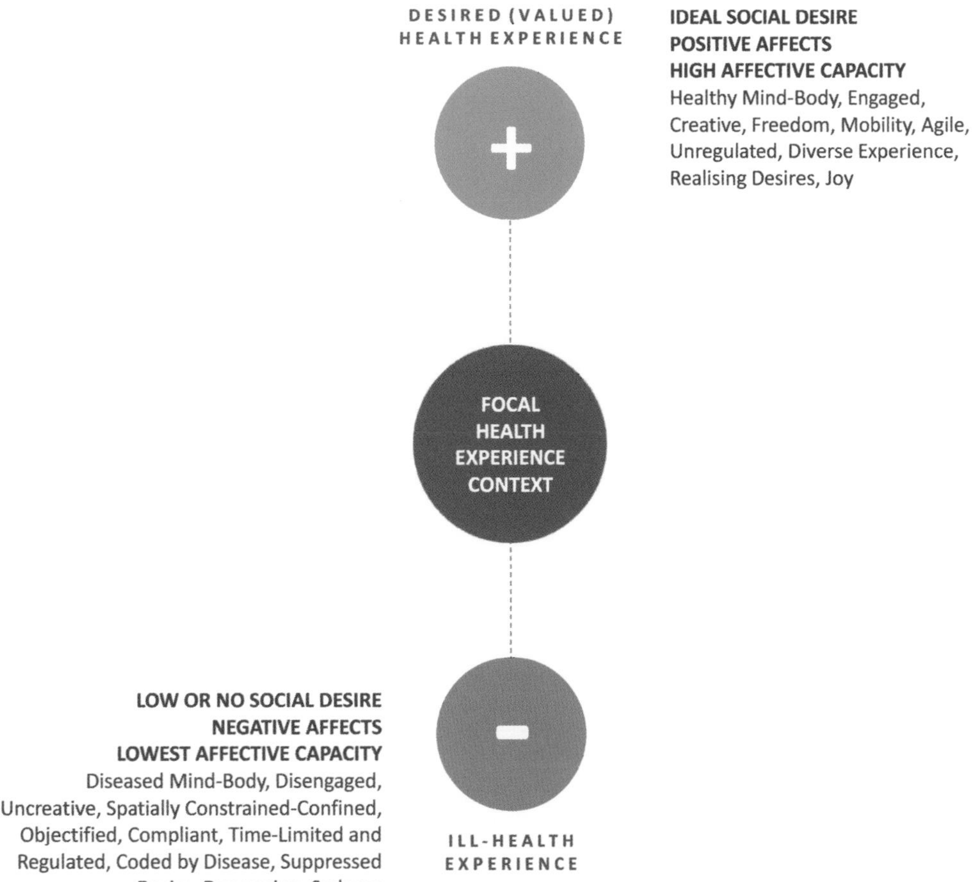

Figure 1.11: Poles of affect and capacity for any focal health experience context

Table 1.4 – The ten elements of social desire linked to interactional flows as the source of health in the virtual-real forming lived experience

INTERACTIONAL FLOW IN THE SOCIAL WITH NATURAL BODY	AFFECTIVE DOMAIN	TEN ELEMENTS OF SOCIAL DESIRE IN LIVED EXPERIENCE WITH HEALTH									
		1 LIFE DURATION	2 BODILY VITALITY	3 BODILY INTEGRITY	4 CREATIVITY LEARNING	5 EMOTIONAL ATTACHMENT	6 PRACTICAL REASON	7 SOCIAL CONNECTION	8 NATURAL CONNECTION	9 PLAY FUN	10 FREEDOM PARTICI-PATION
BODILY	B-M	●	●	●						●	
MOTOR		●	●	●						●	
SOCIAL (HUMAN)	S-C	●		●	●	●	●	●		●	●
CULTURAL				●	●	●	●	●		●	●
MATERIAL (MATTER-ENERGY)	M-S	●	●						●		
MATERIAL (ARTEFACTUAL)		●	●								●
SPATIAL			●	●		●		●	●		●
PERCEPTUAL	P-C	●	●	●	●	●	●	●	●	●	●
COGNITIVE		●	●	●	●		●			●	●

1. **Desire for a full life duration** - the desire for physical survival and to live to the end of a normal human life, not dying prematurely or to have one's quality of life reduced to the extent that life is not worth living
2. **Desire for bodily vitality** - the desire to have and enjoy good health including reproductive health, to be adequately nourished with access to a variety of healthy foods and to have adequate, safe and secure shelter
3. **Desire for bodily integrity** - the desire to be move freely from place to place, to be secure against physical or sexual violence or abuse, to have opportunities for sexual freedom and satisfaction and to have choice in matters of reproduction
4. **Desire for experiencing, creativity and learning** - the desire to imagine, explore, think and reason in a human (not machine-like) way that is informed and cultivated by an adequate education and that allows a desire to experience, create and produce ideas, thoughts, works and events of one's own choice and interest, guaranteed by political, religious, spiritual and artistic freedom of expression and exercise of mind without non-beneficial pain
5. **Desire for emotional attachment** - the desire to form and have attachments to things, places, spaces and persons outside ourselves; to love those who love and care for us, to grieve, to experience longing, gratitude and justified anger and to develop emotions free of fear and anxiety in relationships with others
6. **Desire for practical reason** - the desire to conceive of the good, to engage in critical reflection of one's experiences and to plan and conceive of purpose and to change one's own lived experiences in the future
7. **Desire for social connection and engagement** - the desire to live for, with and towards others, to recognise and show concern and empathy for others, to form social connections and interactions and to be treated by others with dignity and without discrimination.
8. **Desire for connection and engagement with nature** - the desire to live and act with concern for nature and to form a mutually beneficial connection with non-human species and the natural environment
9. **Desire for play and fun**- the desire to laugh, have fun and enjoy recreational, sports and leisure activities
10. **Desire for equal recognized participation and free rights (freedom)** - the desire to have freedom over one's environment, including political freedom and freedom of expression of political ideas and self, to hold property and rights to material goods on an equal basis, and to access and have work on an equal basis and recognition with other workers without exploitation, bias or injustice.

Consider again lived experience with chronic pain. For persons living with chronic pain (defined as pain lasting longer than three months and typically much longer), some are able to achieve a degree of sustained freedom from pain and to live well. They have a more positive lived experience despite their ongoing pain. Others however become severely debilitated and isolated by their pain. Their capacity to affect their pain is limited. We can visually represent these contrasting affect qualities and capacities. Figure 1.12 depicts the negative ill-health lived experience of someone who is limited and controlled by their pain. They have a debilitating, chaotic and socially isolating pain experience, characterised by affects of (amongst others) episodes of unpredictable undiagnosed intensive pain (in the bodily-motor affective domain), poor sleep and increased fatigue, low energy, a reduced capacity to plan ahead, to work and to socialise and a loss of a sense of purpose. For this person, external forces are strongly negative, lived experienced time (real duration) has slowed down and their affects forming experience are stuck, intense and confined (shown conceptually in the centre of the model). The person has become over-coded by their pain and their affective capacity is poor.

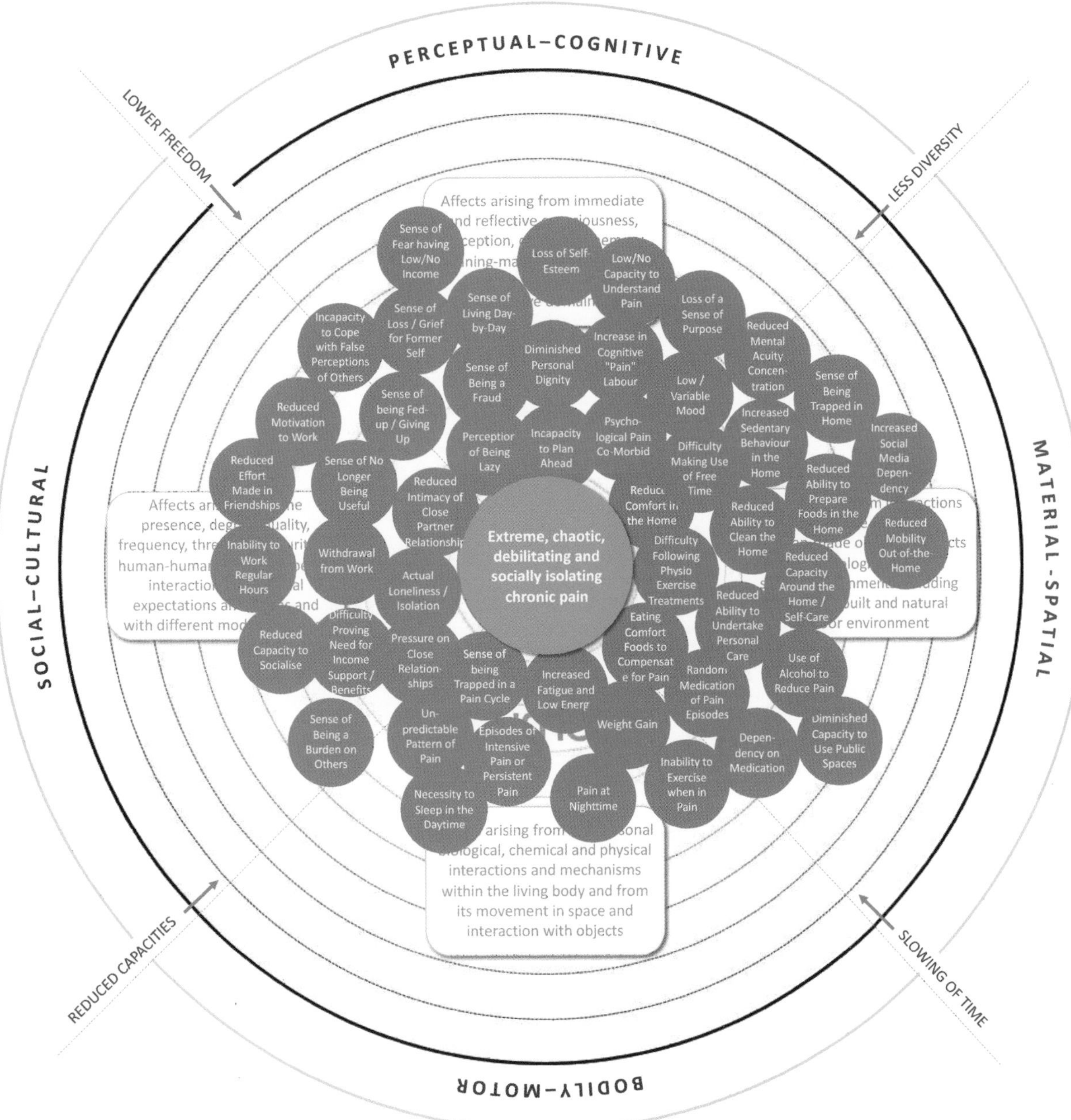

Figure 1.12: Affects (feelings, sensations and affective capacities) of a debilitating, chaotic and socially isolating experience when living with chronic pain

By contrast, Figure 1.13 depicts the experience of someone who is able to live well with chronic pain and enjoy a degree of sustained freedom. They have a well-developed affective capacity that has allowed them to overcome the determinism and tendencies of their pain, a capacity characterized by (amongst others) lower pain intensity, better sleep at night-time, more active social engagement, an improved capacity to work, greater cognitive understanding of their pain pattern and overall a greater sense of hope for the future.

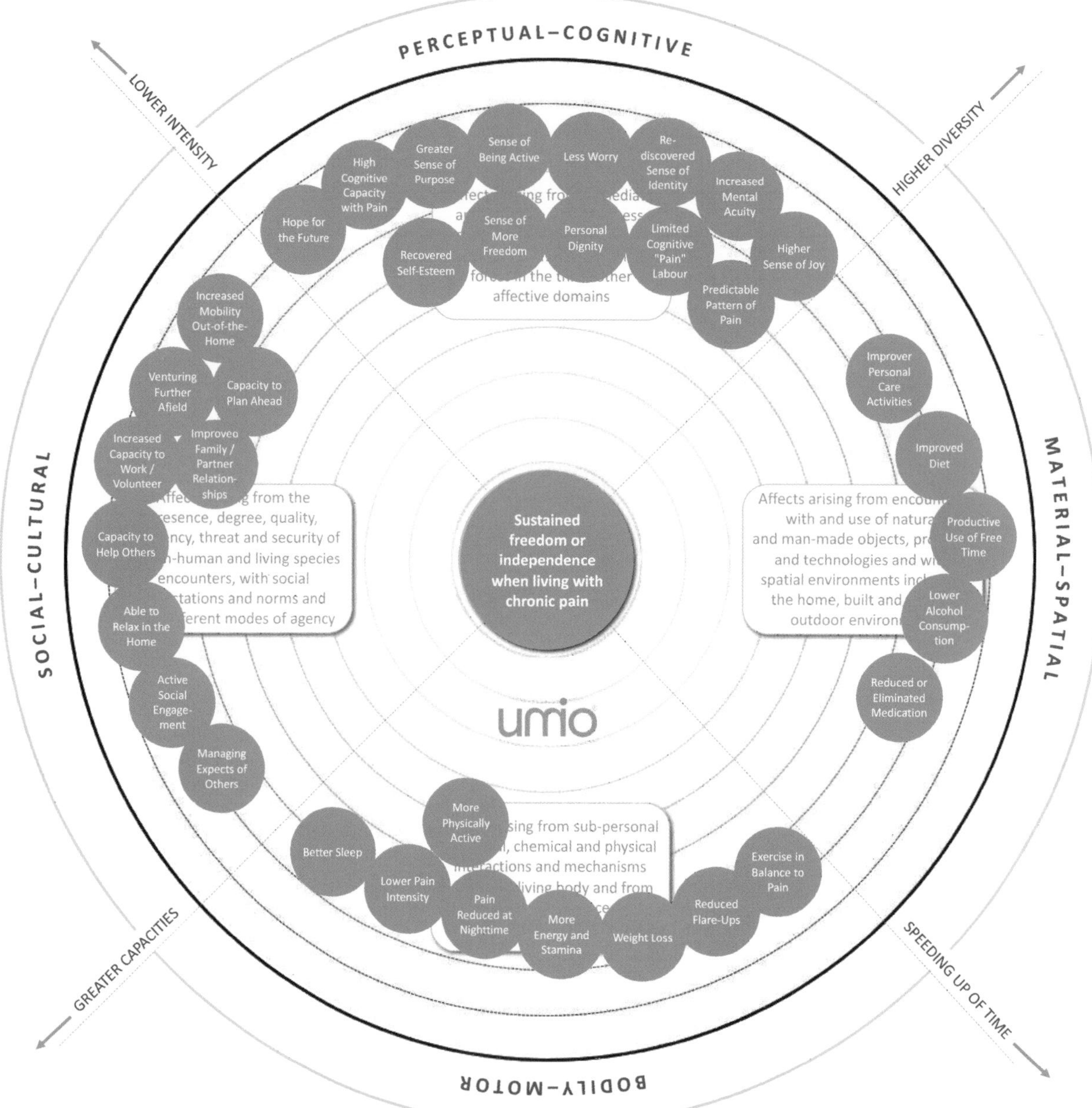

Figure 1.13: Affects (feelings, sensations, qualities and capacities) of living well with chronic pain and enjoying a degree of sustained freedom from pain

A model of interior quality and capacity of lived experience with health

Note that in the pain example, difference in lived experience is defined by affect quality and affective capacity rather than more typical objective, quantitative measures of pain. Usually, pain is distinguished and defined by a pain score, an intensity with an underlying condition. In an affect view of lived experience, however, affect quality and affective capacity transcend quantitative measures by defining not only an individual's general state of lived experience but also their potential capacity to recover or improve their lived experience. This is true for any condition context. For example, obesity is usually defined by a BMI score rather than affect and affective capacity. The experience of depression can by defined by affects and affective capacity, such as to experience joy and positivity in everyday interactions or to deal with stigma and hopelessness, rather than by PHQ-15 scores or low, medium and high categories of depression.

Through the lens of social desire, I now propose a model of the intrinsic interior elements forming a particular dynamic state of affect quality and capacity of actual lived experience with health for an affectee (benchmarked to the ideal of social desire) together with their interrelations. In the model (Figure 1.14 and examples in Figures 1.15A, B and C), the coloured 3D spheres indicate a given state of quality of affects and affective capacities in each of the four affective domains as follows:

- The smaller the size of the sphere, the lower is an affectee affective capacity; they have less capacity to create or transition their lived experience in interactional flows
- The closer any of the spheres is to the centre of the model, the more negative are the affects forming their lived experience for the affective domain. In other words, the more diseased or "dis-eased" (a sense of unease), objectified, hopeless, confined and stuck is the affectee's lived experience (like the example of chronic pain experience in Figure 1.12).
- The further any of the spheres is to the edge of the interior of the model, the more positive, desired and subjectively valued are the affects forming their lived experience. In other words, the more health, freedom, creational capacity, mobility and unregulated life that is enjoyed.
- The white or red transparent space connecting the position of the spheres shows the total amount of health. The more space, the greater the health and wellbeing of the affectee. Figure 1.15C shows the greatest amount of health compared with Figure 1.15A which has the least.
- Note that an affectee can have low capacity in one affective domain yet still have a relatively good quality of lived experience. For example, Figure 1.15B shows an affectee with poor bodily-motor affects and affective capacities yet more positive affects and capacities in the other three domains.

I have placed ill-health in the centre of the model due to dominant tendencies in Western societies for lived experience to be attracted towards ill-health rather than desired, valued health (or social desire). Such tendencies arise and are present in the tendential forces of capital with labour such as unnecessary consumption, excess work, stress, withdrawal from nature, presenteeism, regulation and routinization. Sadly, the natural attractor is not health contained in the ideal of social desire, but ill-health contained in the idea of negative desire; a desire of passion, want, of absence whose lack can lead to ill-being or poor-quality lived experiences with health. How else can we explain rising incidences of obesity, cardiovascular disease, stress, depression and chronic pain amongst many others? Arguably these are all diseases of a lack of affectee capacity to counter the negative tendencies of capital-with-labour forces.

Summary

In summary, foundation four states that for any focal lived experience with health context, we can identify poles of positive and negative lived experience defined by states of affect quality and degrees of affective capacity.

Foundation Four
For any focal lived experience with health context, we can identify poles of positive and negative lived experience defined by states of affect quality and degrees of affective capacity

The next foundation describes the dynamic relational aspects of different states of quality and capacity of lived experiences with health within any focal lived experience with health context.

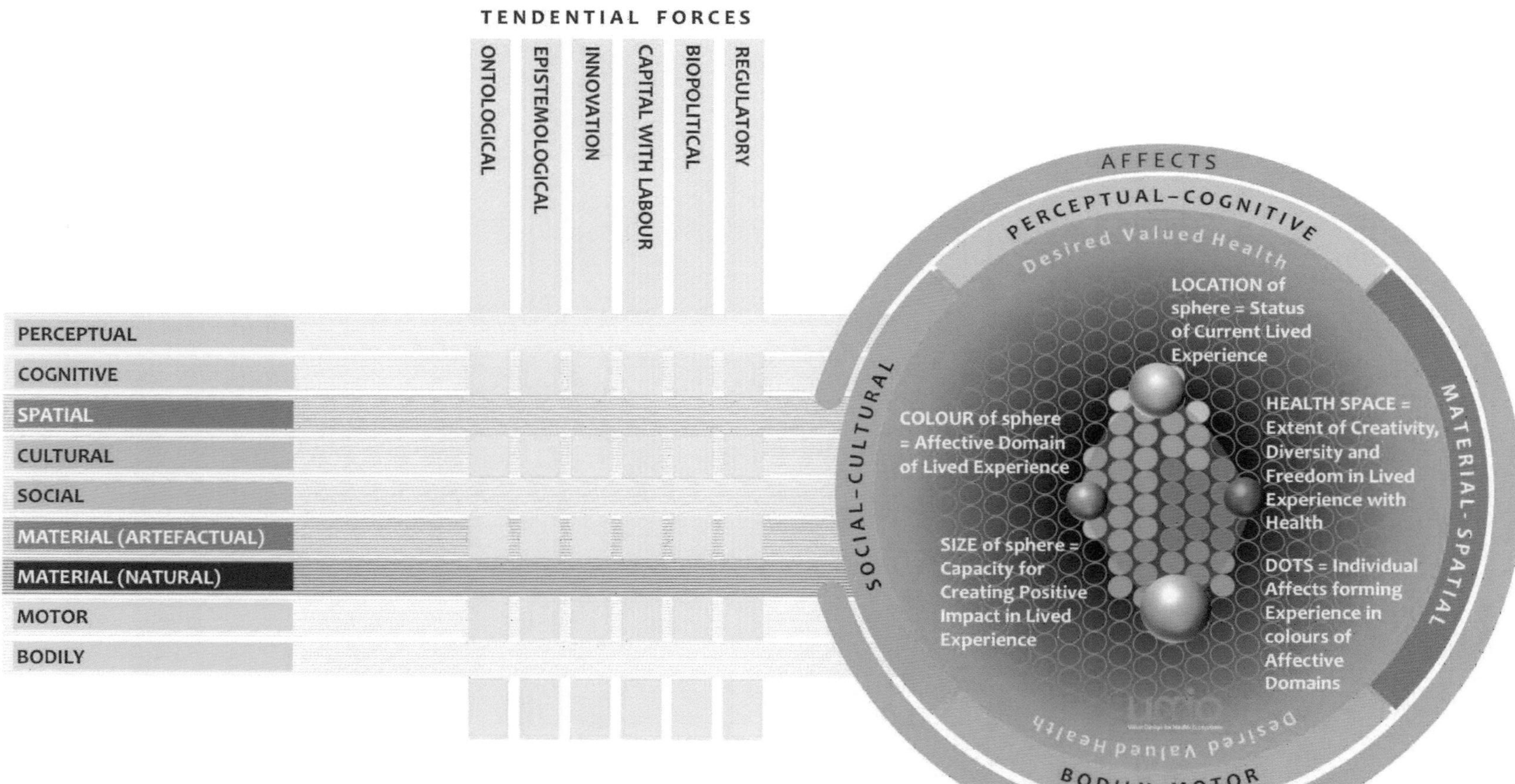

Figure 1.14: Model of interior lived experience with health (quality of experience and affective capacity)

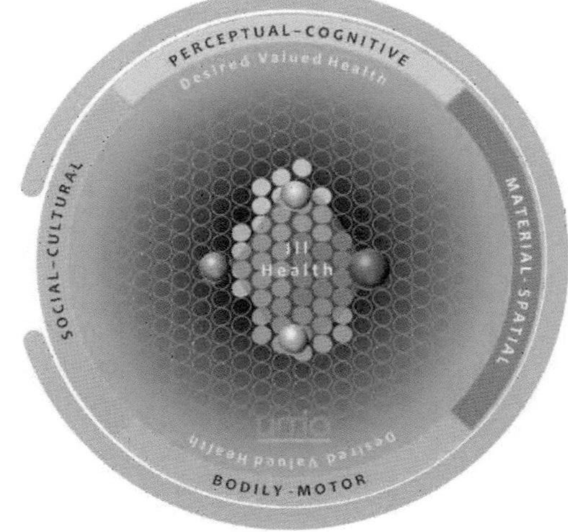

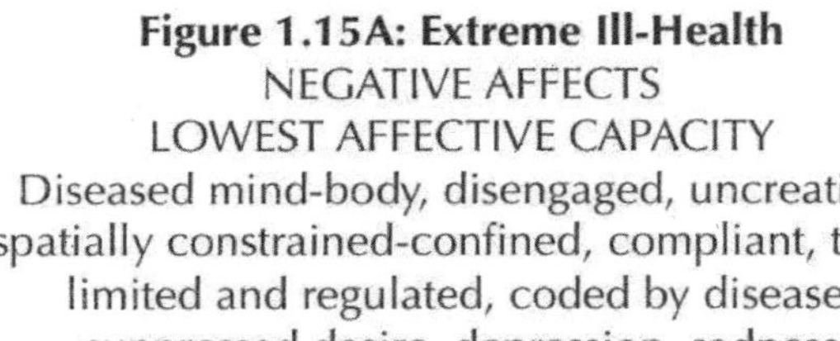

Figure 1.15A: Extreme Ill-Health
NEGATIVE AFFECTS
LOWEST AFFECTIVE CAPACITY
Diseased mind-body, disengaged, uncreative, spatially constrained-confined, compliant, time-limited and regulated, coded by disease, suppressed desire, depression, sadness

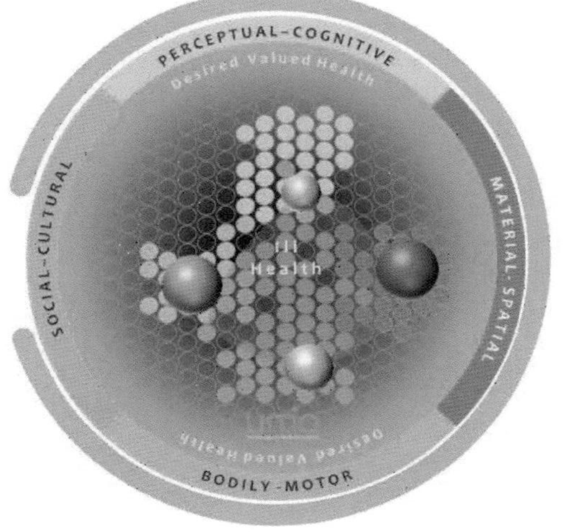

Figure 1.15B: Bodily Constrained Health
NEGATIVE BODILY AFFECTS (e.g., PAIN)
DEVELOPING SOCIAL-CULTURAL AND MATERIAL-SPATIAL AFFECTIVE CAPACITY
Emergent creativity, greater freedom and mobility, developing cognition of experience

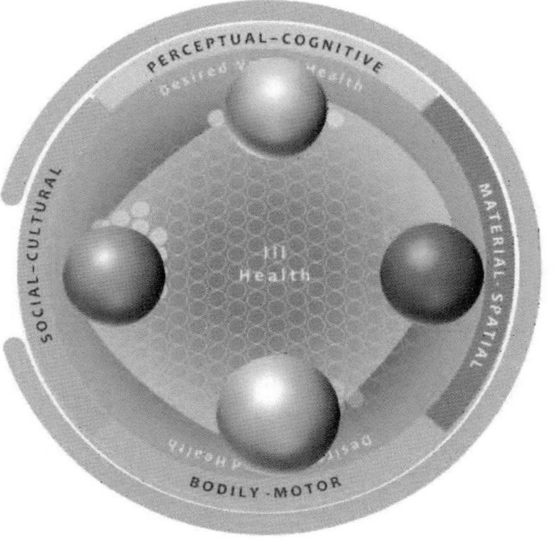

Figure 1.15C: Extreme Good Health
POSITIVE AFFECTS
HIGH AFFECTIVE CAPACITY
Healthy mind-body, engaged, creative, freedom, mobility, unregulated, diverse experience, realising desires, greater joy

Foundation Five | How can we identify different states and transitions of actual lived experience with health within the same context?

Foundation five identifies the existence of distinct yet contingent and variously recurrent dynamic states of affect quality and capacity *between* the two poles of ill-health and desired, valued experience described in foundation four. It defines how similar states and capacities of lived experience for a focal lived experience with health context can originate, emerge, differenciate, persist and may decline over time. Also, it helps to see movements from one state to another and the tendential forces in interactional flows that can power those movements, stabilise or hold them back. In short, foundation five introduces a novel view of the formation and emergence of an entire dynamic virtual space of distinct lived experiences for any focal lived experience with health context.

In Figure 1.16, I distinguish six universal lived experience with health states along with the (greyed out) transition phases between them. These states are (moving towards the negative pole) *at risk, worsening* and *chaotic* and (moving towards the positive pole) *emerging, building* and *stable* (note that these state descriptions can be tailored for any given context of experience being studied. Also, it is possible to zoom into a single state and find further differentiated states, along with their processes of differenciation.)

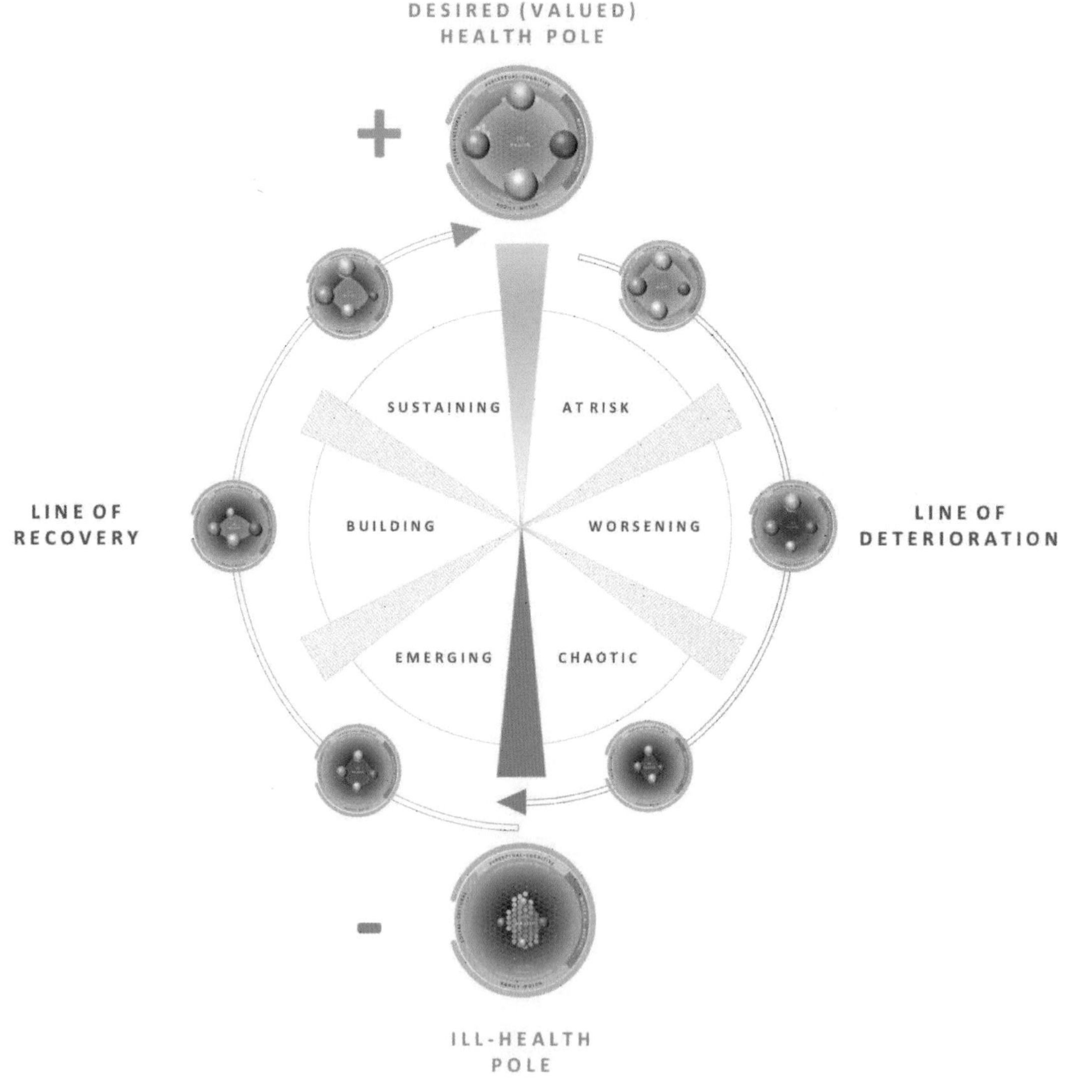

Figure 1.16: States, transitions and lines of becoming in lived experiences with health/disease

Figure 1.16 also depicts two pervasive "lines of becoming" that denote the primary directions of movement or transition between states and capacities for a focal health experience context. These are:

- A (red) **line of deterioration** from the at risk to the chaotic state (on the right-hand side)
- A (blue) **line of recovery** from the chaotic state to the stable state of living well (on the left)

We can also envisage points of stabilization of experience that serve to hold or to prevent transition out of a state. They can lock an experience in either a positive (healthy stability) or negative (ill-health stuck) state or somewhere in between.

Applying a dynamic model of states of lived experience with health

Using this model of states, transitions, lines of becoming and points of stability or "stuckness", we can understand how lived experiences for any health, disease or illness focal context arise, emerge, differenciate, persist and change over time. Such a developmental view supports a series of insights that I now describe.

Ask questions of how different lived experiences come to be and persist in a wider context

First, we can explore why certain lived experiences, especially negative ones tend to *originate* and also why they *tend to persist*. We can use the model of contingent distinct states of relatively homogenous affects and affective capacities generated within virtual interactional flows and tendential forces to enquire into the origins, emergence and persistence of the different states along with the potential for movements of affectees between the states. Such questions are often neglected within health systems in favour of those concerned with how to recover or care for an already negative lived experience, usually with illness or disease.

Understand the distribution of affectees within states of lived experience

Second, we can determine the *distribution* of affectees within different states for a focal lived experience with health context, i.e., the number and percent of *affectees* in the *at-risk* state, the number and percent in the *worsening* state, the number and percent in the *chaotic* state, and so forth (see Figure 1.17 for an example lived experience distribution of the chronic pain population in Northern Ireland). This insight supports a more informed review and potential reallocation of resources within a health system for a focal experience context.

See new patterns of affects forming different states of lived experience (for a focal context)

Third, we can discover and better understand the *quality, intensity and patterning* of affects and affective capacities that are present and actualized within particular interactional flows flowing within and across the states between the poles. Having knowledge of these supports a more nuanced and differentiated view of the design, types, fitness and value of human and non-human resource deployments within the different states. Table 1.5 shows example affect and affect capacity differences for the six different states of chronic pain identified in my Northern Ireland study.

Understand flows and forces of state stability and transitions

Fourth, we can look at and compare *degrees of stability* within and the rates of transitions between the different states. We can explore the affects and tendencies in interactional flows and the tendential forces that stabilise individual states (in a positive enabling or a negative stuck sense) and also that could or do transition an affectee from one state to another, whether towards or away from the positive or negative poles. For example, if there is a high rate of transition of affectees from the at-risk to the chaotic state (e.g., more and more young people in the US becoming more obese), then clearly more effort is needed to discover which interactional flows and tendential forces in whole lived experience are producing this transition and what can be done to slow or reverse them.

Discover how the distribution of lived experience knowledge limits capacities for impactful action

Fifth, we can identify *gaps in current knowledge* of the different states of lived experience. Also, we can see where *existing knowledge* of lived experience is held by particular affectors (for example knowledge of the ill-health experience state is held by professional actors in the healthcare system whereas knowledge of the at-risk state is held by professional public health system actors). We can then learn how the availability and pattern of knowledge ownership and use translates into epistemological and innovation tendential forces and how these exert influence on priorities of action within the different states. We can see and compare what we know to what the model of states of lived experience tells us we should know. We can then rethink individual, organizational and system-level priorities, responses and capacities for addressing interactional flows and tendential forces of differenciation and transition in experiences with health.

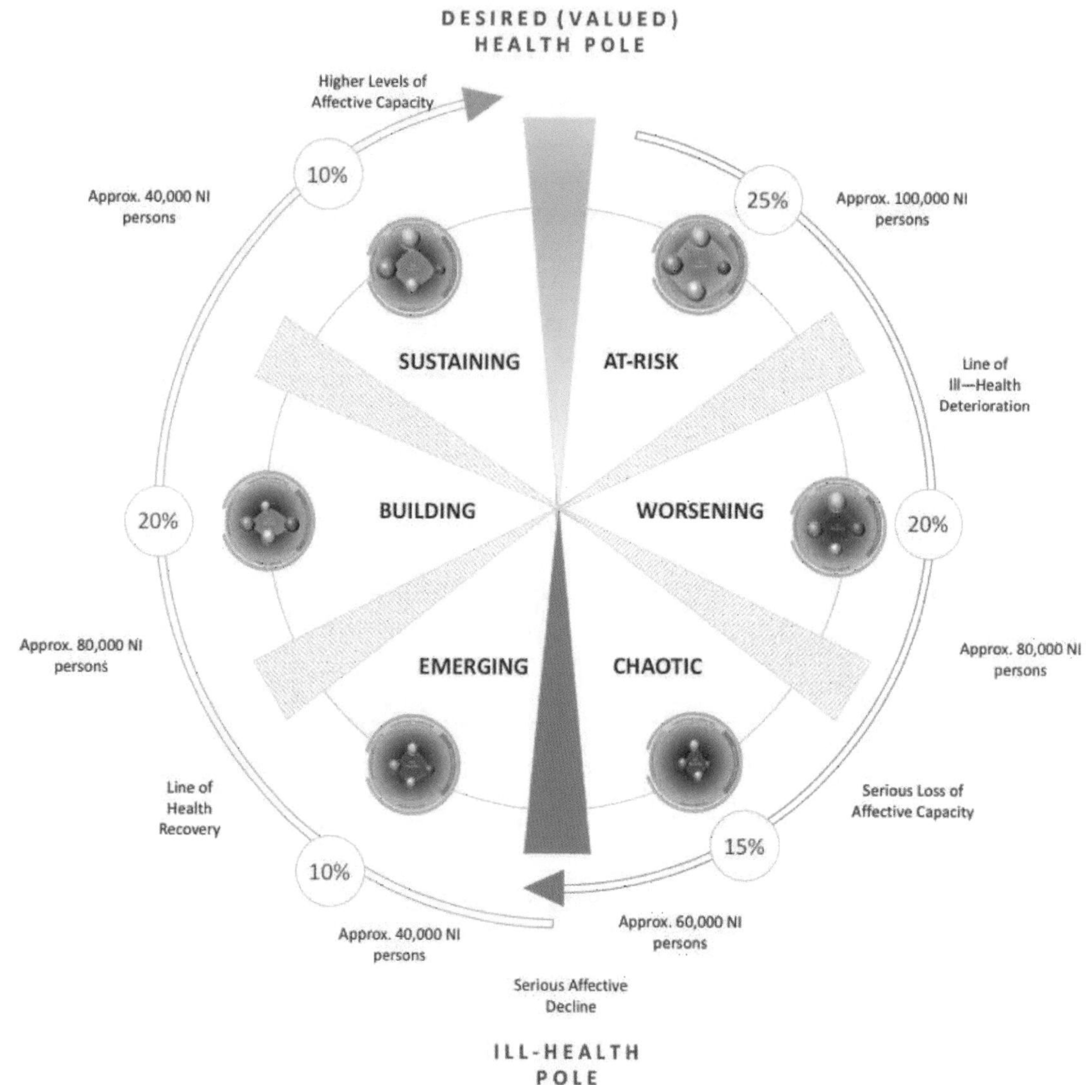

Figure 1.17: Distribution of chronic pain population of 400,000 persons in Northern Ireland across the six states of lived experience (affect quality and capacity)

Understand the influence of, modify and overcome (or boost) tendential forces

Finally, we can learn how, where and why tendential forces present within different states of lived experience can blind us to *seeing novel paths and possibilities* for transitioning those states. We can identify which tendential forces are stuck, which to change and which to pursue new paths within a whole model of differenciated experience states spanning qualities and capacities of more health and ill-health for a single focal health experience context.

Summary

In summary, foundation five states that for any focal experience with health context, there exist distinct relatively homogenous yet dynamic states and capacities of lived experience, each formed of similar affective capacities arising from patterns and frequencies of interactions within particular interactional flows modulated by tendential forces.

Foundation Five
For any focal experience with health context, there exist distinct relatively homogenous yet dynamic states and capacities of lived experience, each formed of similar affective capacities arising from patterns and frequencies of interactions within particular interactional flows modulated by tendential forces

Having defined a view of distinct states of affect quality and capacity for a focal lived experience with health context, along with the nature of movements or transitions between them, the next foundation defines the process whereby dynamic agencial bodies originate, differenciate and variously reproduce distinct states of lived experience with health in a focal experience context. These bodies are known as assemblages.

Table 1.5 – Summary of distinguishing affect qualities and affect capacities within the six chronic pain states of lived experience

	AT RISK	WORSENING	DECLINED	EMERGING	BUILDING	STABLE
PER CENT	**% (100k)**	**20% (80k)**	**15% (60k)**	**10% (40k)**	**20% (80k)**	**10% (40k)**
PERCEPTUAL-COGNITIVE	Low understanding of possibility of chronic pain; some pain-denial; low-level anxiety, hope in cure; sense of trust in health and care service	Worsening mood; anger and frustration; growing anxiety and stress; increasing sense of boredom; developing negative thoughts; low-level cognitive pain capacities; fear of exercise and movement; low acceptance and low pain information / support search; managing on tactical, day-to-day basis; declining self-esteem; losing sense of purpose; feeling useless; sense of distrust / disappointment in health service / GPs.	Depression or very low mood; sense of giving up; very limited pain sense; resignation but no motivation; loss of self-esteem, identity, purpose, personal dignity; low sense of enjoyment in life; withdrawal; low sense of hope; high tension; lower health literacy	Realising that things can be done to address the pain; Emerging from low mood and possible depression; developing acceptance and understanding of personal pain experience; building a strategy of baseline activity and flare warning signals; developing early-stage commitment to living with pain; building up personal tolerance levels	Reducing stress, tension and anxiety; achieving regular states of calm; building sense of control over pain; reducing mental attention on pain; improving mood; reduced anxiety; developing effective cognitive pain capacities; reducing fear of exercise and movement; developed acceptance and understanding of pain; forming personal strategy; improving self-esteem; greater sense of purpose; sense of possibility of living with pain; some ongoing frustration with slow pace; feeling more useful	Power to affect is greater than affects of pain leading to sense of real purpose and responsibility recovered; sense of personal achievement and possibility, growth; strong acceptance to drive powers of acting in mental space beyond the pain; sense of near control of pain; balanced body with mind understanding; predictive, cognitive capacities that can link activities with pain response; sense of joy and frequent laughter; less worry about making pain worse; more sense of free time. Clear understanding of capacities in context;
MATERIAL-SPATIAL	Just started taking medication; Ongoing bad encounters with pain-inducing entities such as sitting for long periods in an office, vehicles, doing physically heavy work etc.; Acute post-trauma, operation, infection or sickness encounters; increasing uses of NSAID, paracetamol and opioid medication; frequent, inconclusive visits to GP. Maybe still at or returning to work, following mostly normal daily routine; regular work habits and routines but more frequent days off work at home	Becoming more dependent on partner finances, resources dwindling; may have some access to savings yet increasing possibility of welfare dependency; some pain technology used but it's not helpful; not using a toolkit or other materials; Acute care, physiotherapy and pain specialist use but long waiting times. Progressively higher doses of medication; possibly developing opioid addiction. Mostly at home, possibly movement confined to garden and immediate community, local shops; local environment quality has importance; safety of local community a factor too.	High drug dependency; consuming alcohol for pain; medicating for pain; complex medication needs; possible opioid addiction; poor diet, smoking; illicit drug use / exchange where available; few leisure activities; Limited means to access technology resources; low financial resources; likely on PIP/DLA. Confined to home; poorer communities with lower social cohesion and high tension; more rural, remote areas	Changing with a view to optimising medications; experimenting alternative group and human therapies; may use a pain management digital technology or manual toolkit Becoming more confident, leaving the home and venturing out-and-about in local places and spaces	Optimising use of medications and slowly reducing dose; using toolkits and technologies as reminders; engaging with objects to take mind off pain, e.g., hobbying Widening places and spaces of activities; using own transport to get ahead; walking longer distances in public	Reducing or eliminating medication use altogether; encounters with more spaces. Places of negative affect are fewer; exploring new places; wider travel horizons;
SOCIAL-CULTURAL	Maybe working still; relatively active socially; belonging to a team or group	Reduced capacity to work; may have give up work and have retired early; reducing contact with friends and family; more frequent sleeping in daytime; losing partner intimacy; declining personal mobility; everything tried is making the pain worse	Fewer social / friend encounters; real social isolation; much less likely to be working; low ability to work; dependent on partner for care (if they have one);	Getting value from new peer connections of from pain clinic; reducing dependency on informal carer, family; finding it difficult to communicate improvements	Increasing level of social engagement; building peer-network and relations with other pain persons; improving social relations with family and friends; possible return to work but volunteering in the meantime.	Maybe offering help to others; managing expectations of others such as family, friends and colleagues; finding new friends; having fun with a wider social circle
BODILY-MOTOR	Early-stage pain signals, developing post-acute or post-trauma pain; intermittent and maybe unnoticed; inflammatory pain from ageing and pressure on joints with pain at nighttime; some low-level fatigue; some decline in exercise and movement; low-level compensatory actions; Increasing impact on behaviour and personal/social activity; some sleep disruption; undertaking activities not conducive to mitigating risk and pain;	More bad days of pain than good ones; unexplained flare-ups; weight gain; loss of muscle strength and fitness; higher levels of fatigue; becoming trapped in pain cycle; activities not conducive to pain relief;	Significant debilitating, intense pain; psychological pain co-morbidity; post-severe trauma, complex multi-type pain; may lack a diagnosis; other co-morbidities, e.g., obesity, CVD, COPD; persistent flare-ups; high level of sedentary behaviour / no exercise or movement; frequent bed / pajamas days	Set-backs and flares less frequent; having higher number of good than bad days; still a tendency to be overconfident and overdo activities leading to flares; or doing too little for fear of increasing the pain; experimenting with light exercise and relaxation	Pain flare-ups may still occur randomly; pain persists yet seems to occupy mind and time less; Doing more enjoyable personal and social activities within cautious limits; Increasing use of exercise and social activities in balance to pain intensity becoming appropriately confident; not overdoing light activities leading to flares; sleep quality improving	Pain persists but takes up less "mind space"; more energy; better stamina to cope with pain; fewer aches and pains; Successful pacing of personal and social activities; doing more fun and pleasurable activities; using physical activity to release endorphins

Foundation Six: How do different states of actual lived experience with health within the same context originate, differenciate and persist?

Foundation six identifies a dynamic body of affectors (human and non-human entities) and affectees having creational force or agency to originate, actualize, differenciate and variously stabilise and reproduce distinct lived experiences with health, illness and disease. Interacting with interactional flows, this virtual body (not a human body I emphasise) is termed an *assemblage*[21].

Looking again at Figure 1.17, we can say that each of the six lived experience states forming the whole population of persons living with chronic pain in Northern Ireland is an assemblage of affects, capacities, affectees and affectors interacting within a virtual-real natural and social body of interactional flows bearing tendential forces. Each assemblage defines a certain affect quality, intensity and stability, and affective capacity of lived experience (in this case with chronic pain) within a territory or place (Northern Ireland). In the model, on the line of deterioration, there is an at-risk assemblage, a worsening assemblage and a chaotic/declined assemblage – the most ill-health state - and on the line of recovery, an emerging assemblage, a building assemblage and a sustaining assemblage, close to the desired, valued pole of lived experience.

I now define an assemblage, its properties, components and entities and explain its mode of action in lived experience.

Defining assemblages of lived experience (with health)

An assemblage is an agencial body producing a lived experience state of a certain quality, intensity, capacity and stability for a focal lived experience with health context. To give its full definition, an assemblage is:

> *An agencial emergent open body consisting of an ensemble of heterogenous, self-subsistent and variously stabilized components and entities whose arrangements of interaction may create, differenciate, repeat and/or recover a state of lived experience (with health) ... of a certain content and expression of affect capacity and quality, stability, duration and impact in the lived journeys of affectees (whether persons, families, groups, communities or places)*

The first half of this definition (up to the three dots) defines the properties of assemblages and their component entities that put into motion agencial mechanisms acting within and upon interactional flows and tendential forces coursing over the virtual natural with social desire body. The second half identifies the actual qualities of lived experience that are created and differentiated by these properties and mechanisms (affect quality, intensity, stability, duration and impact) of the kind listed in Table 1.5. Next, I briefly explain the properties and mechanisms of the components (in the front half of the definition).

Agencial

As described in foundation three, affectees and affectors have varying affective capacities to create or modify their and others' lived experiences. An assemblage has affective capacity too; they are agencial[22] meaning an assemblage's power of acting on interactional flows and tendential forces that course over the natural with social body. Over time, the agencial capacities of assemblages may be limited by tendential forces in interactional flows (as I described in foundation three). Nevertheless, like an arterial stent, new tendential forces can unblock diseased assemblages. Regulatory tendential forces may be modified to lift limits and standards

[21] Assemblage is an English translation of the French word "agencement" or the process of arranging, organising and fitting together. It was elaborated by Deleuze and Guattari. Agencement, with the same root as agency, are arrangements endowed with the capacity of acting in different ways depending upon its combination of heterogeneous components, interrelated to one another in a way that brings about evolving lived experiences. This explanation is provided by DeLanda.

[22] "Agencial" rather than "agential" emphasises the agency of assemblages rather than the human and non-human agents working within them. I am grateful to Venkat Ramaswamy and Kerimcan Ozcan (2016) for this distinction.

that constrain assemblage agencial capacity and potential. New epistemological tendential forces may be developed to generate new knowledge and novel organizational modes in capital-with-labour tendential forces can unblock interactional flows to help realise more sustained impact.

Through an agencial assemblage view, we can overcome the inclination in structure-oriented social theories (and related ideas such as the social determinants of health) to locate structure somewhere separate from and causal of agency when pursuing explanations of social phenomena such as disease. Instead, with assemblage thinking, we can substitute notions of fixed, deeper and separate structures with that of tendential forces (biopolitics, capital with labour, ontology, epistemology, etc.) that are present within flowing and dynamic interactional flows. Assemblages operating within and acting upon these flows in the virtual domain have varying agencial powers to produce, differenciate and repeat lived experiences. Thus, by affording a view of structure as conjugated with agency within interactional flows, assemblages offer an alternative ontological basis with which to see, understand and intervene in powers and patterns of the creation, differenciation and recurrence of lived experiences with health.

Emergent

Whole properties of assemblages emerge from interactions between their component entities. These whole properties, such as an assemblage's agencial powers and degree of stability or transience cannot be reduced to the properties of their components (e.g., individual entities, affectees, affectors, flows and forces in the assemblages) but can act back on those components. In short, the whole properties of any assemblage are greater than the sum of the properties of its component entities.

Open

Like most systems on earth (outside the laboratory), assemblages are open and relational systems; they do not contain parts or mechanisms that are closed off from other systems. Thus, an assemblage is open to new components becoming attached to it. Also, parts of one assemblage may move to other assemblages as well as be present simultaneously in other assemblages. Assemblages have more or less exterior properties although a higher degree of openness does not necessarily relate to having greater agencial capacities.

Ensemble

Ensemble means that assemblages are arrangements of contingent component entities that come together to produce, differenciate and repeat a particular quality, capacity and identity of lived experience when acting on interactional flows modulated by tendential forces.

The following three terms explain the properties of components and entities in assemblages.

Heterogeneous

An assemblage is formed from a diversity of components and entities: four domain affects, affect capacities, presence, interactions and intensities of material, social, semiotic and natural entities in the nine interactional flows modulated by six tendential forces, and diverse affectees and affectors.

Self-subsistent

As in the explanation of "open", an assemblage component or entity can "unplug" itself from one assemblage and plug itself or be plugged into another assemblage having a different affectual, spatial, temporal and processual context, identity, quality, capacity and tendency of lived experience. In other words, assemblages do not have a "totality" in that their parts are autonomous; they are not mutually and instrumentally dependent on one another and if removed, then cease to function (like most living organisms).

Stabilized

An assemblage can be in a more or less transient or stable state depending on the power of tendential forces acting within and on interactional flows within them. Like the river metaphor I used in foundation three, a whole assemblage may contain fast-changing components along with stuck, slow-moving components, or it may be more homogenously fluid or stable. Stability in an assemblage can produce positive or negative lived experiences; positive in the sense of enabling the free creation of positive affects (social desire) or negative in the sense of concentrating and repeating stuck poor affects as when an ill-health assemblage "acts back" on itself to further intensify and repeat the stuck affects and tendencies.

Assemblages as the primary unit of enquiry of dynamic lived experience

An assemblage is not only a creational agencial force driving various qualities and degrees of differentiation, recurrence, stability and transition in lived experience in the virtual social with natural body, but it also acts as a practical unit of enquiry for pursuing concrete analysis and thicker explanation of different contexts of lived experience, situations and outcomes. It serves as a research tool as well as novel conceptual frame to explore and explain origins, difference, change and stability in lived experiences with health for a focal experience context. Also, assemblage thinking tells us why, where, what and how to intervene to positively prevent or recover ill-health experiences and to create and improve desired (valued) experiences (the positive and negative poles of experience quality and capacity).

Complete assemblage model of whole unified lived experience with health

Figure 1.18 depicts the complete dynamic assemblage model of lived experience with health showing the different elements and their relations that form, differenciate and variously stabilise lived experience. In its "living" version (viewable on the Umio website), all the blue-grey circles spin at different speeds in a clockwise direction. The outer dotted circle contracts into the centre and expands out again to imitate the centripetal and centrifugal nature of affective capacity or the capacity to affect and be affected in interactional flows. Around the perimeter of the model are the primary contexts used by Health Ecosystem Value Design to frame a study.

Summary

To summarise foundation six, the unit of enquiry and discovery in Health Ecosystem Value Design is not the individual person (typically the objectified or categorized "patient") but an assemblage, an emergent agencial body of heterogeneous components and entities differenciating and variously stabilising a state of lived experience of a certain quality and capacity, content and expression.

Foundation Six
The unit of enquiry and discovery is not the individual person (typically the objectified or categorized "patient") but an assemblage, an emergent agencial body of heterogeneous components and entities, differenciating and variously stabilising a state of lived experience of a certain quality and capacity, content and expression

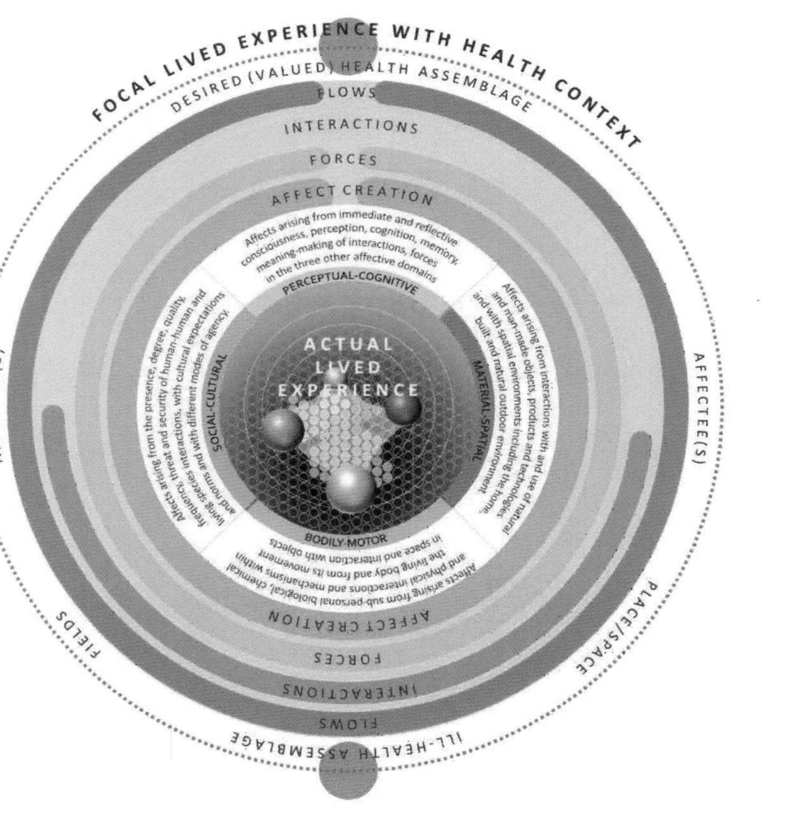

DYNAMIC ASSEMBLAGE ELEMENTS

ELEMENT	DESCRIPTION
(INTERACTIONAL) FLOWS	An interactional flow is a dynamic moving body of natural, material, social and semiotic entities bearing virtual affects, capacities and tendencies. When an interactional flow is interacted with, the pre-experience affects, capacities and tendencies it contains are actualised in a process of creative enactment producing a state of a certain expression, content, quality, intensity and stability of lived experience.
INTERACTIONS	Affectee and affector interactions within interactional flows modulated by tendential forces generate intensive movements or transitions in lived experience
(TENDENTIAL) FORCES	Tendential forces contain tendencies that direct, limit, stabilise or sediment affects and capacities in interactional flows. They have power to originate, attract, moderate, regulate, promote or otherwise influence interactional flows
AFFECT CREATION	The circle indicates the creation of affects forming actual lived experience from affectee and affector interactions in tendential forces and interactional flows. Affects created (unlocked, modified, stabilised, emergent) are of two kinds: Sensations and Capacities. **Affects as sensations (dots in centre of model):** Affects are sensations, feeling states and impressions that mark transitions within and between lived experience states. Actualised via interactions in the four affective domains (bodily-motor, perceptual-cognitive, social-cultural, material-spatial), affects themselves interact, combine and can fuse together to qualitatively differenciate and variously stabilise and reproduce lived experiences with health. **Affects as capacities (coloured spheres in model):** Affects are also a capacity to affect or be affected by and in interactions within the four interaction domains in the model of whole lived experience, or affective domains. As a capacity, affects are also a force or a power for creating and acting in and upon lived experience. They are also a capacity to be affected or be acted upon or within desired or often undesired interactions. I term these affecting and being affected dimensions of affect, affective capacity.

ASSEMBLAGE FRAMING CONTEXTS (SHOWN IN PERIMETER)

ELEMENT	DESCRIPTION
FOCAL LIVED EXPERIENCE WITH HEALTH CONTEXT	Qualitatively distinct and recurring lived experiences defined by a particular type and relation of affects and affective capacities.
DESIRED (VALUED) ASSEMBLAGE	An assemblage characterised by the most ideal or normatively ideal affect qualities and capacities of lived experience for the focal lived experience with health context. For example: Healthy Mind-Body, Engaged, Creative, Freedom, Mobility, Agile, Unregulated, Diverse Experience, Realising Desires, Joy
ILL-HEALTH ASSEMBLAGE	An assemblage characterised by the worst affect qualities and capacities of lived experience for the focal lived experience with health context. For example: Diseased Mind-Body, Disengaged, Uncreative, Spatially Constrained-Confined, Objectified, Compliant, Time-Limited and Regulated, Coded by Disease, Suppressed Desire, Depression, Sadness.
AFFECTEE(S)	A type of individual person, a family, neighbour(s), a community or a social group of any kind (ethnic, gender, age, political or religious affiliation, patient group) or even a place or space that is experiencing affects and capacity for the Focal Lived Experience with Health Context.
AFFECTOR(S)	An individual person, family, neighbour, community, social group or organisation that is directly or indirectly responsible for generating or influencing affects and affect capacities experienced by the affectee for the Focal Lived Experience with Health Context. An affector may also be a non-human agent affector such as a drug, technology, piece of data, natural matter, or cultural sign or signifier of health or disease
FIELDS	A selected domain of focus or intersection of interactional flows and tendential forces, affectees and affectors of particular interest in an HEVD enquiry.
PLACE-SPACE	A place, spatial or geographical setting of the Focal Lived Experience with Health Context, whether real / physical or virtual, natural or man-made / built.

Figure 1.18: Complete Umio model of assemblage of creation of lived experiences with health showing circular interactional creation elements, framing contexts in the perimeter and table of definition of all terms

Foundation Seven: How do we see and define experience ecosystems of interactional creation of health?

The final foundation defines an open space or "cut out"[23] of the virtual social (desire) with natural body within which contingent yet distinct agencial assemblages form and interact with interactional flows to originate, differentiate and reproduce distinct states and qualities of lived experiences with health, disease and illness for a focal experience context. I call this cut out a focal experience ecosystem environment or FEEE. An open loosely bounded domain of the total virtual-real domain, each FEEE is framed and defined using a focal lived experience with health and other contexts. Template 1.0 in HEVD is used to frame a FEEE. The individual framing contexts are shown in Table 1.6[24].

Table 1.6: Contexts used to frame a cut-out of the virtual-real experience ecosystem environment

Context	Description
Focal lived experience with health context (or "focal context")	As defined in foundation two, a focal lived experience with health context is a qualitatively distinct and recurring lived experience with health, disease or illness defined by a *particular type and relation of affects and affective capacities*. A focal context can be one or combination of a physical chronic disease, mental illness, behavioural problem, chronic multi-disease state, feeling state or a wider-than-health social problem.
Affectee	A type or types of individual person, family, community, social group (ethnic minorities, religious belief, gender, sexual orientation, class, age) that are experiencing the focal context
Affector	Human and non-human agents and entities who directly or indirectly influence and create lived experiences, or act on, modify or seek to help affectees for the focal experience context
Place or space	A geographical territory or setting in which the focal experience context exists (and which may be another type of affectee)
Fields	A selection of a context of interactional flows and tendential forces of particular interest. For example, an HEVD study may select a context of *social interactional flows* and *capital with labour tendential force* to explore issues of bias or exclusion in the allocation of health system resources for particular groups (e.g., black obese persons) or geographies (e.g., rural areas).
Transition purpose	A defined purpose to transition the FEEE towards a future preferred state. A transition purpose usually defines a movement from the ill-health to the desired valued assemblage in a body of assemblages. In chapter two, I discuss movements and transitions in the context of value creation in more detail.

Using the above contexts, a framed FEEE affords a dynamic view and ongoing unit of enquiry into a cut-out of the social with natural virtual body over which interactional flows and tendential forces course and coalesce.

[23] As I explained in foundation three, a river is a cut-out from the virtual natural body of different matter and energy.

[24] Note that when framing FEEEs, particular attention must be paid to the meaning of the terms used in the context descriptions and selections so as to uncover unconscious bias or beliefs that themselves constitute a tendential force.

Via interactions with flows and forces in a FEEE, distinct yet interrelating contingent assemblages of lived experiences with health originate, emerge and become variously stabilized as well as patterned with one another. Each assemblage so produced in a focal experience ecosystem environment has a different agencial force of quality, capacity, tendency and developmental impact in lived experience. Each is constituted by distinctive properties, components and mechanisms of interaction within interactional flows and tendential forces coursing over the social (desire) with natural (matter and energy force) body.

Before I show a model of focal experience ecosystem environments and discuss them further, first I wish to reflect on existing disciplinary perspectives of lived experience.

Overcoming disciplinary fragmentation of focal experience ecosystem environments

Since the birth of the modern clinical sciences around the 1820s, we have witnessed the progressive fragmentation of disciplines and methods for understanding and acting on lived experiences with health, disease and illness (see Figure 1.19). I identify two dominant empirical domains of focus arising from this fragmentation:

1. **Bodily-focused**, dualistic mind-separate-from-body, biological, clinical, medical, neuroscience, technological and healthcare disciplines and practices (shown in the grey in Figure 1.19) which largely adheres to a quantitative empirical realist health science method
2. **Social, cultural, spatial, material, economic and political disciplines and practices** (shown in the green in Figure 1.19) which often tries to emulate the hard sciences in its search for determinacy, cause-effect, prediction and explanation

And on top of this primary fragmentation, there are of course many sub-disciplinary fragmentations, especially within the bodily domain where clinical practice has been traditionally organized by body organs.

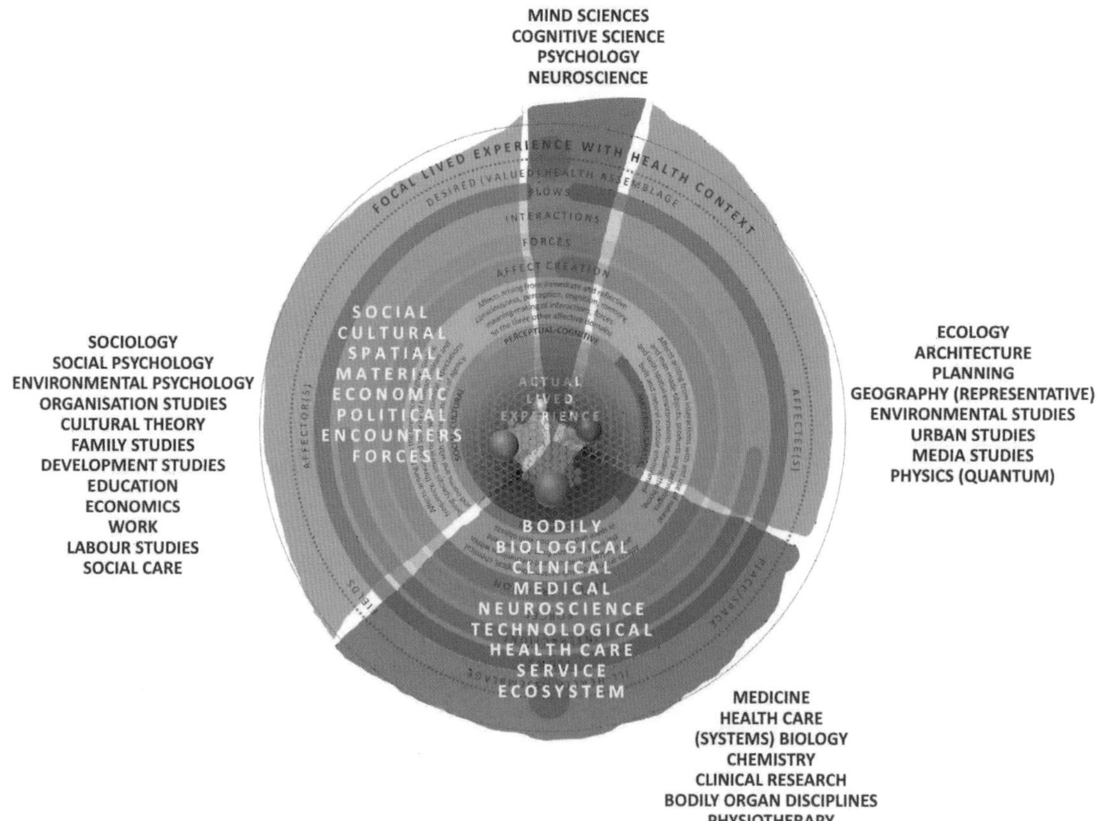

Figure 1.19 – The ongoing fragmentation of lived experiences with health into two primary disciplinary and knowledge domains: bodily-mind (grey) and social-focused (green)

Over time, the largely bodily-focused health domain has expanded incrementally through ongoing advances in research, knowledge, innovation, technology and practice adaptations to become a complex system of ideas, affectors (human and non-human), organizations and routines, each often with competing claims on truth and limited resources. This fracturing has led to many disciplines becoming distant and blind to *whole* lived experiences with health even though it has helped them to get closer to *parts of* actual lived experiences. The result is that many neither perceive nor account for the processes that originate, differenciate and repeat actual lived experience. To address this distancing, HEVD maps the interactions and flows of affectees and affectors in the two disciplinary domains. This helps affectors to see how actual experience is fragmented by their disciplinary and organizational focus and then to find opportunities to converge around a whole unified model of lived experience in a wide focal experience ecosystem environment. Next, I explain the mapping model or base template that is used to do this.

Mapping affectee-affector interactions in a framed focal experience ecosystem environment

Template 3.0 in HEVD supports the mapping of affector - affectee interactions in a framed FEEE along with their allocation to one or more of the nine interactional flows. This divides a FEEE for a focal experience context into two inter-relating sub-domains or ecosystems. These secondary ecosystems are:

- **The health and social care (statutory) sub-ecosystem** – the formal statutory resourced domain of public health, medical, clinical care and social care services consisting of mostly planned and regulated flows of interaction between affectees and professional care affectors, their teams, organizations, representative, overseer and funding bodies as well as non-human regulated affectors such as drugs and other treatments, medical devices and technologies. This is the largely bodily-focused disciplinary domain.
- **The social-cultural sub-ecosystem** – the social domain of affectee interactions with informal or indirect agent affectors, whether human (such as family members, employers, friends, sports coaches and fitness instructors) or non-human entities (such as the air, water, foods, personal technologies, the home and built environment, symbols and representations). This is the domain of actual lived experience occurring in real durations of sensed time. It is where health is created and differenciated and where disease and illness originate, concentrate and variously persist or recur.

Figure 1.20 depicts the base map of health and social affector-affectee interactional spaces for a focal lived experience with health context. Surrounding the focal lived experience with context in the centre are four rings of interacting affectee types, starting with individual person affectees then relations of affectees (e.g., family, extended family) then affectee peers or groups and then affectee communities. Overlaid onto these is a hierarchy of interaction spaces for each of the social and health domains and for each of the four types of affectors, starting with one-to-one affector with affectee interactions, then group/team affector with affectee interactions, then organization affector with affectee interactions, then affector fields (selections of interactional flows and tendential forces of interest) with affectee interactions and finally health overseer or governing affector interactions with the whole domain. The template also incorporates the potential to map affector with affector interactions across all the different levels. Figure 1.21 shows an example of mapped affector-affectee interactions for the chronic pain study in Northern Ireland.

By dividing a FEEE for a focal context into these two ecosystems, HEVD explores where, why and to what degree the two sub-ecosystems are separated from one another in current disciplinary perspectives, research and modes of design, practice and action in the health, life and related social sciences. When mapping affector-affectee interactions for a focal experience context through a whole unified lived experience view, participants in a HEVD program begin to see the collective holistic interactional picture of lived experiences with health. They realise how distinguishing health from the social body is a false distinction and one of the main tendential forces (epistemological) influencing how we perceive, prioritise, organise and act to prevent and counter disease and illness. They overcome the transformative limitations of biomedical reductionism and its "boxing in" and management of lived experience into abstract disease identities, categories, conditions and outcome measures.

Focal experience ecosystem environments and the complete ontology of interactional creation

FEEEs contain all the dynamic entities and elements that combine and interact to originate, differenciate and reproduce states, qualities, capacities, tendencies and stabilities of real lived experiences with health, disease and illness. In Figure 1.22 I display the full model of all FEEE elements and entities and their relation. To conclude the seven foundations, I summarise the ten elements depicted in the model here.

1. **Actual lived experiences**: A whole unified dynamic view of actual lived experience formed from interactions in four affective domains: social-cultural, material-spatial, bodily-motor and perceptual-cognitive made up of nine interactional flows
2. **Affects**: Affects as the generative material forming lived experiences defined as transitions in sensations, feelings and impressions and which may be distinguished within the same four affective domains
3. **Affective capacity:** The capacity of affectees to affect and be affected in interactional flows modulated by tendential forces formed from interactional, creational and valuational capacities
4. **Affectees and affectors**: Affectees are individual persons, families, communities, social groups and places experiencing a focal context of lived experience with health. Affectors are both human and non-human agents and entities having direct and indirect influence on affects forming lived experiences of affectees
5. **Social desire:** A normative idea of human experience that acts a prime circulating energy of force in the social body. It drives a sense of striving, creativity and innovation towards positive health and wellbeing and ideally (but rarely) greater harmony of existence with nature.
6. **Interactional flows**: Nine interactional flows of entities bearing affects, tendencies and capacities that emanate from, course and coalesce over virtual experience ecosystem environments and from which a focal experience ecosystem environment is cut-out for a focal lived experience with health context
7. **Tendential forces**: Six tendential forces bearing tendencies that modulate interactional flows and can restrict, sediment or stabilise their capacities and affects: ontological, epistemological, innovation, capital with labour, biopolitical, and regulatory
8. **Lived experience qualities within social desire for a focal context**: Poles of experience quality, ranging from positive desired (valued) experience (ideal social desire formed of ten elements) to negative ill-health experience
9. **States and transitions in lived experience for a focal context**: The existence of differentiated states of affect quality and affective capacity between the positive and negative poles for any focal lived experience with health context, and the mechanisms of transition between them
10. **Agencial assemblages:** Contingent agencial emergent open bodies consisting of an ensemble of heterogenous, self-subsistent and variously stabilized components and entities whose arrangements of interaction create, differenciate, repeat or recover a state of lived experience (with health) ... of a certain content and expression of affect quality, stability, duration and impact in the lived journeys of affectees (persons, families, groups, communities, places)

Together, these ten elements constitute a complete virtual interactional creation ontology of lived experiences (with health), an ontology that surfaces and explains the origination and differenciation of lived experiences into contingent states of affect quality, intensity, capacity, stability and recurrence of a certain content and expression. Deploying this ontology, HEVD helps to improve how we see, understand, design and act to create more health and wellbeing, and to prevent and recover illness and disease and wider related social problems.

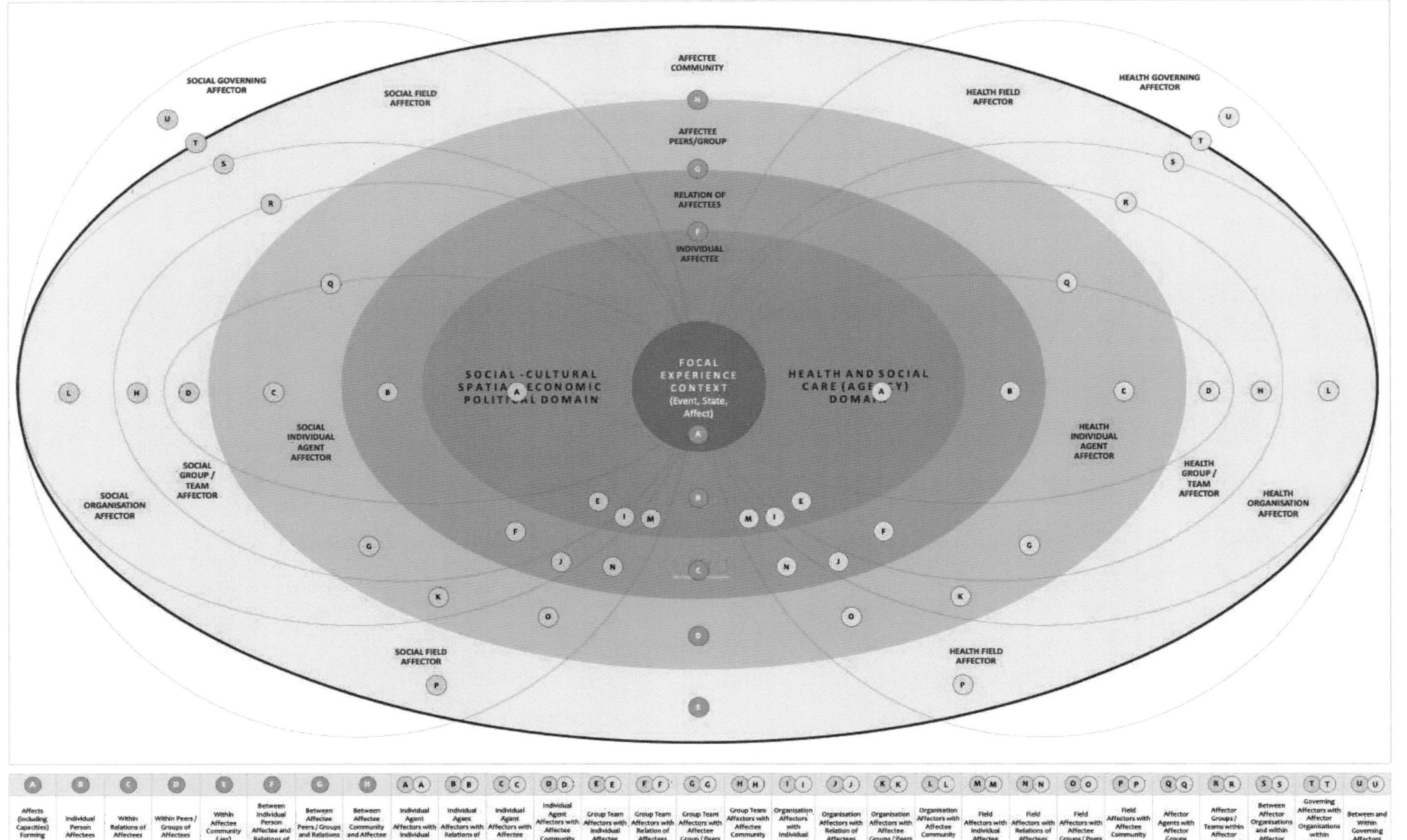

A	B	C	D	E	F	G	H	A A	B B	C C	D D	E E	F F	G G	H H	I I	J J	K K	L L	M M	N N	O O	P P	Q Q	R R	S S	T T	U U
Affects (Including Capacities) Forming Experience	Individual Person Affectees	Within Relations of Affectees	Within Peers / Groups of Affectees	Within Affectee Community (-ies)	Between Individual Person Affectee and Relations of Affectees	Between Affectee Peers / Groups and Relations of Affectees	Between Affectee Community and Affectee Peers / Group	Individual Agent Affectors with Individual Affectee	Individual Agent Affectors with Relations of Affectees	Individual Agent Affectors with Affectee Group / Peers	Individual Agent Affectors with Affectee Community (-ies)	Group Team Affectors with Individual Affectee	Group Team Affectors with Relation of Affectees	Group Team Affectors with Affectee Group / Peers	Group Team Affectors with Affectee Community (-ies)	Organisation Affectors with Individual Affectee	Organisation Affectors with Relation of Affectees	Organisation Affectors with Affectee Groups / Peers	Organisation Affectors with Affectee Community (-ies)	Field Affectors with Individual Affectee	Field Affectors with Relations of Affectees	Field Affectors with Affectee Groups / Peers	Field Affectors with Affectee Community (-ies)	Affector Agents with Affector Groups	Affector Groups / Teams within Affector Organisation	Between Affector Organisations and within Affector Fields	Governing Affectors with Affector Organisations within Affector Fields	Between and Within Governing Affectors

Figure 1.20: Focal experience ecosystem environment base template made of two domains: Health and the Social and with a focal health experience context at the centre and showing the individual spaces of interactions (circles with letters matching the key. NB Individual affectors may be human or non-human).

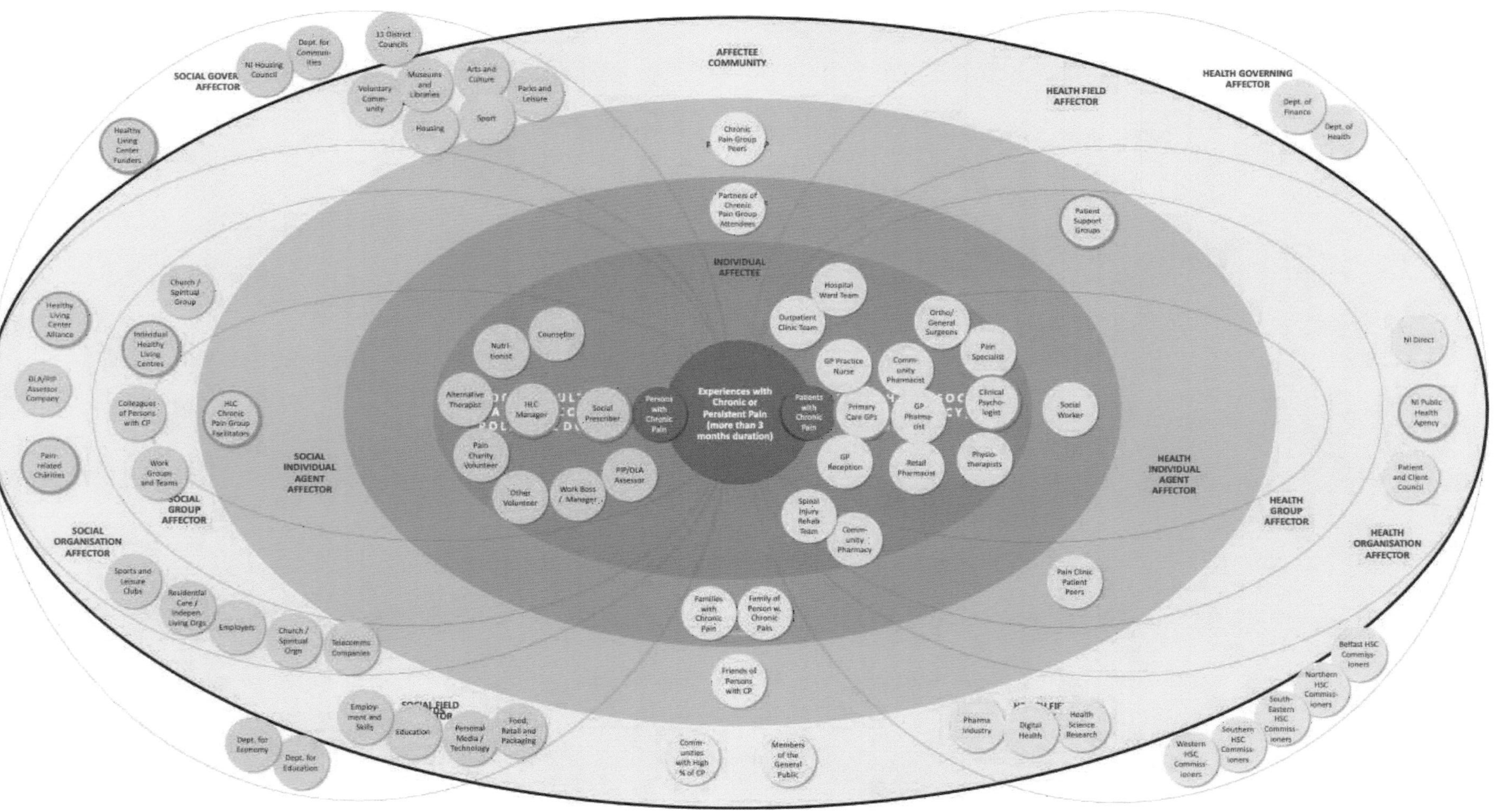

Figure 1.21: Example focal experience ecosystem environment of affectors for the chronic pain focal lived experience with health context (Northern Ireland)

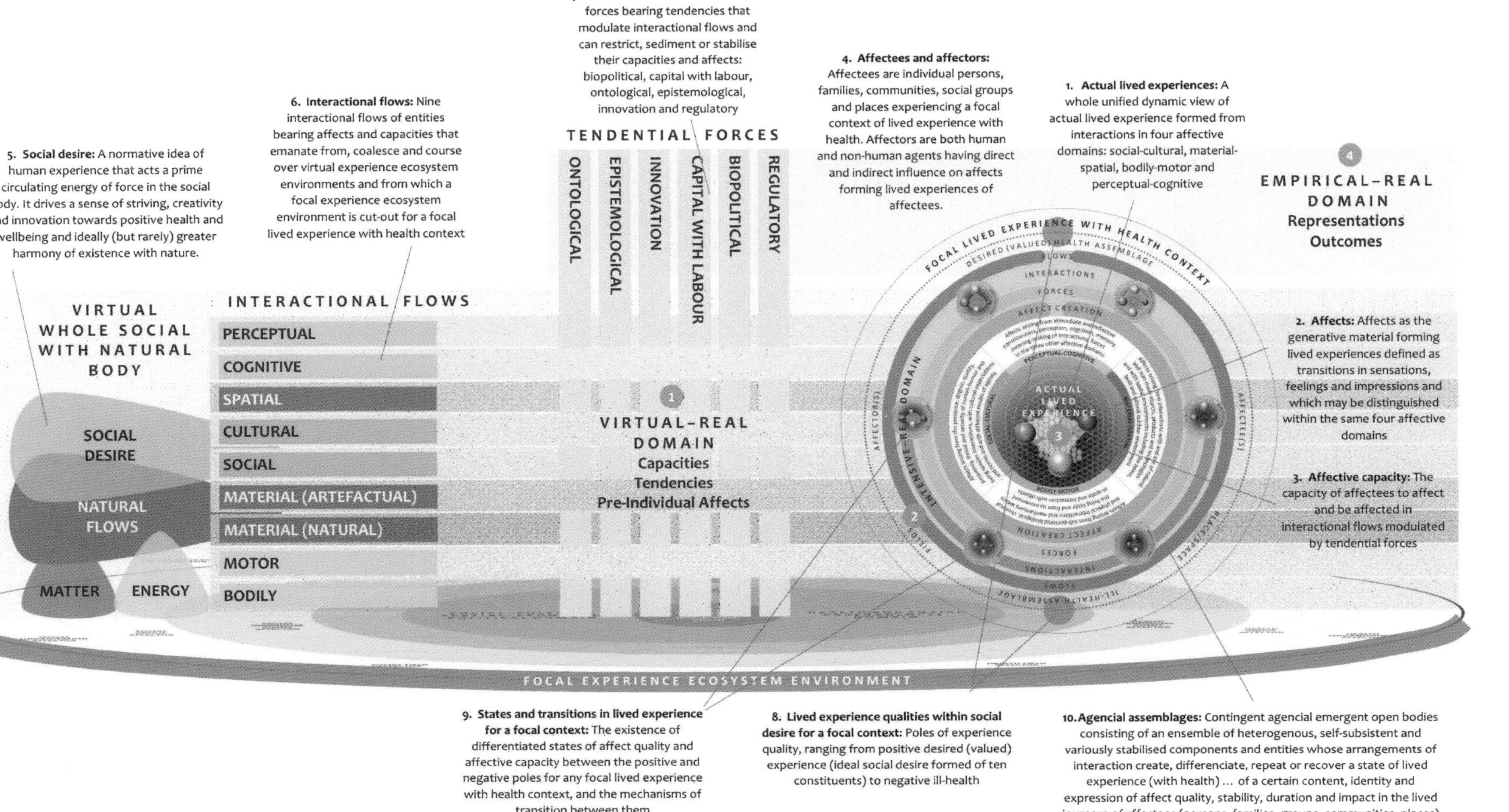

Figure 1.22 – Complete annotated model of an experience ecosystem environment showing interactional flows and tendential forces producing, differenciating and variously stabilising assemblages of states (quality, tendency, capacity) of lived experiences with health along with the four real domains of the virtual, intensive, actual and empirical

Summary

In summary, the final foundation seven states that a focal experience ecosystem environment (or FEEE) is an open system or "cut-out" of the virtual social (desire) with nature body within which contingent yet distinct agencial assemblages form and interact with coursing and coalescing interactional flows and tendential forces of potential affect, capacity and tendency to originate, differenciate and reproduce distinct states and qualities of lived experiences with health, disease and illness.

Foundation Seven
A focal experience ecosystem environment (or FEEE) is an open system or "cut-out" of the virtual social (desire) with nature body within which contingent yet distinct agencial assemblages form and interact with coursing and coalescing interactional flows and tendential forces of potential affect, capacity and tendency to originate, differenciate and reproduce distinct states and qualities of lived experiences with health, disease and illness

The seven foundations forming an interactional creation of health in experience ecosystems ontology

Below in Table 1.7 I repeat the seven foundations forming an interactional creation ontology of experience ecosystems. In the next chapter, I explain how I deploy the seven foundations to rethink and redefine health and value, and to create positive sustained impact in focal experience ecosystem environments.

Table 1.7 – The Seven Foundations forming an Interactional Creation of Health in Experience Ecosystems Ontology

No.	Foundation
1	Whole lived experiences with health, illness and disease are embodiments of the occurrence, force, content and patterning of human interactions in four intersecting domains, social-cultural, material-spatial, bodily-motor and perceptual-cognitive
2	Actual experiences with health, disease and illness are formed from individual and multiplicities of affects - defined as sensations, feeling states and impressions having real duration (sensed in psychological time over lived journeys) that mark a transition in an experiential state, as well as affective capacities defined as the capacity or power to act and to create affects and to be affected in interactions in four affective or interactional domains
3	Affects forming experience are actualized from affectee and affector capacities for affecting and being affected in interactions with individual and combinations of interactional flows and tendential forces that course over a virtual social with natural body and which bear capacities, degrees, intensities and rates of creative affect realization
4	For any focal lived with experience with health context, we can identify poles of positive and negative lived experience defined by states of affect quality and degrees of affective capacity
5	For any focal experience with health context, there exist distinct relatively homogenous yet dynamic states and capacities of lived experience, each formed of similar affective capacities from interactions within particular interactional flows modulated by tendential forces
6	The unit of enquiry and discovery is not the individual person (typically the objectified or categorized "patient") but an assemblage, an emergent agencial body of heterogeneous components differenciating and variously stabilising a state of lived experience of a certain quality and capacity, content and expression
7	A focal experience ecosystem environment (or FEEE) is an open system or “cut-out” of the virtual social (desire) with nature body within which contingent yet distinct agencial assemblages form and interact with coursing and coalescing interactional flows and tendential forces of potential affect, capacity and tendency to originate, differenciate and reproduce distinct states and qualities of lived experiences with health, disease and illness

Chapter Two

Rethinking health, value and the task and method of their interactional creation in experience ecosystems

The matter and life which fill the world are equally within us; the forces which work in all things we feel within ourselves; whatever may be the inner essence of what is and what is done, we are of that essence. Let us then go down into our own inner selves: the deeper the point we touch, the stronger will be the thrust which sends us back to the surface.

Henri Bergson

Chapter Two | Rethinking health, value and the task and method of their interactional creation in experience ecosystems

Introduction

In chapter one, I set out seven foundations forming an interactional creation ontology of health experience in a virtual social (desire) with natural body defined as an experience ecosystem. Using this ontology, I propose we can better see the creational mechanisms driving the origin, emergence, differenciation and recurrence of real lived experiences with health, illness and disease. Once we see these mechanisms and their different impacts in actual individual experiences and in focal experience ecosystem environments, I suggest too that we can engender novel collective and individual capacities to create and emerge the lived experiences with health that we desire and value and prevent and recover the dis-eases, diseases and illnesses that we do not.

In this chapter, I explain how the seven foundations in the ontology underpinning HEVD help us to rethink four fundamental drivers of perception, method, design and action in the health, life and the related social sciences. I then describe how this perspectival renewal helps us to see, create, enable and emerge more positive sustained impacts in our individual lived experiences with health, and more widely in focal health experience ecosystems. Following roughly the sequencing of the seven foundations, I ask four questions:

- How do we rethink *health and individual lived experience with health?*
- How do we rethink *value and its creation in individual lived experiences with health?*
- How do we rethink *health, value and their creation in experience ecosystem environments*?
- How do we rethink the *task and method of interactional creation in experience ecosystem environments*?

I then summarise how the Health Ecosystem Value Design framework addresses all four questions. I start with how we can rethink health and its individual lived experience.

How do we rethink health and individual lived experiences with health?

Implicit in the first five foundations described in chapter one is a view of individual health as holistic, embodied and enactive and as constituting a mode and capacity of interactional agency in lived experience. Also implicit is an idea of the human body as homo ecosystemus "folded" into the virtual social and natural body. By that I mean that the exterior world of social interactions, possibilities, relations, mores, values and rituals in which we participate in our thoughts and actions, and the natural world of matter and energy particles, flows and forces which we need to exist are both inside our human bodies; they form our subjectivities and the material and organistic processes that constitute our actual lived experience with health, and when it goes wrong, with disease and illness.

In this sense of the outside being inside, lived experiences with health are not seen as separate from exterior socio-environmental contexts, from social determinants of health or from underlying social structures (as is typically the case in much public health discourse and empirical realist method). Rather, these forces are present in potential pre-individual, pre-personal affects, tendencies and capacities in interactional flows and via their interaction, are actualized in our actual lived experience. Such a view moves us away from a rather vague "context-is-everything-yet-nowhere" view of disease and illness causation and also from a separating "upstream" force and "downstream" outcome model. In their stead is a transcending whole view of affects and capacities forming experience from the interactional creation of difference in interactional flows.

The interactional whole lived experience perspective of HEVD contrasts with prevailing views of individual human agency, action and experience found in the mind (cognitive science, neuroscience, psychology[25]) and behavioural sciences. Embracing a form of methodological individualism where behavioural scientists focus on intention-action outside the mind, and the mind sciences look inside the mind using a computer processing metaphor, they both detach the mind from the body and the environment in which it is situated. In doing so they negate the dynamic situated interactions of all three in forming lived experiences. But we know from biology that the body embodies and senses movements of affect in the form of changing sensations, feeling states and impressions. Also, we know that we perceive and experience the world and create meaning via intercorporeal interactions with other human bodies, with material entities and also through our movements in space. Yet both the mind and behavioural sciences tend to reduce the role of the body in producing and recording (in its own memory) states and transitions in lived experience. They do not see the body as an element of mind operating together as one dynamical system of powers, sympathies and sensitivities situated in and interacting with its environment.

Further, prevailing normative, rational goal-driven models of homo economicus individual agency tend to assume a straight-line of agential-centric reasoning from goal to decision to action and then a valuation loop back again in which the human agent assesses performance against an original intent. In this closed system model of individual rational agency, little consideration is given to the developmental properties of capacities that emerge in the "becoming of lived experience" in search of novelty, difference and possibility. Contrary to intentional agency models, humans are not goal-driven rational decision-making machines but rather they trial, enact, learn and reuse their capacities in everyday interactions. A creational capacity is therefore immanent to agency when it is viewed as an ongoing affective capacity for connection, growth, change and development in the pursuit of different or novel lived experiences.

---

[25] For the past five or six decades, the cognitivist mind sciences (neuroscience, psychology, cognitive science) have embraced a computer-based metaphor of the mind. Locating the mind within the brain, they hope to match the structure of complex problems with the brain mechanisms that compute how we anticipate, reason, decide and act upon them (such as how we are likely to respond when inexplicably finding ourselves in the middle of a fast-flowing river). Deploying an information processing view of the mind, they hope to create hypotheses, build theoretical frameworks and develop predictive models that link problem content and contexts with specific brain-mind functions and with certain types of response or action.

The HEVD perspective

HEVD looks beyond computational brain mechanisms and motivation-behaviour models to ask more systemic questions concerning the origination, divergence and persistence of different lived experiences and the capacities and tendencies in moving flows and forces influencing them. Whilst it may seem that the prevailing mind and behavioral sciences have full coverage of a beginning (intention, goal), middle (brain mechanisms) and end (behaviour), all omit the essential underlying continuous qualitative becoming reality of lived experience in their formulations and methods. All three are based on the search for similarity and generalization, not explanation of difference. Each leads to an abstraction of experience that fails to account for the energies, creativities, capacities and diversities of real lives. In essence, they all struggle to account for the origins, conditions and contexts as well as the real possibilities of actual lived experience.

In contrast, HEVD views mind as an embodied and creational system. The transcending qualities of our embodied minds contain and generate a capacity to create, interact and act. If the mind were machine-like, it could not sense and respond to risk and opportunity in the interactional flows of the social and natural body nor with the open-ended and dynamic nature of interests motivating our perception-actions. Rather, the very capacities that enable the mind to interact in flows of possibilities also allow it to wander beyond them, imagining opportunity yet to be created and discovering new connections in a virtual-real domain that is beyond the horizon of our individual actions.

Embracing a whole enactive and situated view of the human body, HEVD therefore redefines action and agency as follows:

- **Action** or interaction is an embodied creation, transition or movement in affects producing experience and experienced events.
- **Agency** is the affective capacity to create (as opposed to act per se) within interactional flows and tendential forces of affect in pursuit of an individual sense of desired, valued experience. It entails the capacity to improve life conditions or avoid threats by assessing a situation relative to what is expected and then acting on it in a directed and more or less efficient manner.

With these views of action and agency as the dynamic mechanisms in lived experience enacted and embodied in interactional flows and forces, affects and affective capacities become the basis for seeing patterns of the emergence, persistence and concentration of states of qualities of experience in types of individuals, communities, social groups and places over time.

Beyond an abstracted logic of quantified experience states of health and disease

An important perspective on health and its lived experience embraced by HEVD addresses a dominant view in the empirical health sciences and especially in clinical practice. This concerns the use of an abstracted logic that divides actual experiences with health into ordinal representational states. Viewing these states as "things", they are usually distinguished using a measure or category of quantity or intensity for a given state. For example, a pain score, a BMI of obesity, a score of depression, a stress scale and so on. Assuming these quantitatively ordered and distinct states of lived experience with health, disease and illness actually exist, the empirical health sciences then apply the logic of rational agency to assess the nature, effect and outcome of individual human and other affector (human and non-human, e.g., technology) actions upon these states. Then, by examining changes across intervals of experience states (such as a reduction in a pain score from 7 to 5) in relation to certain actions taken with affectors, agency too is broken down into a series of episodic time-bounded actions with discrete ends marked by outcome points, with each action rationally considered, enacted and evaluated in a mindful stepwise manner.

Many have argued about the flaws of quantifying lived experience and of an associational model of agency and action that is derived from this abstraction[26]. They posit that by substituting quantity for quality of experience, spatial ordering models of experience get trapped in an unproductive cycle of experimental verifications of quantitatively differentiated states of experience that do not actually exist. The truth is they suggest, there is no direct equivalence between quality of experience and its quantitative measurement and ordering. When we substitute quantity for quality, we can only ever work with poorly analysed reductions and composites of actual lived experience and then when we act using these approximations, our interventions are inevitably blunted, fail, are sub-optimal or miss their actual target.

To address the shortcomings of a quantitative fragmenting logic of lived experience with health and as I described in foundation two (and depict in the model of interior lived experience in Figure 1.14), we must conceive of actual lived experience as a continuous flow in real sensed time made up of a multiplicity of affects that move, combine and fuse like different notes forming a chord or a melody in a song. In this view, an action does not delimit and transition experience from one distinct state to another but rather embodies a movement of affects over *gradations in qualitative states of experience*. In this flow sense of experience therefore, action can be further reconceived as the embodied creation of a *gradational movement in intrinsic affects* forming experience (via interaction within interactional flows), a creation that may shift experience in three directions or lines of becoming: positive towards ideal desired (valued) experience, negative towards ill-health experience or stabilizing or stuck within recurrent experience.

With action viewed as an embodiment of an intensive creation of movement of affects in lived experience and agency as creational affective capacity (see above), HEVD pays more attention to sensory-motor perception-action, intuition, memory, heuristics and tendencies in capacities acting in interactional flows as the underlying mechanisms driving real lived experience. All replace rational cognitive reasoning and machine-like information processing as the engines of action and agency. No longer is experience reduced to intentions, observed actions, quantitative states and outcomes. No more do we rely on the study of the linear relation of goal to reason to decision to action. In their place is a qualitative creational interactional model that foregrounds perception-action, intrinsic affects, qualities, capacities and their embodied enaction in creations and transitions of interactional flows of lived experience. Whilst the cognitive neurosciences may tell us how things are solved by the brain as a computer, the behavioural sciences may inform us about observable patterns of health behaviour, and health economists (anticipating my arguments about value below) can make forward projections of the future value and impact of new entities and resources in health systems, all three lack understanding of the actual interactional mechanisms of creation and differenciation of actual lived experiences with health. How do we overcome these limitations? By starting with a new definition of health itself.

A new definition of health in individual lived experience

Combining the above critical analysis, I now redefine health itself. In doing so, I go beyond the dominant biomedical, reductionist and individual behavioural agency / person-centric view of health as normal baseline functioning, end-state absence of disease, risk mitigation and a resource for living. Rather I define health as a whole affective capacity or power for creating desired valued and meaningful lived experiences that (using the ten dimensions of social desire described in foundation four in chapter one) are expressed in summary form as a full expected life, bodily vitality and integrity, creativity, belonging and attachment, social purpose, human connection, connection with nature, play and freedom.

In this perspectival *relocation*, health is no longer a separate object existing outside of our self-perception but rather is now brought fully into or inside our whole actual lived experience. In this perspectival *expansion*, health is no longer seen as an objectified and quantified functional end in itself to be normalized or repaired but rather is viewed as a means to create and realize the desired, valued experiences we seek. Health therefore

[26] I base my arguments again on those of Henri Bergson.

is regarded as a whole potential capacity for positive, normative striving in lived journeys of experience; it is a creational force for individual and as we shall see, collective being and becoming. With this view of health as inside and whole to our experience, the freedoms, creations, belongings and connections that we seek, together with their absence and the forces enabling or preventing them in our environment become the objects of study, design, intervention and action. Health has therefore moved firmly into the centre of our critical social science. Health is lived experience.

Redefining health at the level of individual personal lived experience
Health is a whole affective capacity or power for creating desired valued and meaningful lived experiences expressed as a full expected life, bodily vitality and integrity, creativity, belonging and attachment, social purpose, human connection, connection with nature, play and participatory freedom

Next, I reconceptualize value using the above affect and affective capacity-based and social desire-seeking view of health in whole lived experience.

How do we rethink value and its creation in individual lived experiences with health?

In the prevailing view of individual rational agency held by the mind, behavioural and empirical health sciences, and deployed in economic exchange-based models of value, human (or homo economicus) actions are said to be undertaken intentionally, rationally and evaluatively in relation to a definable goal, the exchange and use of material (products) or human resources (services), and the impact of the action measured with quantified outcomes. This is a functionalist view of human agency and also of capacity that is directed by intention and motivation, decided through information-based reasoning and problem-solving, enacted by a mind separate from the body and isolated from the environment in which choice and action occur. The following are the main characteristics of this prevailing view of individual agency:

- **Purposeful intention.** Conscious deliberative guided action is directed towards an outcome from use of an entity in the form of a product, technology, service or human resource; action that can be distinguished from merely reflexive reactive responses to external stimuli in the environment
- **Causal information-based reasoning**. Goal- and object-directed options, decisions and modes of action are filtered through a rational linear causal reasoning information process
- **Freedom of choice**. Human agents act with freedom of choice in how, where and when to act and with what object or thing. Freedom is conceived in individualistic terms as an inalienable right or private property of an isolated passionate individual.
- **Mind is separate from the body.** Agency is a cognitive rational mind-centred (or more specifically brain-centred) process that occurs independently of the human physical body. The body is an external separate object of directed intentional action. This is why an individual agency view regards a bodily disease or illness as a thing to fight or battle with; it is objectified and distinguished from the mind.

Adopting this model of agency, research methods in the health, care and related social sciences pursue law-like analysis and prediction of complex health, disease and related social phenomena via empirical realist method and through study of individual people's intentions and motivations, goals, choices and actions. Such methods have their roots in the social science doctrine of methodological individualism, an epistemological perspective originating in the nineteenth century in the work of J.S. Mill and later elaborated theoretically by Max Weber (1922). Taken into an economic realm by late nineteenth century neoclassical rational action/choice theory, articulated by the celebrated economist Joseph Schumpeter (who was Weber's student) in 1908 and taken up by Karl Popper (1945) who boldly called it an "unassailable doctrine", MI holds a positivistic, functionalist, utilitarian view of human agency. Although not as bounded to a pure form of doctrine of MI as others, Schumpeter (1954: 888) explained the rationale for his focus on the individual as the primary unit of analysis:

> *"the self-governing individual constitutes the ultimate unit of the social sciences; ... all social phenomena resolve themselves into the decisions and actions of individuals that need not or cannot be further analysed in terms of super-individual factors."*

Insofar as public health, healthcare professionals, health economists and policymakers hold an underlying shared epistemological perspective, methodological individualism is the most prevalent and influential. Embracing the rational view of individual agency described above, value in the health, care and related social sciences is assessed in terms of the *property* of an entity in *relation* to its potential effect on health, disease or illness outcomes when used by an agent. To elucidate both,

- **A property** in the sense of the "valued" property or properties of the external entity, object, person, service or other resource used in an agent action and,

- **A relation** in the sense of the relation of the entity and an action to a desired goal, intention and/or change in a state of health or illness that is determined by an outcome for which an action is directed.

Such relational properties of value can be of four types:

1. **Utilitarian** where an entity (object or person or service) helps an agent to perform an action linked to a state of health and a goal-intention (e.g., a pain drug to relieve pain)
2. **Instrumental** where it contributes to another entity's performance of an action linked to a state of health and goal (e.g., a device to deliver a pain drug)
3. **Inherent** if it adds value during the agent reasoning process prior to its acquisition or use in an action for a state of health (e.g., the contemplation of having a more powerful drug to relieve excess pain), or
4. **Contributory** if it supports a wider context of action of which it is part (e.g., being able to sleep without pain).

Similar to methodological individualism, this relational property-based logic of value in health has its origins in late nineteenth century neoclassical economics built on marginal utility and equilibrium theory of markets. It has persisted ever since. In the health care disciplines, the logic of an exchange-based view of a relational value runs as follows:

1. Capital (industry or state-provided investment) joins with labour (healthcare workforce, employees, patients) (a tendential force if you recall) to infuse potential value (one or more of the four relational valued properties) in health-creating or disease-mitigation or treatment entities – whether products, persons, services, technology or data or their combination - in relation to evidence and estimates of their efficacy, need, demand and the cost of their manufacture, distribution and use/deployment.
2. The infused properties of value in the entity become actualized either before an entity is acquired (inherent property), when it is exchanged (contributory property) or when it is actually used in action (utilitarian or instrumental property)
3. Third-party agents (payers and regulators who may never use the entity) undertake valuations of an entity linked to their own goals and outcomes along with societal, ethical, economic and practical considerations in relation to its cost compared with other entities
4. Imbued with these properties, entities are exchanged at a cost with the end-user agent or with intermediate agents relative to their valuation
5. Individual end-user agents use the entity to unlock its infused value and perform a valuation linked to their own goals and intentions

Using this linear logic of value creation, health economists predict trajectories of valuation and value realization using results from controlled clinical research and other tests based on future interventions of resources and agents in health systems. Since the birth of health economics and outcomes research as a discipline in the 1960s, there is a strong tendency to value disease or illness-treatment products, technologies and services and scarce resources based on future clinical decision-making, exchange- and potential outcome-based terms. Today, this remains the primary mode of research and valuation shaping priority, organization and practice in the health sciences.

In Figure 2.1, I pare and fragment the original base model of lived experience (Figure 1.1 in chapter one) to illustrate the position and relation of the defining characteristics, methods and views of value-in-exchange and value-in-use held within a functionalist individual agency view.

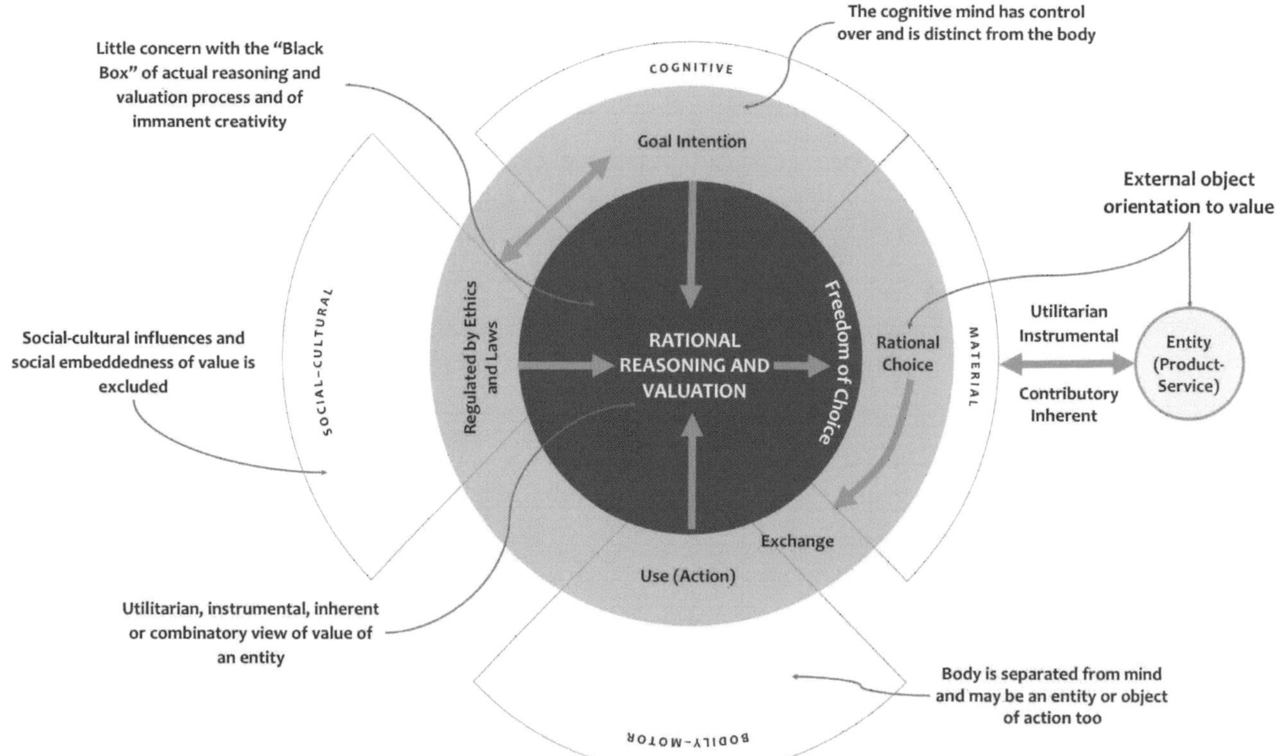

Figure 2.1 – Modified model of whole unified lived experience showing primary characteristics and relations of the individual agency view of value and method in health and social sciences

Having explained the individual-agency-based view of value and how it shapes prevailing research methods in the health, care, health economic and related social sciences, I now offer my reconceptualization.

A new definition of value and its creation in individual lived experience

In HEVD's view of health as whole affective capacity for creation of meaningful desired valued experiences and of action as an embodied interactional movement or transition in lived experience, we see that our view of value and its creation changes too. Value is no longer an objective property of an entity that is exchanged in relation to its perceived or actual value, whether utilitarian, instrumental, inherent and/or contributory compared to another entity and its cost. Nor is value-creation focused on achieving improvements in functional outcomes of disease at lower cost, using rudimentary quality of life scores and vague notions of wellbeing and flourishing. Instead, we now see value and its creation in individual lived experience to be,

a) *embodied* in intensive interactional creations, movements and transitions in affective capacity,
b) *experienced* in the actualized events of affectees, and
c) *effectuated* in the impact of events in the real duration or sensed time of lived journeys of affectees (and also human affectors).

In this conception, value is a dynamical construct of potential affective capacity creation and realization in lived experience. In individual lived experiences with health, it is the interactional creation of surplus and/or novel social-cultural, material-spatial, perceptual-cognitive and bodily-motor affective capacities having potential to create and sustain affects of desired, valued experiences expressed (through the normative ideal of social desire) as a full expected life, bodily health and integrity, creativity, belonging and attachment, social purpose, human connection, connection with nature, play and freedom. Here, value is no longer located in the relational properties of an external entity but rather has moved to the interior of individual lived experience. What we can call *value-in-interactional creation* is the inside event transition or movement of intrinsic affects and affective capacities that have the potential to create more desired valued lived experiences.

Redefining value and its creation in individual lived experience
Value-creation in health is the interactional-creation of surplus and/or novel social-cultural, material-spatial, perceptual-cognitive and bodily-motor affective capacities having potential to create and sustain affects forming desired, valued experiences expressed (through the normative ideal of social desire) as a full expected life, bodily health and integrity, creativity, belonging and attachment, social purpose, human connection, connection with nature, play and participatory freedom

To visualize value as the interactional creation of affective capacities in lived experience, over the next two pages I annotate two examples of the interior model of whole unified lived experience shown in Figure 1.14. The first is for chronic pain lived experience and the second for work-related cognitive and physical stress leading to burnout. Each entails a four-way holistic creation of affective capacities and affects. Briefly I set the context and explain both examples.

Chronic pain lived experience

Chronic pain affects about 40 per cent of the adult population in the UK, the same proportion as most Western nations. At any given time, approximately 14% of the total UK population experience pain that is either moderately or severely disabling. Women are more likely to experience chronic pain than men and prevalence increases with age; two-thirds in those over the age of 75 suffer from pain. In those with chronic pain, 87% have at least one other chronic physical or mental health condition. Significant disability and loss of role functioning is often a consequence.

The model in Figure 2.2 depicts the four-way interactional creation of affective capacities forming whole lived experience with chronic pain for persons who are badly affected and debilitated by their pain. In Table 2.1, I list a selection of potential means to enact these creations and the affects they produce to generate improvements in lived experience with pain. An important *affective capacity is found in social-cultural interactional flows* (the "D" interactional creation) that connects persons with chronic pain with each other (especially those who are now able to live well with pain and can pass on their knowledge), and with persons and groups who can help them with both pain-centric and non-pain related daily needs and activities through new forms of community-level interactional creation in social engagements.

Work-related cognitive and physical stress leading to burnout

The costs and health impacts of work-related burnout are huge. In the UK, the cost of presenteeism is estimated to be £15.1bn per year, dwarfing the £8.4bn cost of absenteeism (UK Centre for Mental Health). The European Agency for Safety and Health at Work cites stress as a factor in at least half of all lost working days and Gallup reports 41% lower health-related costs for employees with thriving wellbeing, compared with those who are struggling. More than ever before, worker wellbeing is now good business, providing an advantage for organizations intent on competing successfully. The return is high for forward-thinking organizations that invest in the whole lived experience of their people by thinking about it interactionally and incorporating it as part of their business strategy.

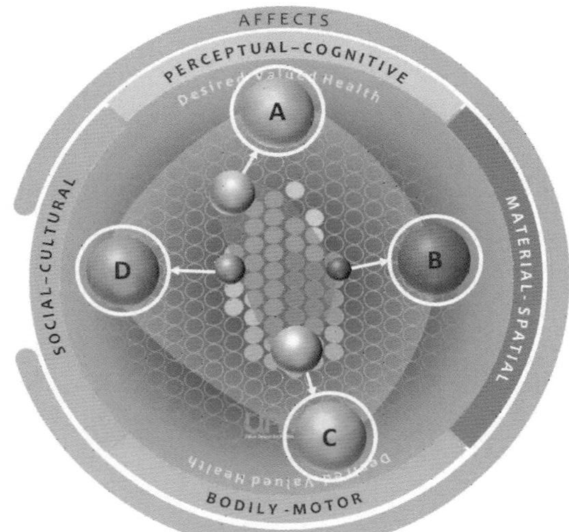

Figure 2.2: Example of value-in-interactional creation in individual lived experience with health for person with extreme debilitating chronic pain

NB: The letters A B, C and D indicate transitions in four interactional affective capacities. The red space indicates a current lived experience with health (in this case with chronic pain). The grey space indicates the target improved lived experience with health.

Table 2.1: Targeted creations in affective capacities in lived experience with chronic pain

Creation and description	Example means to enact creation in affective capacity	Example target affects to transition
A. Creating affective capacity in PERCEPTUAL-COGNITIVE interactional flows	• Make a person's experience and progress living with pain more visible • Create a personal "Living with Chronic Pain" progress index • Co-create predictive pain flare models for use by pain persons • Identify and overcome limiting individual perceptions of pain	• Sense of a lack of progress • Sense of confusion about why a pain episode has occurred • Sense of fear of flare-ups leads to movement paralysis • Sense of a loss of power • Sense of diminished capacity to concentrate
B. Creating affective capacity in MATERIAL-SPATIAL interactional flows	• Co-create capacity to choose suitable places and spaces to visit or navigate in built environment for persons with pain • Co-create collective model of environmental factors with episodes of pain, e.g., daily weather, seasons	• Sense of foreboding about a change in the seasons bringing pain • Sense of worry about an environmental factor causing pain, e.g., weather change • Sense of unwanted dependency on a digital pain technology • Sense of anxiety when outdoors • Sense of confinement in the home
C. Creating affective capacity in BODILY-MOTOR interactional flows	• Support optimization of pain medication use • Develop capacity to take compensatory actions to reduce pain that work consistently • Co-create capacity to understand relationship between intensity of activity and a pain response	• Sensation of pain that arises from a particular resting body state • Sensation of pain arising from a load on part of the body • Sensation of pain linked to changes in weather • Sense of losing control of pain medication use
D. Creating affective capacity in SOCIAL-CULTURAL interactional flows	• Co-create pain persons / GP interaction / question skills • Include family members in community Chronic Pain programmes • Define community volunteering pathways for Chronic Pain persons • Develop peer-peer co-creation of social capacities	• Sense of being not taken seriously • Sense of being perceived as untruthful by others (about the pain) • Sense of being a burden / dependent on others • Sense of being blamed for having chronic pain • Sense of loss of connectedness / belonging

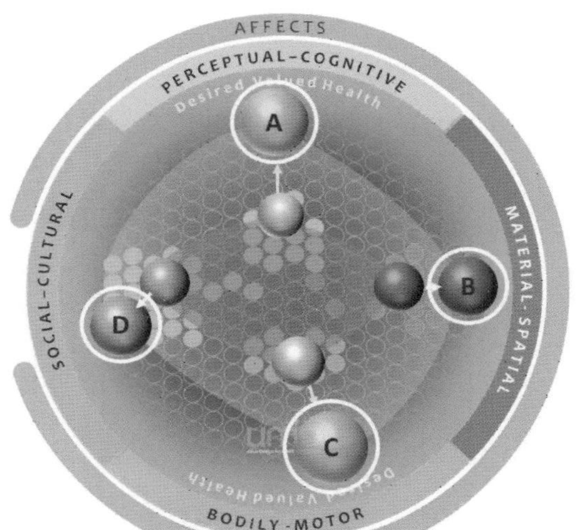

Figure 2.3: Example of value-in-interactional creation in individual lived experience with health for person with work-related cognitive and physical stress leading to risk of burnout

The letters A B, C and D indicate transitions in four relational affective capacities. The red space indicates a current lived experience with health (in this case with risk of burnout). The grey space indicates the target improved lived experience with health.

Table 2.2: Targeted creations in affective capacities in lived experience with workplace stress

Creation and description	Example means to enact transition in affective capacity	Example affect transitions
A. Creating affective capacity in PERCEPTUAL-COGNITIVE interactional flows	• Support more creative freedom and self-expression at work • Increase variety of types of work undertaken • Support shift from work perfection and keeping up pretenses to emotional openness • Encourage personal expressiveness • Offload routine tasks into the work environment	• Sense of failing to cope with tasks • Sense of acting with greater risk to self and others • Sense of diminished creativity • Sense of feeling no longer useful to others
B. Creating affective capacity in MATERIAL-SPATIAL interactional-flows	• Introduce "soft" home-like environments at work • Provide quiet spaces for reflection • Adapt workspace for flexible types of work	• Sense of being confined in the same space • Sense of limited choice about where to work • Sense of excess workspace noise having undesirable effects
C. Creating affective capacity in BODILY-MOTOR interactional flows	• Help employees monitor their bodies to detect early signs of stress and pain at work • Increase degree of bodily movement at work • Encourage a variety and change in body postures at work in varied locations in the workspace • Recover the downward trend in neck and shoulder position	• Sense of developing pain • Sense of fatigue • Sense of frustration at lack of time to exercise • Sense of body slowing down • Sense of pain in the upper extremity, especially neck and shoulders
D. Creating affective capacity in SOCIAL-CULTURAL interactional flows	• Increase shared beliefs through purpose- or "calling-driven" organizations • Create shared meaning or sense of community at work • Design workspaces for transparency, so people can see and be seen and build trust	• Sense of not belonging to work and with colleagues • Sense of work being routine and functional • Sense of a lack of trust and team support at work

The model in Figure 2.3 shows the four-way interactional creation of affective capacities forming whole lived experience of persons suffering from work-related burnout. In Table 2.2, I list a selection of potential means to enact these creations and the affects forming experience that are transitioned. Key *affective capacities are found in perceptual-cognitive and material-spatial interactional flows* (the "A" and "B" transitions) that aim to create work and workplace environments and cultures where positive affects can form and thrive. Whilst physical wellness is an important area of concern, focusing only on bodily-motor affective capacities and especially the ergonomics of posture and movement at work misses the bigger opportunity. Whilst most companies rely on hunches or trial-and-error approaches to workplace wellbeing, this interactional model affords a whole systemic view of potential transitions in wellbeing and reduction in burnout through a wider definition of health and an embodied affect-based view of work-related interactional flows in actual lived experience.

Having redefined health and value at the level of individual experience, next I widen our perspective to describe how we can also redefine them and their creation at the level of focal experience ecosystem environments or FEEEs (defined in foundation seven in chapter one).

How do we rethink health, value and their creation in experience ecosystem environments?

Covid-19 has shown us that health, illness and disease are and were always a collective phenomenon. Today more than ever, health is no longer within the control of the individual person acting as an intentioned rational agent but rather is now shaped by an intensifying and accelerating mesh of interactions amongst an increasingly diverse body of health affectors and other affectees, each often pursuing and enacting their own interests. The state, corporations, employers, insurers, media, communication and information technology providers, urban planners, building architects, vehicle manufacturers, non-governmental and social organizations and community groups to name a few, as well as traditional health system actors, their government funders and regulators, all are entangled in a complex confluence of affective capacities and affects in assemblages of interactional flows and tendential forces shaping our lived experiences with health. Add a non-human entity such as a deadly virus into the mix and the reality of a convergent interactional and collective "being in the world" picture of health, disease and illness creation comes starkly into view.

Accelerating the interactional nature and the possibility of new modes of creation of lived experience with health is ongoing digitalization. A recent McKinsey survey of nearly 900 global C-level executives in a mix of industries and functions found that Covid-19 has rapidly hastened their investments in digitalized offerings[27] by as much 7 to 10 years. In the first half of the 2020s, we can expect further rapid convergence of physical and digital interactions that distribute, democratize and de-centre health and value-in-health interactional creation, communication and information-sharing across all hierarchal levels of society. From individual persons through families and communities to social groups, industry, health organizations and governing bodies, all shall be participants in emergent flows of co-creation enabled by increasingly digitalized, platformized and resourced capabilities in experience ecosystem environments.

Yet the full potential of this interactional mode of health creation risks being held back by prevailing rational individual agency models and associated ideas of value and of health itself. Dominant conceptions and methods do not align with an intensifying *co-creational* picture of diverse, open affectee and affector flow interactions; they do not see or can capture all the promise of an emergent reality of a multi-actor, not-just-human interactional picture of health, disease and illness in lived experience co-creation. Nor do they always consider how an individual person's idea of their health and their value is co-extensive with social ideas of health and value, and how both are always changing, as we have witnessed and continue to observe with Covid-19.

Reflecting on the above developments and the gap in perception and understanding of potential opportunities, I now offer my "rethinking" of value and first health at the level of focal experience ecosystem environments.

Rethinking health and its creation at the level of experience ecosystem environments

Building on the definition of health at the level of individual human lived experience, within the wider frame of focal experience ecosystem environments (FEEEs) we can now problematise health as a *collective affective capacity* to co-create social desire in lived experiences with health, with social desire now expanded and expressed as the ecosystems of lived experience of full expected lives, bodily health and integrity, creativity, belonging and attachment, social purpose, human connection, connection with nature, play and participatory freedom.

In this definition, our perception and frame of health and also of agency and action is enlarged to that of a focal experience ecosystem environment, and our view of affective capacity expands to the capacity of all affectors (human and non-human) and affectees to co-create surplus potential and/or novel social desire. With this expansion, we now explore and address differences in health affective capacity within affectees at all levels

[27] https://www.mckinsey.com/business-functions/strategy-and-corporate-finance/our-insights/howcovid-19-has-pushed-companies-over-the-technology-tipping-point-and-transformed-businessforever (last retrieved January 2nd, 2021)

(individuals, families, communities, social groups, places and populations) and we focus our learning efforts on understanding where potential affective capacity exists, where it is being generated or enacted, where it is stuck and where it is absent in different agencial assemblages acting upon interactional flows and tendential forces coursing over the virtual social and natural body.

Redefining health at the level of focal experience ecosystem environments
The collective affective capacity to co-create social desire in lived experiences with health, with social desire now expanded and expressed as the ecosystems of lived experience of full expected lives, bodily health and integrity, creativity, belonging and attachment, social purpose, human connection, connection with nature, play and participatory freedom.

Having defined health at the level of experience ecosystem environments, I now augment this conceptualization by redefining value and its creation through the lens of interactional creation ontology.

Rethinking value and its creation at the level of experience ecosystem environments

The acceleration of technology and digital offerings in the next decade that I described above should herald a perspectival, methodological and practical shift in value and its creation in lived experiences with health (and indeed in all lived experience contexts). Yet the full potential of an interactional mode of health creation risks being slowed by existing largely functionalist individual rational agency thinking, the use of abstract quantified and interval-based models of lived experience with health states (especially in disease and illness diagnosis, guidelines and standards) and their related ideas of action, intervention and value (exchange and use) and of health itself. Methodologically speaking too, prevailing modes of co-creation risk retarding future possibilities. They do not perceive, learn, design, assess and act within an experience ecosystem frame of assemblages of diverse, heterogeneous open interacting affectee and affectors acting in interactional flows. They do not see how value is created by a plurality of human and non-human agent entities with diverse affective capacities and where everybody and everything is a co-creator of value in different degrees.

Before defining value and its co-creation in the interactional creation ontology of HEVD, first I briefly describe two prevailing modes of co-creation thinking presently deployed in health and most other design and value creation contexts. I do so to draw the key distinctions between them and the interactional creation perspective. The two modes of co-creation are project-based design thinking and service dominant logic.

Co-creation in project-based design thinking

In many health-oriented design thinking efforts, co-creation follows a functionalist, project-based model enacted through stakeholder and end-user (patient) collaboration, idea generation, prototype product and service creation and experimentation, all usually directed towards a goal determined and measured by outcomes. Here, as per rational individual agency, the view of value held by actor participants is largely utilitarian, instrumental, contributory and inherent and the model of valuation itself is largely economic.

In this mode of co-creation, participants capture expert inputs and build empathy-based narratives with affectees to pursue rapid experimentation of potential product and service solutions. With less time spent on systemic problem framing, learning and immersion, this design-focused method of co-creation assumes it can generate a "learning multiplier" when expert participants from different disciplinary backgrounds and affectees with first-hand lived experience perspectives share narratives, ideas and their knowledge.

In its quest for rapid action through experimentation, project-based design thinking tends to use established categories of health problems when co-creating ideas and concepts. Using existing empirical representations such as disease types, abstracted experience states, quantities, symptoms and standard outcome measures, the tendency is to seek and work with actionable generalizations of experience rather than the harder-to-see differences in actual lived experiences. This cognitive preference for the empirical, the same and the known explains why many ideas and solutions generated or co-created in this way fail to have much impact; they lack sufficient breadth (reaching beyond traditional problem boundaries and assumptions) and depth (reaching down into differences within problem frames). Indeed, project modes of co-creation find it easier to stay "close to the status quo" rather than exploring the "adjacent possible". They can suffer a bias towards the reasonable and the doable, rather than the transformative in their ambition. The forces and flows present in experience ecosystems are too intangible or unknowable and are difficult to work with in a design process that emphasises speed of experimentation, action and iteration.

Service-ecosystem and -dominant logic mode of value co-creation

In service-dominant logic (SDL) thinking[28], multiple actors create, access, share, interact with and integrate their resources to achieve or realise a service purpose (such as to prevent, screen, diagnose, treat, monitor a disease, etc.) and outcome. In SDL, these actor interactions occur in a service ecosystem focused on a beneficiary actor, the actor with a need or problem such as a patient. A service ecosystem is defined as a "relatively, self-contained, self-adjusting system of resource-integrating actors connected by shared institutional arrangements and mutual value-creation through service exchange."[29] Service ecosystem value emerges from beneficiary, service and overseer actor resource integrations, from the influence of contexts, material resources, capabilities and knowledge, and from their arrangement and co-ordination in roles, practices and organizations. In any service ecosystem, practices of co-creation of resource integration appear, emerge, self-sustain, rigidify and decline at different rates.

In service dominant logic, value is originated via actor-generated co-ordinations (through project-based design thinking perhaps) and institutional arrangements that support resource integration. It is then "released" during service-based exchanges of actors with beneficiary actors. Value co-created in this way is heterogeneous, meaning-laden, diversely understood, held, derived and determined by ecosystem actors in varying contexts. Value is determined phenomenologically by beneficiary actors, incorporates the context of present experience in use, is always co-created and has an emergent property that comes into view in a temporal and contextual manner.

Emphasis on the "co" not the "creation"

In both project-based design thinking and service-dominant logic modes, co-creation is concerned with the activities, resources, integration and outputs of collaborating human actors (whether in design studios or service ecosystem practices) rather than with the mechanisms of creation involved in actually producing value. In them, the emphasis is more on the prefix "co" rather than the suffix "creation"[30]. They are more concerned with questions of "who creates value?" and "who is the value created for?" rather than the actual processes of "creation" itself. Indeed, beyond these two modes a focus on the "co" has led to identification and classification of a wide variety of modes of co-creation including: collaboration with users as innovators, user customization of products and services, co-production, knowledge learning and solutioning within business networks and multi-firm partnerships. Again however, all undertheorize and do not define, specify or work with the inherent

[28] Service-Dominant Logic was the basis of the first version of the Health Ecosystem Value Design framework released in 2017. This framework is still available from the Umio website.

[29] Vargo, S. L., and Lusch, R. F. (2016). Institutions and axioms: an extension and update of service-dominant logic. Journal of the Academy of Marketing Science, 44(1), 5-23

[30] Venkat Ramaswamy and Kerimcan Ozcam (2018), What is Co-creation: An interactional creation framework and its implications for value-creation. Journal of Business Research 84 (196-205)

"creational" mechanisms and interactional dynamics by which value gets "co"-created, especially at the ecosystem level. All favour an activity-, human actor- and resource-integration view of value in co-creation.

As the name implies, the interactional creation perspective corrects these shortcomings by shifting the focus to the problematization of creation itself. I now expand on the ontological conceptualization of value-in-interactional creation that is deployed within HEVD.

Value-in-interactional creation in focal experience ecosystem environments

Interactional creation ontology is concerned with the origination, emergence, differenciation, repetition and various stabilization of phenomena forming heterogeneous lived experiences with health, disease and illness. It offers a transcendental, processual, virtual-to-actual-to-virtual via empirical view of reality that seeks to explain how human and non-human agent interactions in distributed, de-centred interactional flows modulated by tendential forces engender diverse affects and capacities of lived experiences in the lived journeys of affectees and affectors. In doing so, it shifts the locus of thinking on value co-creation from design projects, actors, activities, resources and their integration in the pursuit of quantified outcomes to the immanent mechanisms of creation and differenciation enacted by assemblages acting in/on interactional flows that course and weave over the virtual social with natural body. Further, it sees all actors as "interacted" creational experiencers immersed in a virtual world of interactional flows.

Central to its quest for an expanded, richer conceptualization of interactional value creation and the emergence of difference at the level of focal experience ecosystems is the notion of affective capacity, the core driver of creation, differenciation, heterogeneity, recurrence and stability in affects forming lived experiences with health (and all lived experiences). By conceptualising affective capacity as a power of creation and acting in and upon lived experiences with health (as in the definition of health above) and by identifying its immanent creational, interactional and valuation mechanisms, we can begin to specify and examine the actual dynamics by which value is interactionally "created". We can begin to see and explain variations in capacities, affects and impacts of affectee lived experiences in experience ecosystems and of affectors influencing or seeking to change them. Then, once we see differences, we can determine where and how to generate, (re)distribute, focus and improve affective capacities for the co-creation of desired valued lived experiences with health at the level of focal experience ecosystem environments. In other words, we discover how to co-create real lived experience value.

In this perspective, I now define value-in-interactional creation in experience ecosystem environments as the win-win-win sustained creation of affective capacity by agencial assemblages with the potential to generate surplus potential and/or novel social desire in lived experiences (1st win) that engenders equitable developmental impacts in the social body (2nd win) and ecologically balanced developmental impacts in the natural body (3rd win).

Redefining value-in-interactional creation at the ecosystem level
Value-in-interactional creation in experience ecosystem environments is the win-win-win sustained creation of affective capacity by agencial assemblages with the potential to generate surplus and/or novel social desire in lived experiences (1st win) that engenders equitable developmental impacts in the social body (2nd win) and ecologically balanced developmental impacts in the natural body (3rd win)

In this conceptualization of interactional creation of value and of health, the introduction and use of *impacts* in the definition calls attention to what can be *realized or impacted* from the creation of affective capacity in experience ecosystems and not of health outcomes as an end in themselves. For example, what impacts does an improvement in chronic pain lived experience generate in a chronic pain experience ecosystem environment? What impacts does an improvement in workplace wellbeing generate in a work experience ecosystem environment? This shift to *impact beyond outcomes through capacity creation* at the level of focal experience ecosystems heralds a more transformative purpose that is no longer limited to the more immediate observable and measurable ambition of a norm or baseline of bodily health for everyday functioning. Rather, purpose now rises far beyond this baseline by aiming for the creation of surplus potential and also *equally distributed* and *ecologically balanced* impacts arising from the ecosystem-level creation of social desire.

The 6E flow of creation and differenciation in experience ecosystem environments

In the visual of the complete interactional creation ontology of lived experience, (Figure 1.22 in chapter one) I identified all the dynamic entities and elements that combine and interact to originate, differentiate and reproduce states, qualities, capacities, tendencies and stabilities of real lived experiences with health, disease and illness. Within this model I identified four domains of the real that together define the total space of lived experiences with health along with the creational dynamics of their origination, differenciation and recurrence, namely the virtual-real, intensive-real, actual-real and empirical-real.

Using these elements and the four real domains, I am now able to identify six phases in a generative flow of the creation and differenciation of lived experience running over the virtual, intensive, actual and empirical real domains constituting an experience ecosystem environment. Each phase in the flow distinguishes a particular mode, content and expression of creation. I summarise these six different phases in the creational flow, each of which begins with the letter E.

Emergent creation

In the virtual-real domain, social desire is the creational force that originates interactional flows of pre-individual affects and capacities and generates tendential forces that course and coalesce over the social body. Like the river before we jumped into it in chapter one, the interactional flows bear virtual affects, capacities and tendencies of experience that are distributed or sedimented in various degrees by the effect of natural and social tendential forces. In short, the flows contain the original generative material of lived experiences prior to their differenciation (or becoming actual) in lived experience, material that is always emerging and differencing.

Enacted creation

In the virtual-real domain also, agencial assemblages of affectors, affectees and affective capacities interact with the interactional flows and tendential forces to enact ongoing processes of differenciation of lived experience. Assemblages produce, differenciate and variously stabilize lived experience states of a certain quality, intensity and capacity for a focal lived experience with health context. Assemblages collect and sediment tendencies leading to stratification of the social body into hierarchies. Different levels of the hierarchy contain variable powers of affective capacity in interactional flows producing recurring tendencies of organization, method, practice and action in health systems.

Embodied creation

In the intensive-real domain, the embodied actions of affectees in interactional flows and tendential forces (at different levels of hierarchy in the social body) produce intensities of affects in human bodies. Affects are the embodied sensations, feelings and impressions arising in the four affective domains that mark a transition in whole unified lived experience. Recall that action is an embodied creation, transition or movement in affects producing experience and experienced events, and agency is the affective capacity to have potential to create affects within interactional flows and tendential forces in pursuit of desired, valued experience.

Experienced creation

In the actual-real domain, the actions that produce embodied intensities and recurrences of affects generate actual qualities and events of lived experiences of affectees in their lived journeys. These qualities, having a certain content and expression, sit somewhere between the poles of positive desired (valued) experience (ideal social desire) and negative ill-health.

Effectuated creation

The actual experienced events and outcomes of affectees generate impacts back in the virtual-real domain in both the social and natural body. They also act back on interactional flows and tendential forces by modifying affects, capacities and tendencies and by generating a memory of the impact of agencial assemblages in an experience ecosystem environment.

Evaluated creation

Finally, in the empirical-real domain, the flow and impact of creation and differenciation of lived experience is evaluated by affectees and affectors. It is often quantified, costed, categorized and ordered in generalized and static representations that may not see the above flow of creation from emergence to effectuated impact. How experiences are seen and evaluated is a creational mechanism itself, forming ontological and epistemological tendential forces which build a virtual memory of *the value of actions* and their impact in interactional flows. These tendencies may harden or sediment interactional flows shaping further the emergent generative loop of creation in experience ecosystem environments.

Summary

Putting all the 6E's together, we can say that creation and differenciation of lived experiences with health, disease and illness in experience ecosystem environments occurs in a generative looping flow of inter-relating phases of emergent, enacted, embodied, experienced, effectuated and evaluated creation. This flow acts upon a virtual body of pre-experience affects, tendencies, affective capacities and interactions having diverse potential to yield different lived experiences, events and impacts. Figure 2.4 overlays this 6E flow of creation of lived experience onto the full interactional creation ontology model (Figure 1.22 in chapter one).

To co-create enhanced value in lived experiences, defined as the sustained win-win-win creation of affective capacity having the potential to generate surplus potential and/or novel equitable and ecologically balanced social desire, we can now link the flow of the "6Es" of creation of difference to the flow of interactional creation itself. In the final part of this chapter, I therefore describe the task of HEVD and its method for value-in-interactional creation in the flow of the 6Es.

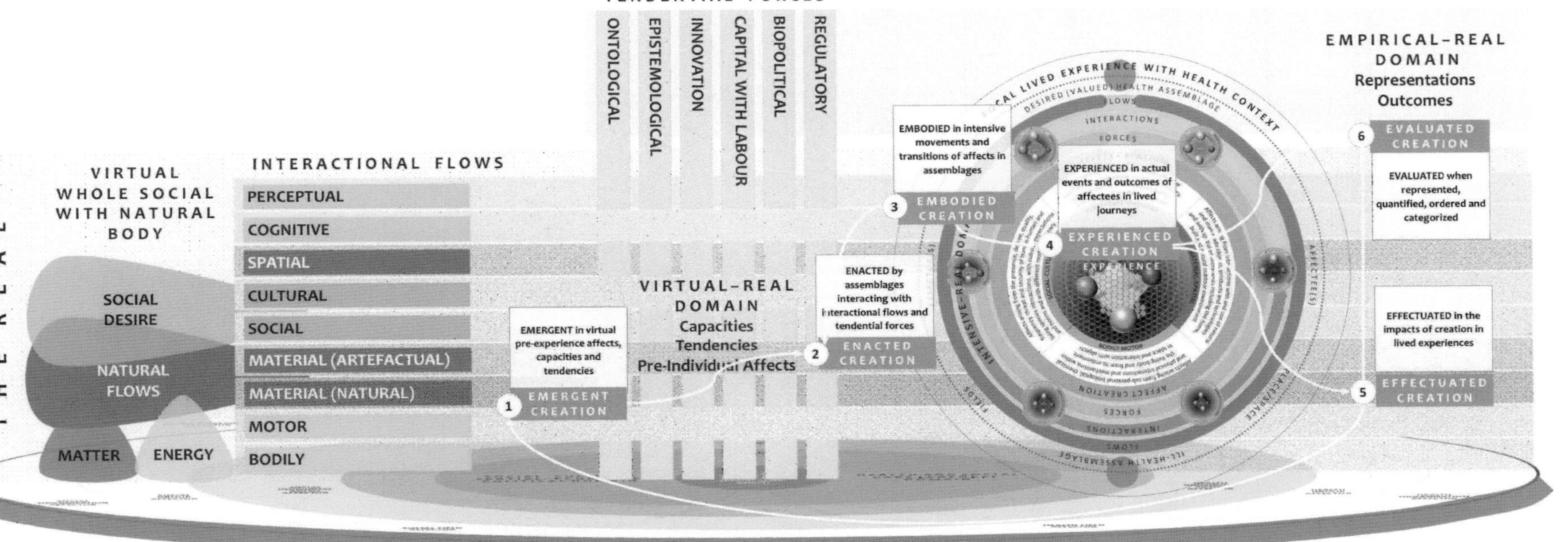

Figure 2.4 – The 6E flow of creation in an experience ecosystem environment

How do we rethink the task and method of value creation in focal experience ecosystem environments?

Before I describe how HEVD organises the method of value-in-interactional creation in the flow of the 6Es of creation in experience ecosystem environments, first I describe the distinctive capacities and capabilities needed to drive the co-creation of desired, valued lived experiences through the lens of HEVD and its ontology.

Capacities of value-in-interactional creation in experience ecosystems

In foundation four of chapter one, I described the three immanent types of capacities constituting and driving affective capacity and that determine and differentiate an affectee's potential and powers of acting and creation of social desire in affectee lived experience. These were interactional, creational and valuational capacities. The same three immanent capacities underpin and define the focus and task of value-in-interactional creation in focal experience ecosystem environments of agencial assemblages too. Each denotes and defines the potential capacity of a focal experience ecosystem (of assemblages of affectees and affectors wishing to transition their and others' lived experiences) to create desired lived experiences for a focal context, or of enacting desired transitions in the agencial force of assemblages (that are central to my redefinitions of health and value provided above). Without or with a shortfall in these capacities, value-in-interactional creation in any focal experience ecosystem environment is limited and can lead to the production and reproduction of disease, illness, social inequality and ecological imbalance and decline. Briefly, I describe each of the three immanent capacities.

Interactional capacity

Interactional capacity is the potential capacity of assemblages to democratize, de-centre and distribute engagement and interactions with and between affectees and affectors within interactional flows in an experience ecosystem environment. It defines the capacity to enact and facilitate flows, exchanges, absorption, assimilation and transformation of data, ideas, perspectives, narratives, knowledge, valuations, information and materials across disciplinary, organizational, cultural and social group boundaries to improve protection, cooperation, coordination and understanding. Interactional capacity supports new ways for affectees and affectors to associate with other affectees and affectors and to defy the limits of prevailing social and cultural boundaries, identities and contexts. It supports recognition and acceptance of the "otherness of others" by supporting interactions that are more inclusive and bias-free, that promote and enable care, empathy and dignity and that respect cultural differences.

Creational capacity

Whilst creation is the immanent force of differenciation of lived experience, creational *capacity* defines the potential to invent, pursue and realise one or more transitions supporting growth, development and novelty in experience ecosystem environments. The counterforce to routine and non-reflexivity in definition and representation of problems, thought and action, creational capacities are determined by the ability to enlarge perception to the level of experience ecosystems, envision a desired future, define, state and invent true problems conducive to the creation of desired valued lived experience, sense the reality of lived experience and its conditions, uncover origination, emergence and recurrence stories of differenciation and actualization of lived experiences and generate and support the means for assemblages of ecosystem affectees and affectors to co-create solutions.

Valuational capacity

Valuational capacity is the capacity to identify, review and reflect upon the conditions and possibilities of actual lived experience of affectees produced from interactions in interactional flows and tendential forces in the focal experience ecosystem environment. Through more intimacy, directed intuition, sympathy and new modes of interaction with affectees, it is the capacity to evaluate actual states of lived experience linked to a normative idea of social desire. Especially, it defines the capacity to discern the impact of individual and relations of entities, tendencies, interactions and events on actual lived experiences in any of the ten elements of social desire. To do so requires reflection on epistemological tendencies of value and of valuation practices, especially of how value is perceived, defined, measured and distributed in a focal experience ecosystem environment.

Capabilities and the task of value-in-interactional creation in experience ecosystems

As drivers of ecosystem-level affective capacity, interactional, creational and valuational capacities are the core generative mechanisms shaping the potential to transition lived experiences with health in an experience ecosystem environment. To discover, create and distribute surplus and more potential affective capacity requires the enactment by an ecosystem orchestrating enterprise of three inter-relating *see, enable* and *emerge* experience ecosystem capabilities or SEE capabilities. Each is made up of distinct capabilities that define a certain task, purpose and focus of creational, interactional and valuational capacity generation in agencial assemblages. Each must be resourced to see, enable and emerge affective capacity and to effectuate sustained developmental impacts in a focal experience ecosystem. In short, resourced SEE capabilities act on the three immanent mechanisms of affective capacity to enact interactional-creation of value. In Figure 2.5, I depict this capability-capacity relationship and also portray the individual capabilities in the three SEE wheels. Note how the three wheels of capabilities can be rotated to allow the match-up of different capabilities in each. Experimenting with different match-ups helps to define different design challenges, purposes and tasks for ongoing value-in-interactional co-creation in assemblages in any focal experience ecosystem. I now describe each of the three dynamic capabilities and their constituent capabilities.

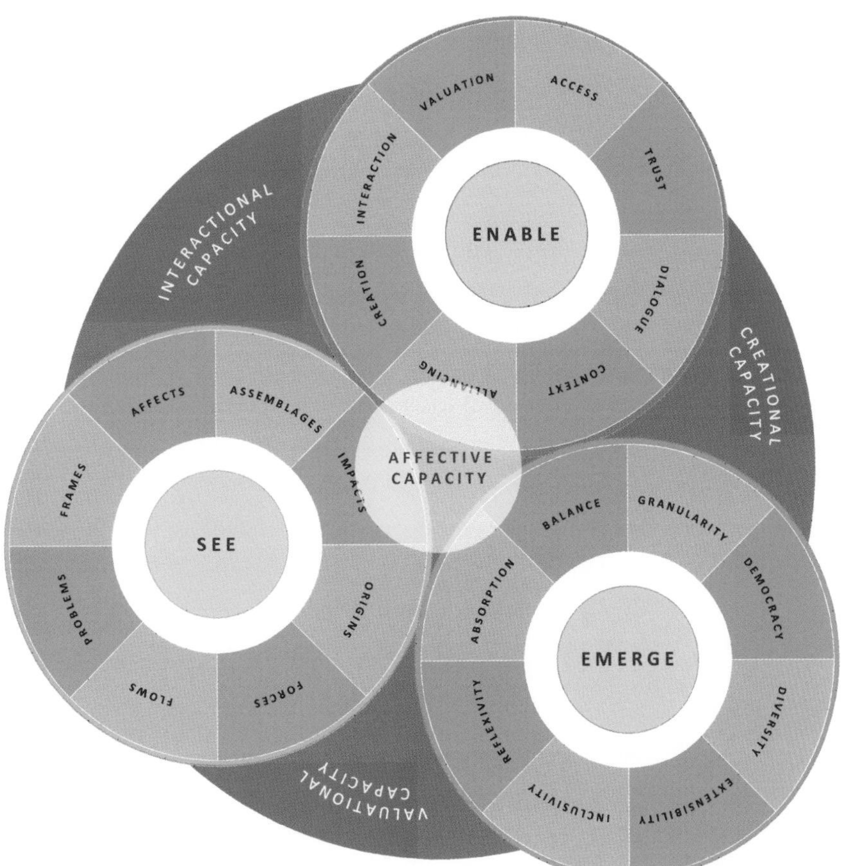

Figure 2.5 – See, enable and emerge dynamic capabilities and their eight constituent capabilities interacting to generate affective capacity formed of interactional, creational and valuational capacities

See dynamic capabilities

See dynamic capabilities enact an elevated, extended and transcending empiricism and perception of experience ecosystems, agencial assemblages, actual human lived experiences and the capacities and events that define them. They define the capability for affectees and affectors to go above and beyond existing institutional structures, disciplinary conventions and boundaries to see wholes and differences in experience ecosystems and in lived experiences. They support research and organise more holistic understanding of real conditions and possibilities of experience that is presently hidden by prevailing systems of ideas, organization, categories and representations. A see capability starts with the acceptance of difference as a given beneath representation. It acknowledges singularity and ongoing change as the fundamental constants of the dynamic nature of lived human experience. It does not therefore pursue order and generalization by taking a snapshot of differences for analysis purposes but rather accepts that difference is always becoming more different; the goal then is to see and determine patterns of flux, emergence and recurrence of lived experiences that are different in kind from other experiences on the basis of different assemblage and affectee capacities or powers to act and create social desire.

There are eight constituent capabilities of a *see* dynamic capability. These are:

1. PROBLEMS – The capability to find, see, state the terms of and invent "true problems" that are conducive to seeing difference and its emergence, the definition of a transition purpose, and the design and creation of capacities of desired valued lived experience (social desire)
2. FRAMES – The capability to enlarge perception to the level of focal experience ecosystems and to frame for a transition purpose aligned to a focal context of a whole lived experience with health
3. AFFECTS – The capability to sense, discern, gather data on and relate affects within a whole interactional frame of lived experience formed of four affective domains of nine interactional flows
4. ASSEMBLAGES – The capability to see differences in affectee affective capacity from closer intimacy and sympathy, to identify sources and enablers of surplus and potential capacity and to develop a view of different agencial assemblages acting upon interactional flows in the virtual social-with-natural body
5. CURRENT IMPACTS – The capability to see present impacts and especially different impacts in types of affectees across the focal lived experience context, and how different assemblages of capacity, force, tendency and affect generate and can sustain these differential impacts
6. ORIGINS OF DIFFERENCE – The capability to explore and understand the origination of different lived experiences for a focal context within the framed experience ecosystem. Seeing patterns of origin and divergence helps to discern the interior tendencies and forces present in entities in interactional flows, and that when interacted with diverge lived experiences and can lead to their recurrence.
7. TENDENTIAL FORCES – The capability to discern ontological, epistemological, innovation, biopolitical, capital with labour and regulatory tendencies and presuppositions, their forces and influences in flows of lived experience, and their relation and translation into prevailing ideas and ideologies, powers, priorities and practices of action and interaction in the focal experience ecosystem environment
8. VIRTUAL FLOWS – Finally, the capability to discriminate entities and relations of entities in virtual flows of interaction and their varying presence, intensity and sedimentation in places and other contexts of a focal experience ecosystem, affording different potential creational, valuational and interactional capacities of affect

Without a see dynamic capability, any effort to transition to an experience ecosystem environment through value-in-interactional creation will have limited success.

Enable dynamic capabilities

Enable dynamic capabilities unlock, de-sediment and mobilise assemblages of affectors and affectees in focal experience ecosystems; they enact the agencial capacities of assemblages by democratising, de-centring and distributing new modes of interaction, creation, co-operation and engagement to generate desired affects and capacities of lived experiences towards social desire. They generate the movement and transitions of assemblages by equipping affectees and affectors with greater creational, interactional and valuational capacities from resourced capabilities, all leading to higher levels of potential affective capacity. The following are the eight capabilities forming an *enable* dynamic capability.

1. CREATION - Creation is the key capability that enables assemblages of affectees and affectors to imagine, discover, ideate, invent, design, experiment and generate novel affects in interactional flows with the potential to realise elements of social desire. A creation capability is enabled by supporting affectees and affectors to individually and collectively visualise, simulate, experiment and prototype ideas and concepts for creating and realising affects of lived experiences. It also supports the search, exploration and discovery of useful concepts, services and products that have been created and used by others, and by empowering the sharing of ideas, designs and feedback.
2. INTERACTION – Also core, an interaction capability enables assemblages of affectees and affectors (both human and non-human) to access, enter into, engage in, collaborate, dialogue and sustain interactions and relations in interactional flows to generate and actualize positive affects forming a potential of social desire. Most likely but not exclusively enabled by digitalized interactive platforms, it is also the capability to help affectees be protected from, avoid or leave an undesirable or no longer useful interactional flow.
3. VALUATION – Another core capability, a valuation capability enables assemblages of affectees and affectors to interactively identify, assess, value, reflect, store and recall valued, neutral and unvalued affects in interactional flows in their lived experience, and to offer feedback and measure of the human and non-human agent affector entities they use. Value and valuation perception, method and measurement are enacted within the widest context of ten elements of social desire forming health. The valuation practices of agents and entities are themselves a co-creation. All are valuers on an ongoing basis; the enabling mechanisms of value are co-created by affectees and affectors. Valuation as a co-creation (of interactional creation) occurs in three overlapping distinct temporal contexts: pre-enactment, enactment and reflective valuation of experiences, events and impacts.
4. ACCESS – The capability to offer access to all types of affectees to participate in interactional creation of social desire in assemblages in a focal experience ecosystem environment. Access fosters the conditions and provides the resources for hitherto excluded, remote or disadvantaged affectees to enter into novel or effective modes of interaction to develop their practical capacities for creating and improving their lived experience. Access opens up opportunities for all affectees to enter into new relations and encounters on a sustained basis.
5. TRUST - The capability to create and engender trust and fairness in novel social and disciplinary bonds in agencial assemblage interactions through transparency of motive, pooling of resources and open sharing of ideas, data, knowledge and valuations. Transparency to engender trust supporting cooperative creation and experimentation requires a clarity of purpose and role of different agents and entities within interactional flows within agencial assemblages.
6. DIALOGUE – The capability to create shared meaning and understanding from open richer dialogue between affectees and between affectees and affectors in assemblage interactions. Dialogue is de-centred, lightly mediated and centres on the exchange of issues, ideas and valuations of lived experiences to support, along with access and trust, the creation of meaningful and valued lived experiences.

7. CONTEXTUALIZATION – The capability for affectees and affectors to access contextual information, tools, expertise and skills to tailor their creation, interactions, value and valuation, events and experience in assemblages within focal experience environments is essential to value-in-interactional creation.
8. ALLIANCING – The capability to form and mobilise alliances and networks of partner organizations to enable new modes of contextualized interaction in assemblages acting in the focal experience ecosystem

Emerge dynamic capabilities

Emerge dynamic capabilities support the evolution of emergent properties of assemblages enabling further affective capacity creation within and beyond a focal experience ecosystem environment. They do so by adding to, extending, integrating and further relating affectees, affectors, concepts, qualities, capacities, textures, mechanisms and entities in assemblages to engender greater viability and more sustained developmental impact. Emergence is the process of the becoming of new experiences generated from novel relations of pre-existing virtual affects, capacities, tendencies and concepts; experiences which could not have been induced or deduced prior to their actualization. Through emergence, the agencial force and capacity of assemblages evolves from novel interactive combinations of their parts and not merely from the parts themselves; their whole is greater than the sum of their parts (as I described in their definition in foundation six in chapter one). The following are the distinct capabilities forming an *emerge* dynamic capability.

1. GRANULARITY - The capability to continually emerge, accommodate and address heterogeneity in the qualities and capacities of lived experiences within a universal transition purpose of a focal experience ecosystem. Granularity defines the non-finite capability of agencial assemblages to incorporate and act upon a "microsociology" of diverse lived experiences within a single focal context. Whilst an experience ecosystem may focus initially on a particular homogenous context of capacity and qualities of lived experience, over time, its reach and scope widen to include more heterogeneous states, capacities and qualities. In other words, an ecosystem de-territorializes its original focus and context of agency and impact over time.
2. DEMOCRACY – The capability to break down hierarchies of organization and associated power relations within a focal experience ecosystem. To sustain interactional creation of value, powers and possibilities of creation and innovation become distributed, democratized and de-centred across and within assemblages of affectees and affectors in interactional flows.
3. DIVERSITY – The capability to support a diversity of styles of creational interaction practices formed of varied assemblages of affectors and affectees. Styles diversify according to the roles, purpose, activities and modes of interaction of affectee and affector participants in interactional flows of creation. They range from professional affector modes of technical co-creation to impersonal, one-way service provider-consumer modes to more intimate one-to-one partnering modes of empathic creation, for example between a sick person and a health care professional. In each, the context of value that emerges and the valuational mode of experiencers differs markedly depending on the interactional context, its purpose and content.
4. EXTENSIBILITY – The capability to stretch focal experience ecosystem environments by incorporating new affective domains and lived experience contexts composed of different relations, possibilities and potentials of affective capacity, for example to extend the focal experience ecosystem context of obesity from a narrow bodily-motor and material (food input) view to one that incorporates social-cultural interactional flows and tendencies of bias and discrimination against obese persons
5. INCLUSIVITY – The capability to widen access and inclusion to disadvantaged affectees of all capacities and qualities of lived experience in the focal lived experience with health context. This

capability defines how an experience ecosystem avoids insularity in its reach and scope and reduces inequality and inequity in the social body.

6. REFLEXIVITY – The capability for agencial assemblages of affectees and affectors to "act back" onto the experience ecosystem and for their valuational feedback to shape ongoing creation, adaptation and emergence of interactions. Reflexivity shapes the creational capacities of agencial assemblages. Affectees gain learning of potential events and emergent experiences, and affectors learn about emergent actions and tendencies that could be helpful in their interactions.
7. ABSORPTION – The capability to acquire, share, assimilate and absorb know-how and learning of events and experiences as well as the impacts enacted by assemblages in the experience ecosystem.
8. BALANCE – Last but not by any means least is the capability of a focal experience ecosystem to create and sustain ecological balance and ideally ecological benefits in its impacts

The above model of see, enable and emerge dynamic capabilities and their twenty-four constituent capabilities acting on underlying interactional, valuational and creational capacities applies equally to platformized digital experience ecosystems as well as non-digital agencial assemblages of creational arrangements of affectors.

Example of affective capacity creation in a focal experience ecosystem environment

In Figure 2.6, I depict an example of targeted assemblage transitions in affective capacity within the body of contingent assemblages in the Northern Ireland chronic pain experience ecosystem environment. Altogether, there are five assemblage transitions with priority given to the *isolated chaotic* most ill-health pain assemblage, in which approximately 15 per cent of the total population of persons with chronic pain in the country are stuck. Here, the transition targeted is a creation in assemblage affective capacity engendering a movement of affectees and their lived experience with pain from the most ill-health (A) to the emerging assemblage (B); a movement onto the line of recovery that will create emergent affective capacities and support improvements in qualities and stabilities of life when living with pain. Below the transitions in the assemblage model chart is a summary of the developmental impacts realized from enacting the A-B and other transitions. In example templates 8.0 and 9.0 on pages 163 and 166 in Part Two of the book, you can see the different propositions that were designed to enact the A-B and other transitions (in the Enacted Creation phase in the 6E flow of creation).

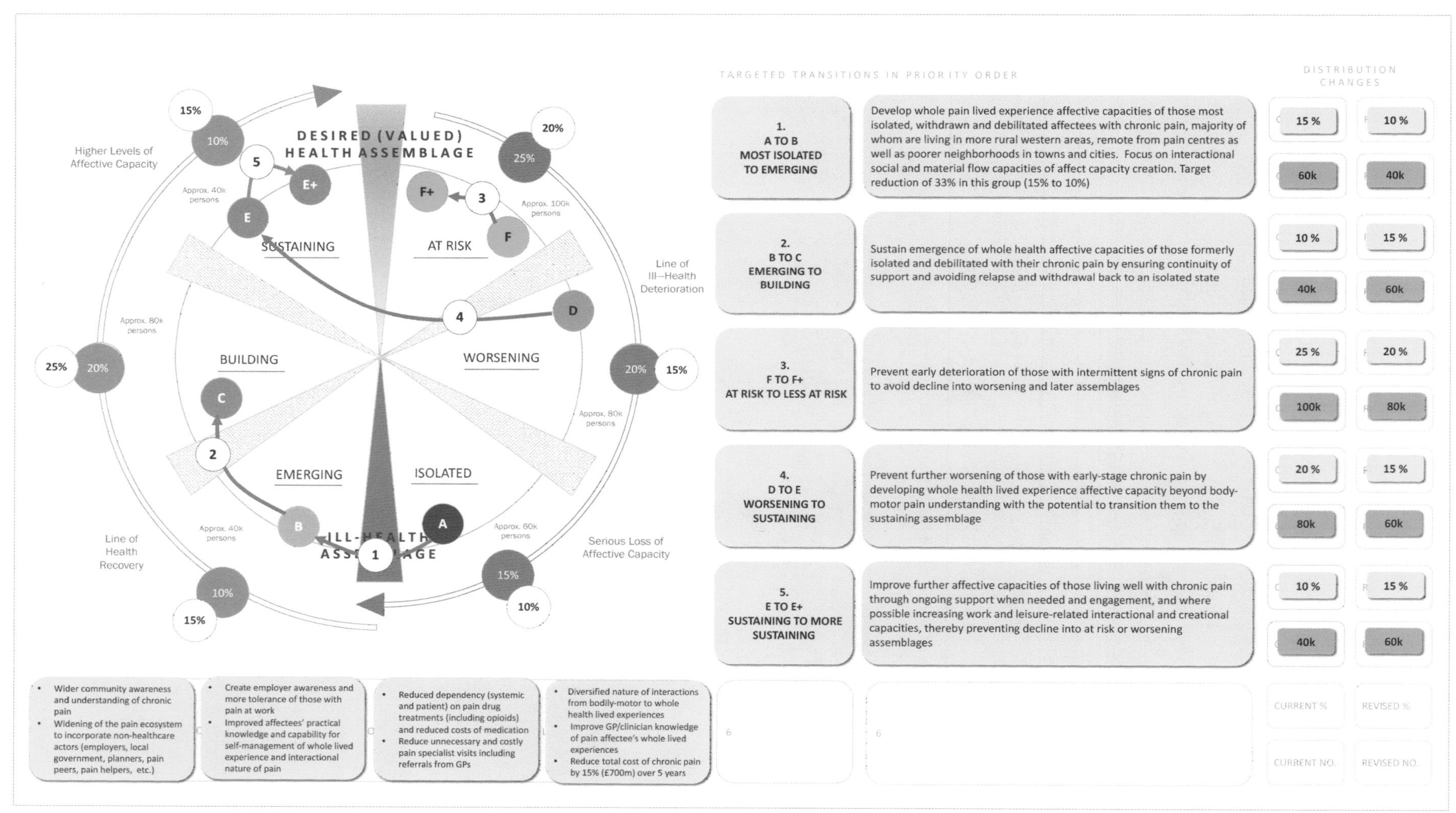

Figure 2.6 - Example of targeted assemblages and transitions within a contingent body of assemblages and showing potential effectuated impacts realized from the movement (bottom left four boxes)

The flow of interactional creation of value in HEVD

An interactional creation ontology demands novel creational capacities in an epistemological sense. It requires us to transcend established empirical representations, generalizations and categories of health, disease and related phenomena by working with novel open frames of whole lived experience in experience ecosystem environments. It asks us to define the true nature and extent of problems in order to seek thicker explanations and stories of the origination and recurrence of ill-health experiences. It requests us to conceptualise and work with capacities, flows, forces and tendencies in the virtual realm and the affects that emerge from them and become embodied in actual lived experience. It requires us to see and determine the impacts that differential agencial powers of assemblages have when acting upon these flows, forces and tendencies. Absence of such creational capacity is one of the main reasons for the failure of "emphasis-on-the-co" project-based design thinking and service dominant logic modes of value co-creation.

When adopting an affective capacity view of health, a transition purpose is centred on a focal experience ecosystem context and is enacted via the resourcing of capabilities that build creational, interactional and valuational capacities to support realization of desired valued experiences. To support an orchestrating organization to embark on such a transition, HEVD defines a "reverse parabola" learning and design flow that runs from the present actual to the virtual past in memory and then forward to the future. This parabolic backwards reach into the memory of the virtual social with natural body of interactional flows and tendential forces runs in the opposite direction to most design methods that tend to start in the present, envision a future through ideation and then seek to realise it through resource creation and exchange. The reason for going in the other direction is to first discover hidden actualized differences in the affective capacities of affectee lived experiences with health in context, discern the agencial assemblages of differential states, force and capacity, and then at the furthest distance from the present, enact a deep phase of reflection on current tendencies and implications of extant design, method, knowledge and action practices. Armed with reflective knowledge of difference, assemblage and tendency, the method then springs forward through the design phases to generate novel value-in-interactional creation propositions of all kinds to enact the desired transition.

In Figure 2.7, I illustrate the reverse parabolic flow method undertaken by HEVD and in Figure 2.8 I overlay an unannotated parabola onto the full model of the interactional creational ontology. Next, I summarise the twelve steps shown in the parabola that form the flow of the HEVD method and in doing so, describe the sequence of the HEVD design and creation task.

The twelve steps in the parabola flow of Health Ecosystem Value Design

Step 1.0: Choose and frame the focal lived experience with health context and set transition purpose

In the first step, we decide the focal lived experience with health context of interest and then frame the focal experience ecosystem environment in a collaborative process using provided contexts. Correct framing ensures higher likelihood of discovery and realization of valid novel paths to interactional value creation.

Step 2.0: Identify the affects forming the ill-health and desired (valued) experiences for the focal context

The second step requires direct inputs from a diversity of affectees selected in step 1.0. Here we gather and map the affects forming differences in lived experience for the four affective domains and defined by the poles of qualities of social desire. The goal is to determine the extremes of lived experience within the focal ecosystem environment and to begin to ask questions about why these differences arise and endure.

3.0 Map affector with affectee interactions in the health and social sub-ecosystems

With inputs and an idea of difference in lived experience for the focal context captured from affectees, we then identify and map the human and non-human affectors with whom and with which the affectees with the extremes of positive and negative experience interact. We do so in the two ecosystem sub-domains, the health and the social (See Figure 1.20). The goal is to discern which affectors and types of affectors in the nine interactional flows are driving the differences in lived experience discovered in step 2.0. and also working directly or indirectly to create or improve lived experience. Affectees and affectors are mapped in a hierarchy of affectee and affector interactional spaces in both the health and social sub-ecosystems.

Step 4.0: Explore tendential forces in interactional flows for the focal lived experience context

With affector - affectee interactions identified and mapped, next we start to uncover the tendencies present in the six tendential forces that generate and may sediment or restrict creational, interactional and valuational capacities of affectees and affectors when interacting within the interactional flows. We do so for each of the two sub-ecosystems, the health and the social. Tendencies inform ideas and ideologies, powers, priorities and practices of affectors and affectees that can lead to repetition of problems and ill-health experiences.

Step 5.0: Distinguish assemblages in the focal experience ecosystem environment

With knowledge from steps 2.0 to 4.0, we now build the model of contingent agencial assemblages of states, capacities and qualities of lived experience on the line of deterioration to ill-health, the line of recovery to desired valued health and points of stability in assemblages between the two poles. This model provides a new hidden view of the diversity of affective capacities and affectee lived experiences and the forces of creation, valuation and interaction present within assemblages acting within the focal experience ecosystem environment.

Step 6.0: Determine assemblage and lived experience transitions in the focal experience ecosystem

In step 6.0, we identify the target movements or transitions we wish to make in affective capacities in both individual lived experiences with health (6.0) and within the body of agencial assemblages (6.5). This restates the focus of creation by identifying target assemblages or sub-assemblages and particular states, qualities and capacities of lived experience for the focal context. In this step, we also define the ideal developmental impacts sought from the desired transitions.

Step 7.0: Capture and reflect on the learning so far in relation to the transition purpose

With the previously hidden assemblages, patterns, dynamics and states revealed, we now ask a series of questions to support group reflection of the present situation, of past ideas and of how to achieve the refined transition purpose. We determine the key tendencies present in the target actual lived experiences, in assemblage(s) and that are emerging in the virtual-real domain. We explore how tendencies are variously preventing, limiting or have the potential to enable the transition purpose. We organise these into tendency categories and state them as design challenges. These form the generative design inputs for returning back down the parabola to co-design ecosystem-level value concepts, propositions and offerings in the next steps. Note how the parabola returns down the path to the most desired valued experience state in the assemblage model in Figure 2.7.

Step 8.0: Co-design affectee value propositions to create desired valued lived experiences

We then co-design affectee concepts, ideas and offerings (collectively propositions) in the four affective domains of interactional flows forming whole unified lived experience to address the design challenges defined in step 7.0. These propositions support target affectees to access, acquire and build desired valued lived experiences with health for the targeted movements defined in step 6.0.

Step 9.0: Co-design affector value propositions to build affective capacity in the focal experience ecosystem

We then co-design value propositions in five affector value frames consisting of a diversity of concepts and offerings, but this time to support affectors to unlock and mobilise assemblages to enact and sustain the targeted transitions and to realise the developmental impacts also defined in step 7.0.

Step 10.0: Develop a value-in-interactional creation impact model for the focal experience ecosystem

In step 10.0, we build an indicative health ecosystem value-in-interactional creation impact model consisting of six inter-relating domains of developmental impact generated from affective capacity creation.

Step 11.0: Design the emergence of affective capacity in the focal experience ecosystem

We then identify and sequence the activities needed to enact the propositions and the indicative developmental impacts. We allocate activities into the flow of see, enable and emerge dynamic capabilities and to specific affectee types and affector groups.

Step 12.0: Assess your Health Ecosystem Value Design capabilities for ongoing interactional creation

Finally, to support ongoing loops of co-creation, we assess and diagnose gaps in our capabilities for extending and improving interactional creation.

Following step 12.0, the loop is repeated by reframing the focal experience ecosystem context more narrowly or more widely. In the latter case, adjacent focal experience ecosystems and focal contexts may be brought into the interactional creation task, thereby driving a continual expansion of the focal ecosystem experience environment.

In Table 2.3, I indicate how the steps correspond to each of the 6E phases in the flow of creation coursing over experience ecosystem environments. Note that the 6E steps are shown in reverse order in the second row. This demonstrates the parabolic shape of the flow of HEVD in the body of the table (I would have to reverse the flow of the 12 steps in the first column to reflect the actual shape of the reverse parabola but hope this makes sense).

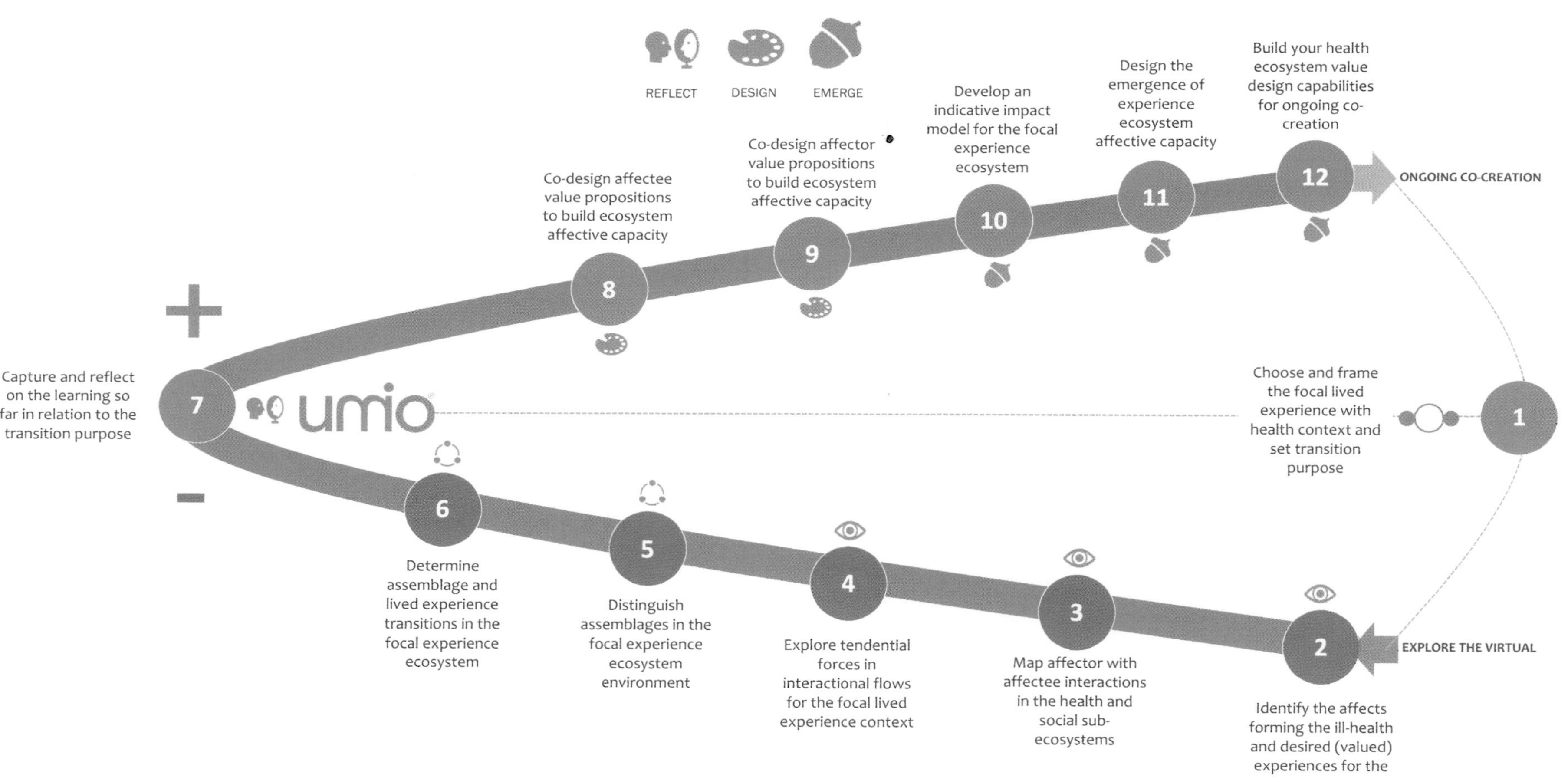

Figure 2.7 – The reverse parabolic flow of the method of Health Ecosystem Value Design

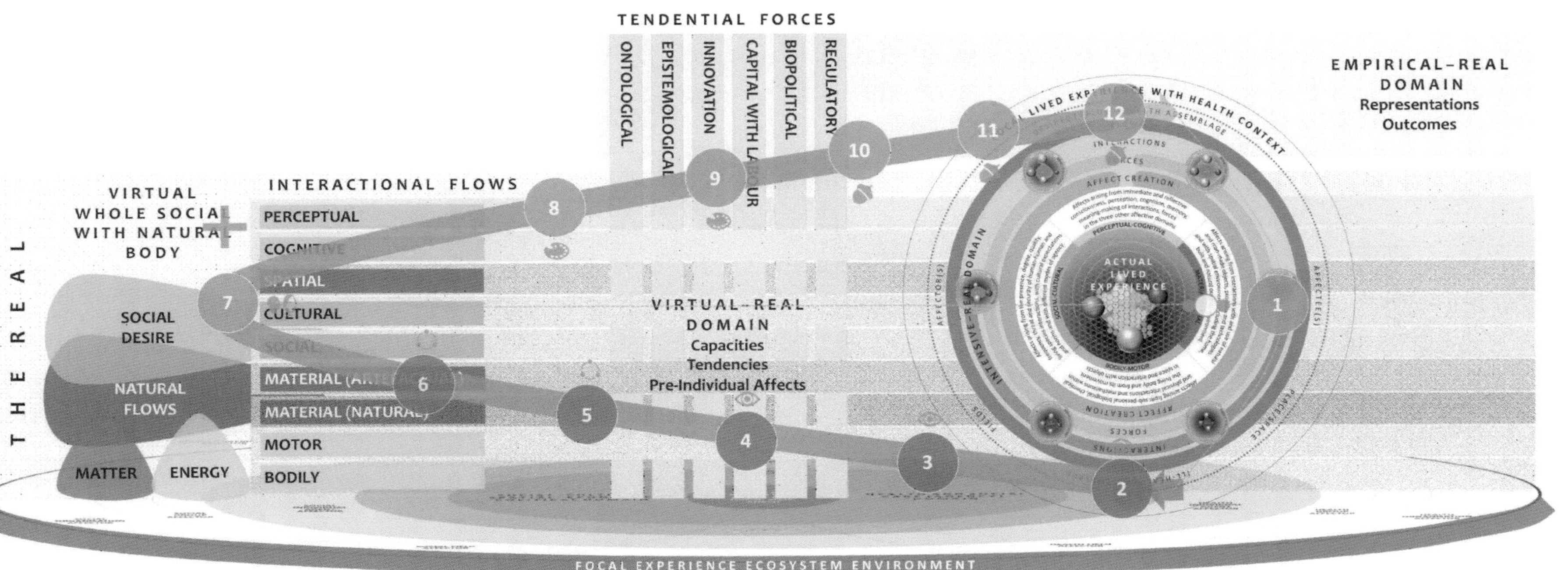

Figure 2.8 – The reverse parabolic flow of the method of Health Ecosystem Value Design overlaid onto the full ontological model of interactional creation of lived experience

Table 2.3: Steps in Health Ecosystem Value Design mapped to the reverse flow of the 6E phases of creation in experience ecosystem environments

	6E PHASE IN THE FLOW OF CREATION IN EXPERIENCE ECOSYSTEM ENVIRONMENTS					
STEP IN HEALTH ECOSYSTEM VALUE DESIGN	6 **EVALUATED** when represented, quantified, ordered and categorized	5 **EFFECTUATED** in the impacts of creation in lived experiences	4 **EXPERIENCED** in actual events and outcomes of affectees in lived journeys	3 **EMBODIED** in intensive movements and transitions of affects in assemblages	2 **ENACTED** by assemblages interacting with interactional flows and tendential forces	1 **EMERGENT** in virtual pre-experience affects, capacities and tendencies
Step 1.0: Choose and frame the focal lived experience with health context and set the transition purpose	Use affectee, affector, purpose contexts					
Step 2.0: Identify the affects forming the ill-health and desired (valued) experiences for the focal context		Determine poles of affect differences				
Step 3.0: Map affector with affectee interactions in the health and social sub-ecosystems			Identify main affectors of ill-health			
Step 4.0: Explore tendential forces in interactional flows for the focal lived experience context				Reveal tendencies in interactional flows		
Step 5.0: Distinguish assemblages in the focal experience ecosystem environment					Build the assemblage states model	
Step 6.0: Determine assemblage and lived experience transitions in the focal experience ecosystem						Decide which transitions to emerge
Step 7.0: Capture and reflect on the learning so far in relation to the transition purpose					Challenge status quo generalizations	
Step 8.0: Co-design affectee value propositions to create desired valued lived experiences				Design individual lived experience		
Step 9.0: Co-design affector value propositions to build ecosystem affective capacity			Define affector creations to fit			
Step 10.0: Develop a value-in-interactional creation impact model for the focal experience ecosystem		Model impact of realized creations				
Step 11.0: Design the emergence of affective capacity in the focal experience ecosystem	Linked to desired transition impact					Synthesize model of creation emergence
Step 12.0: Assess your Health Ecosystem Value Design capabilities for ongoing interactional creation						Prepare for ongoing loops of co-creation

Summary: The power and possibilities of Health Ecosystem Value Design®

There is now no better time to pursue the task of interactional creation of health in experience ecosystems, one that:

- Frames health ecosystems as open experience environments for a focal context of whole lived experiences with health, disease or illness
- Substitutes rational acting homo economicus man with an idea of the human as interactional homo ecosystemus
- Addresses the limitations of economic, exchange- and outcome-based models and modes of value and its (co-)creation
- Widens our view of health as the affective capacity for the interactional creation of individual and collective social desire
- Views agency as distributed in agencial assemblages of human and non-human entities interacting in virtual interactional flows, including natural entities of living species and environmental matter and energy
- Supports transdisciplinary enquiry into the origination, emergence, differentiation and recurrence of diverse lived experiences with health, disease and illness
- Reveals patterns of the occurrence, content, identity and expression of affects forming our lived experience, psychologies and actions
- Identifies how dominant tendencies of health actors embedded in interactional flows drive ideas, priorities and practices in health systems, including public and community health
- Enables the ongoing discovery and interactional creation of health possibilities and their realization

Interactional creation can be enacted in three ways: through a perspective shift, through platformization or via both. The former entails a shift in how we perceive, represent, generalize, organize and act to create health and recover illness and disease (in Table 2.4 that follows, I summarize the ontological and epistemological differences of interactional creation ontology compared with the dominant empirical realism of today's health sciences). The second entails the digital enablement of focal experience ecosystem environments so as to elevate, shape and adapt the flows of creation of social desire and impact.

With Venkat Ramaswamy, I shall be writing more about how such platformization, accompanied with the perspectival ontological renewal and expansion that this book describes, can drive a new form of interactional creational living enterprise; an enterprise with generative purpose to drive valued impacts from experience creation in the lived journeys of affectees and in the experiences of affectors.

Having laid the foundations of an interactional creation ontology and reconceptualized health, value, task and method in Part One of the book, Part Two presents the framework, methods and templates for enacting the interactional creation of value in health experience ecosystem environments.

Table 2.4 – Interactional creation ontology compared with empirical realism in the health sciences

DIMENSION	Empirical Realism (ER)	Interactional Creation (IC)
Notional purpose	• Mastering "the science of life" for the greater convenience and practical interest of action by knowing object and material relations, conjunctions and via an ordering of reality that is instrumentally conducive to human functioning, survival and control of nature and natural matter, including the matter forming and diseasing human bodies. • Solving problems to support mastery of the material (matter, energy and force) of life • Incorporating individual facts into general laws	• Mastering "The art and creation of social desire in life" by understanding the virtual and vital origination, flow and divergence of lived experiences • The exploration of creation, freedom and joy as expressions and capacities of power • Finding, stating and inventing the problem conducive to design and creation of capacities of lived experience (social desire)
Stories explored and told	Stories of the observation and correlation / conjunction of things, events and outcomes and the prediction of their occurrence linked to an action or event	Stories of the formation, differentiation and recurrence of human and non-human entities, observable and non-observable with particular focus on lived experience itself but also going beyond or prior to experience to determine the formative material of experience
View of Reality	• Reality is only what can be and is observed and categorized as "things" or objects. • Relations or conjunctions of categories of things • Absolute reality is unknowable	Virtual whole unified natural with social emergent becoming body as the primary source of creation and differenciation through interactional flows and tendential forces The process of the becoming of reality is knowable
Questions asked	What is, what are, what patterns, what correlates with and what will be?	Why does a social entity (e.g., experience) emerge? Why does a certain entity repeat? How do things come to be the way they are and stay the way they are?
Primary phenomena of interest and assumed	• Inert and organized matter, objects, events and their atomistic conjunction • Visible forms of human beings, "their organs and anatomical elements" (Bergson) • Individual (rational) human actors	• Reality of lived experience • Origins, differentiation, tendency, stabilization, stratification, sedimentation and recurrence of lived experiences through study of intrinsic affects, forces and tendencies
Assumed nature, pattern, level of phenomena of interest	• Exterior representational and generalizable essence of observed phenomena • Observed atomistic events and event regularities of phenomena. • Ordered and quantified abstracted divided sub-states and concepts of lived experience • Seeks generalization and similarity of phenomena • Materialist / object view	• Intensive tendencies and capacities in social and natural phenomena as the interior mechanisms of difference creation modulated by forces in interactional flows • Seeks heterogeneity of phenomena as accepts difference as a given • Dynamism of phenomena • Tendencies in phenomena
Stratification of reality	No – only a sub-divided empirical layer of what can be observed, abstracted, ordered and related as representations, categories and events of matter, conjunctions and observed experience	Yes, but horizontal or rhizomatic that is emergent from interactional creation and differenciation of a virtual one whole being via interactions within interactional flows modulated by tendential forces leading to actualization of experience and through their stabilization, the stratification or territorialization of the social body. Umio HEVD affords a model to see and act within these

		processes for a focal context of lived experience.
View of movements in the phenomena of interest	None – in effect it takes a snapshot of a situation and then analyses it	Inherent dynamic view – study of fluid interactional flows modulated by flowing forces of types of tendencies
Unit of analysis	• Observed / observable external perception events of matter / objects and their conjunctions • Data and quantitative representations of entities within the problem • Category representations of the problem and their notional relation	• Focal experience ecosystem environment • Assemblages of states of experience of a certain quality, intensity, stability and identity, content and expression • Lived experiences of affectees • Lived experience in interactional flows and tendential forces within combinatory and contingent assemblages in experience environments
View of agency	Rational agentic individual person or individual body. There is no such thing as a real separate structure. Implicit behavioural agency and motivation model with limited view and definition of the environment and social body in which behaviour occurs.	Agency and structure conflated into **affective capacity** in experience within assemblages acting upon interactional flows modulated by tendential forces. Affective capacity seen as formed from relations of interactional, creational and valuational capacities.
Knowledge truth and validity	Stable theories and law-like generalizations from observed event regularities; or falsification thereof	Truth is difference as a given yet does exist in forces of differenciation via tendency
Knowledge found in	Categories and via disciplines	• Understanding of concrete lived experience, difference, origin, differenciation and recurrence • Differences in kinds of lived experiences (qualities and capacities) not differences in degrees (quantities and categories) • Transdisciplinary and independent of disciplines through study of types of interactional flows and tendential forces and role in differenciation of lived experience in dynamic models of assemblage formation, movements and qualities, capacities, stabilities and intensities (of lived experience) within focal experience ecosystem environments
View of theory	Theory-building is valid Positivist rationalist model of reasoning and theory-development in pursuit of law-like generalizations	Theory may be possible from introduction of types (of interactional flows, tendential forces and assemblages) into the study of patterns of differentiation and especially of tendential recurrence or routinization in lived experience drawn from multi-parameter probabilities of intensive interactions in assemblages
Knowledge sought	In study of "being", i.e., of stable phenomena, its ordering, categorizing, hypothesizing, correlating, deducing, and predicting In data as representation and intelligence of the problem and	• In study of "becoming" – exploration of creation, differenciation, actualization and recurrence of phenomena in interactional flows and tendencies of actual experience • Through greater intimacy and empathy of actual lived experience • Through intuition of the problem
Discourse	Order words, categories, correlation and predictive logic	Develop a new discourse to help abandon order words, categories and identities of

		representation of lived experience and its conditions and contexts of difference
Mind-Body Relation	Mind and body separate; dualistic model	Mind-body-environment as dynamic interactive system of affect generation
Weaknesses	• Rarely critically reflects on its own weaknesses • Hides differences within phenomena or problems due to over-generalizations • Struggles to explain real lived experience and get close to the actual human condition • Abstraction from real lived experience where intelligence as mode of knowledge is not fully complete or resolved • Relies on universal categories and descriptors of phenomena that hide important differences • Stable categories abstract and hide differences within them; they are "gross resemblances" of phenomena in reality • Use of universal categories may lead to false definition and composition of phenomena in problems by hiding important differences inside and that transcend their representation	• Limited by the ease of explanation (due to its distance from popularly understood and accepted ER) • Transcends disciplines and categories of knowledge and action, and therefore requires an effort of perceptual detachment in order to converge around a new ontology and frame of reality
Strengths	• Socialized deeply as standard practice; "the way we do things around here" • Capable of being shared between humans • Measurable and easy to act upon • Built edifice of practice	• Uncovers origination, emergence and difference stories of differenciation and actualization of lived experiences • Supports holistic view of social with natural body • Reveals differences within generalization • Potential for disciplinary convergence • Requires more intimate contact and sympathy with life on part of researcher
View of value	As a property in relation to exchange or use of a thing or entity and its effect on events and outcomes. Such properties can be one or more of: • Utilitarian • Instrumental • Inherent • Contributory	• Value is interactional experience-centred • Value is multi-level from individual to experience ecosystem environment • Value as a movement in affective capacity • Creating positive affects in lived experience • Creating, moving, transitioning assemblages in experience environments • Impacts in focal experience environments from movements in assemblages
View of health	• As absence of disease • As a norm or baseline • As an object • Reductionist body- and parts-focused • Individual agency behaviour-based	• As a whole affective capacity for creating desired valued lived experiences • As affects of events • In the mind with the mind viewed as a brain-body-environment interactional dynamic system
Measures of value	Bodily and disease outcomes Behavioural change (nudge, etc.) Epidemiological measures	Impacts of transitions in affective capacities of whole lived experience, assemblages and experience environments
Mode of perception	• More cognitivist, intelligence-oriented	• Extended whole sense-perception via intuition of embodied mind, "a vision of the mind by the mind" (Bergson, CM) • Discarding and transcending categories, representations and identities to see different

		differences to gain access to extended perception or a (radical empiricism" (Deleuze)
Methods	• Analytical reductionist approach of observable entities in their categories of representation • Intelligence and knowledge about entities • Use of rules and standards • Surveys • Data analysis • Categorization • Statistical correlation	• Extended, whole and transcendent perception (intuition as method) • Focused Ethnography • Semi-structured interviews • Place interactions • Immersion in context • Affectee self-ethnography • Anthropology
Design approach / habit	• Problem framing – breaking down reality into things and categories of problems including needs • Use of categories to break down and organise understanding of the problem • Relating categories of the problem • Measurement of the problem using categories • Solution design • Iteration	• Enlarging perception to the level of experience ecosystems • Problems as affects and capacities to create them • Context framing and reframing • Difference learning • Difference assembly • Reflection on own assumptions, tendencies and role in how the problem context is understood and addressed • Design of understanding the problem as well as co-creation of how to address the problem • Co-creation of offerings

Part Two
Health Ecosystem Value Design®
Interactional Creation of Health Framework and Templates

Health Ecosystem Value Design® framework and templates

Before introducing the framework and the templates, it is important to state what Health Ecosystem Value Design® (HEVD) is designed to do and also what it is not intended for.

What Health Ecosystem Value Design® is for and not for

HEVD is not designed for the discovery of universal truths and generalizations of lived experience, for precision research and prediction of disease and other outcomes, for revealing repeatable effects from individual causes and interventions or for uncovering indisputable answers to our most complex health problems. I do not believe that any framework that fundamentally explores and seeks to improve the human experience and condition in all its singularities and differences can ever claim to do these things.

Rather, the purpose of Health Ecosystem Value Design is to discover gaps in and build new interactional and creational capacities for individuals, groups and ecosystems of purposeful agents to see, enable and emerge the conditions of potential social desire, defined as greater intensities of health, joy, connection, engagement, freedom and powers to create and act.

By understanding the virtual and vital origination, flow and divergence of lived experiences with health, disease and illness and the tendencies acting upon them all, the framework aims to go beyond the study of *states of being of parts* of lived experience. Instead, it is concerned with the study of the *becoming of whole* lived experience, its creation and differentiation and the past and present conditions of change and possibility. It strives to help us see more clearly the interactional flows, tendential forces, capacities and affects that produce and differenciate ill-health, disease and ill-being, as well as how we collectively and differently perceive, design and respond through various policy, technology, service, community and other interventions.

With its focus on the origin, emergence and recurrence of differences in lived experience in health, HEVD aims to surface some of the shortcomings of prevailing ontology and methods in the life, health and related social sciences. It seeks to advance our collective abilities to acquire a precision intuition beyond situational instinct via elevated and extended perception of the actual lived experience at the level of experience ecosystem environments. To support such higher intuition of the human condition, its differences and transitions, we must pay more attention to how we define and state the terms of problems we seek to address. We must be as concerned with creating the conditions in which solutions can emerge to address correctly stated problems as we are with the solutions themselves. Critically, we must also reflect on our own assumptions, tendencies and roles in how problems originate, are framed, understood and addressed.

HEVD facilitates new modes of multi-actor, multi-disciplinary interactional co-creation of health using a new language and set of tools defined by a novel ontological virtual experience ecosystem perspective. It directs us to ask different questions, challenge our own assumptions and practices, and develop thicker critical explanations of complex health phenomena, all leading to novel, more valid and more sustainable design, positive action and clear developmental impact.

I now introduce the framework and templates to explain how it does so.

Health Ecosystem Value Design® flow

As described in Chapter Two, the reverse "parabola" flow defines the logic and method of Health Ecosystem Value Design®. Each of the 12 steps in the flow contains a template for enquiry into and action in a focal experience ecosystem environment consisting of affectee lived experience, capacities, affects, assemblages, interactional flows and tendential forces. In addition, a summary canvas template is used to organise the key learning, design concepts, impact models and activities to emerge the desired ecosystem transition.

Summary explanation

The task and method of Health Ecosystem Value Design® flows over six phases in two learning and design directions in the reverse parabola.

1. A *learning flow-back* from the initial analysis of difference in present affectee lived experiences for the focal context to explore the origination, emergence, differenciation and persistence of these lived experiences and their differences in interactional flows and tendential forces in the virtual realm.
2. A *design flow-forward* to generate ecosystem-level, assemblage and affectee lived experience propositions and concepts that co-create the desired ecosystem transition purpose and achieve developmental impact.

The six phases are:

1. First, we FRAME the focal health experience ecosystem using provided contexts, paying particular attention to the focal lived experience with health context. Here we set an initial transition purpose of desired interactional creation and health developmental impact in the experience ecosystem.
2. Second, we look differently to SEE patterns and the distribution of states, affects and affective capacities in current lived experiences with health for the focal context and the affector interactions in which they tend to occur, persist and may disappear. We then examine their origin, differenciation (how they become different) and their various stabilization from affectee interactions in interactional flows and their modulation by tendential forces. This is a research phase using any method appropriate to the focal context of lived experience with health.
3. Next, we ASSEMBLE our insights and patterns of affects and affective capacities to identify distinct assemblages of homogenous states, qualities, intensities and stabilities of lived experience in the focal ecosystem that exist between the poles of desired value health (most positive) and ill-health (most negative). We then build the model of contingent assemblages and assess the nature of movement and transition between them. Also, we create "thick" explanations of why these assemblages arise, differ and persist, why the movements occur, and what is preventing the potential to realise the desired transition purpose.
4. Fourth, we REFLECT on phases 1-3 and the discoveries made. We ask why differences in lived experience for the focal context originate, form and persist. We question how and why tendencies in tendential forces have persisted and how they might be undone or modified to release more affective capacity at the level of the experience ecosystem. We build a series of challenge questions to guide subsequent design and emergence phases.
5. We then DESIGN concepts and propositions for building ecosystem-level and affectee affective capacity to support and enable the desired transition. We define an ecosystem value impact model using the concepts generated and the insights from all previous activities.
6. Finally, we EMERGE, lead and sustain the ecosystem transition by defining the sequence of overlapping and reinforcing activities and we assess the Health Ecosystem Value Design® capabilities we need to build for ongoing co-creation.

The Umio "Reverse Parabola" learning and design flow

HEVD deploys a reverse parabolic learning and design flow that runs backwards from exploration of differences in present actual experiences for the focal context into the virtual realm of interactional flows and tendential forces to explore their origins and formation. It then springs forward to design offerings and propositions with the potential to create desired valued experiences for the focal context.

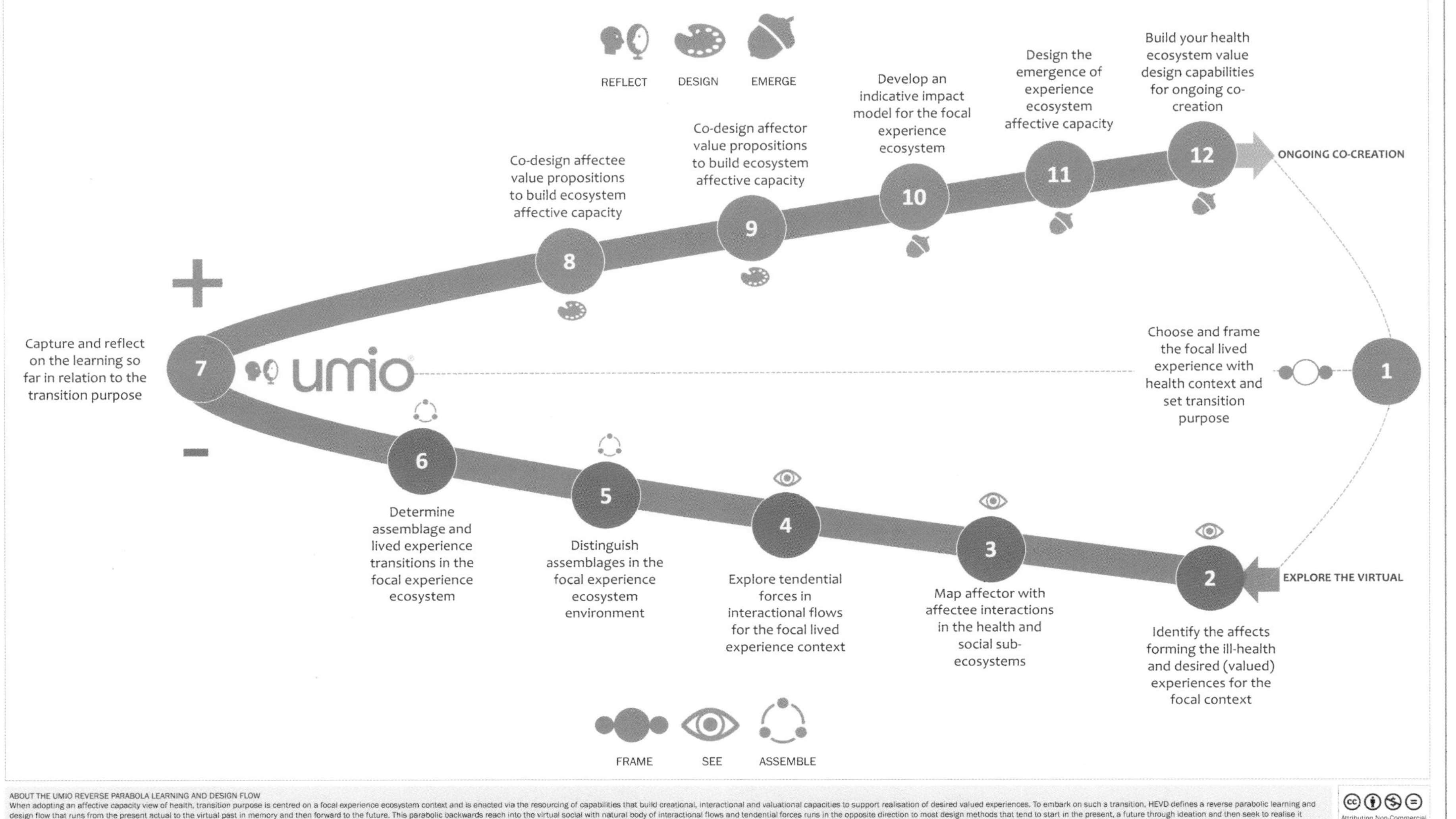

ABOUT THE UMIO REVERSE PARABOLA LEARNING AND DESIGN FLOW

When adopting an affective capacity view of health, transition purpose is centred on a focal experience ecosystem context and is enacted via the resourcing of capabilities that build creational, interactional and valuational capacities to support realisation of desired valued experiences. To embark on such a transition, HEVD defines a reverse parabolic learning and design flow that runs from the present actual to the virtual past in memory and then forward to the future. This parabolic backwards reach into the virtual social with natural body of interactional flows and tendential forces runs in the opposite direction to most design methods that tend to start in the present, a future through ideation and then seek to realise it through resource creation and exchange. The reason for going in the other direction is to first discover hidden actualized differences in the affective capacities forming the lived experiences with health in context, discern the agencial assemblages of differential states, force and capacity, and then at the furthest distance from the present, enact a deep phase of reflection on current tendencies and implications of extant design, method, knowledge and action practices. Armed with knowledge of difference, assemblage and tendency, the method then springs forward through the design phases to generate novel offerings of all kinds to enact the desired transition.

The templates and their purpose

1.0 Framing template

Choose and frame the focal lived experience with health context and set the transition purpose

Decide the focal lived experience with health context of interest and then frame the focal experience ecosystem environment in a collaborative process using the provided framing elements and contexts: affectees, places-spaces, health and social affectors, health and social fields, ill-health and desired (valued) assemblage outlines and the duration to realise the transition purpose.

2.0 Affects template

Identify the affects forming the ill-health and desired (valued) experiences for the focal context

From research with affectees, map the individual affects and affective capacities in four affective domains forming a whole unified interactional view of actual lived experience. Map those forming desired (valued) affects of experience and those forming the negative ill-health experience to visualize the extremes of lived experience within the focal experience ecosystem environment.

3.0 Interactions template

Map affector with affectee interactions in the health and social sub-ecosystems

With inputs and understanding of differences in lived experience for the focal context captured from affectees, identify and map the human and non-human affectors with whom and with which the affectees with the extremes of positive and negative experience interact. Do so in the two sub-ecosystem domains, the health and the social.

4.0 Tendential forces template

Explore tendential forces in interactional flows for the focal lived experience with health context

Uncover the tendencies present in tendential forces that influence the ideologies, powers, priorities and practices of human affectors and affectees in their interactions in interactional flows. Map the forces to the six categories of tendential forces in the outer ring and describe their effects in the inner rings to produce a relational model of forces of tendency present in the focal lived experience with health context.

5.0 Assemblage template

Distinguish assemblages in the focal experience ecosystem environment

Build the model of contingent assemblages of states, capacities and qualities of lived experience on the line of deterioration to ill-health, the line of recovery to desired valued health and points of stability in assemblages between the two poles. Develop a view of the nature and diversity of affective capacities, flows and tendencies of creation and interaction in assemblages within the focal experience ecosystem environment.

There are two sub-templates, 5.1 and 5.2, that split template 5.0 to allow detailed population of affects, states and capacities for the assemblages on the line of deterioration (5.1) and for those on the line of recovery (5.2).

6.0 Transitions templates (assemblages and individual lived experience)

Determine target desired transitions in lived experiences with health of affectees (template 6.0)

Identify the transitions to target in affects and affective capacities in target affectee lived experiences with health and for the targeted assemblages. Do so for each of the four affective domains forming whole unified lived experience.

Determine target desired transitions in assemblages in the focal experience ecosystem (6.5)

Identify the target movements or transitions to make in affective capacities within the body of agencial assemblages. This narrows the focus of creation to assemblages or sub-assemblages of lived experience for the focal context.

7.0 Learning and challenges template

Capture and reflect on learning so far in relation to the transition purpose

With the target transitions decided, reflect on the learning to date for the focal lived experience with health context. Determine the key tendencies that are preventing, limiting or have the potential to enable the targeted movement(s) in the focal lived experience and experience ecosystem towards the transition purpose. Set up the challenge questions to guide subsequent design and ideation of concepts, propositions and offerings.

8.0 Affectee design template

Co-design affectee value propositions to build desired valued lived experiences

Co-design propositions that support affectees to access desired valued lived experiences with health for the focal lived experience with health context. Do so in each of four affective domains forming whole unified lived experiences with health (disease and/or illness).

9.0 Affector design template

Co-design affector value propositions to build affective capacity in the focal experience ecosystem

Co-design value propositions for affectors to co-create greater affective capacity in the focal experience ecosystem environment that is equitable in the social body and ecologically balanced in the natural body.

10.0 Developmental Impact value template

Develop a value-in-interactional creation impact model for the focal experience ecosystem

Build an indicative developmental impact model for the focal experience ecosystem consisting of six inter-relating domains of affective capacity of health value-in-interactional creation.

11.0 Emergent design template

Design the emergence of affective capacity in the focal experience ecosystem

Identify and sequence the main actions, priorities and activities needed to see, enable and emerge the transition purpose to realise the developmental impacts from the design of creational and interactional movements in the focal experience ecosystem.

12.0 Capability template

Assess your Health Ecosystem Value Design capabilities for ongoing interactional creation

Assess and diagnose gaps and discover potential opportunities in your group's capabilities and fitness for ongoing interactional creation of value in a focal experience ecosystem environment.

Summary: Canvas template

Finalise the Health Ecosystem Value Design canvas

Provide a one-page summary view of all elements of your health ecosystem transition and its design.

Each of the 12 templates plus the summary canvas, their purpose, basic instructions and examples are now presented in the remainder of the book.

1.0 Choose and frame the focal lived experience with health context and set the transition purpose

Description

Decide the focal lived experience with health context of interest and then frame the focal experience ecosystem environment in a collaborative process using the provided framing elements and contexts: affectees, places-spaces, health and social affectors, health and social fields, ill-health and desired (valued) assemblage outlines and duration to realise transition purpose.

Purpose of Template 1.0

- To determine the focal lived experience with health context and define an initial transition purpose determined by relevant contexts
- Through collaborative exploration and discussion, to identify, define and describe initial understanding of negative ill-health and positive desired (valued) health lived experiences in order to determine opposing affect qualities and capacities of the focal lived experience with health context
- To identify which affectees – types or categories of persons, families, groups, communities and places - are included and belong to the ill-health and desired (valued) health experience poles
- To preliminarily identify the different health and social affectors (human and non-human) interacting with affectees in the focal lived experience with health context
- To make an initial judgment of the positive, mixed, unknown or negative influence of different affectors and fields of interactional flows on the focal lived experience with health context, especially the most negative ill-health lived experience
- To appreciate how lived experiences with health and disease originate, differenciate and variously stabilize in health / bodily and social, cultural, economic, political and spatial sub-ecosystems
- To determine and agree the anticipated duration over which impact in the experience ecosystem is to be demonstrated
- To reflect on any bias that you may have introduced in the choice and description of the affectees and affectors
- To consider your organization's role and goals in the framed experience ecosystem and the transition purpose.

Template 1.0 summary instructions

1. Discuss, determine and add the eleven ecosystem framing contexts into the template: (1) primary health experience context (2) ill-health experience and related contexts (3) desired (valued) health experience and contexts of the desired transition purpose, (4) affectee(s), (5) place(s)/space(s) of interaction, (6) health affector(s), (7) health fields (8) social affector(s), (9) social fields (10) transition duration and (11) the transition purpose.
2. Describe the desired (valued) health experience and the ill-health experience in the two smaller blue and red circles respectively. Add transition contexts that are important aspects and requirements when enabling the transition purpose around each of the descriptions.
3. Position the different affectors and fields in the red and blue zones of the central wheel based on your collective initial judgment of their negative (red) or positive (blue) influence.
4. Review the selected contexts and reflect on the choices you have made. Ask whether they frame the health ecosystem in a way that helps you discover valid and novel paths to realise the transition purpose.

1.0 Choose and frame the focal lived experience with health context and set transition purpose

Decide the focal lived experience with health context of interest and then frame the focal experience ecosystem environment in a collaborative process using the provided framing elements and contexts: affectees, places-spaces, health and social affectors, health and social fields, ill-health and desired (valued) assemblage outlines and duration to realise transition purpose.

SUMMARY INSTRUCTIONS

1. Discuss, determine and add the eleven ecosystem framing contexts into the template: (1) primary health experience context (2) ill-health experience and related contexts (3) desired (valued) health experience and contexts of the desired transition purpose, (4) affectee(s), (5) place(s)/space(s) of interaction, (6) health affector(s), (7) health fields (8) social affector(s), (9) social fields (10) transition duration and (11) the transition purpose.
2. Describe the desired (valued) health experience and the ill-health experience in the two smaller blue and red circles respectively. Add transition contexts that are important aspects and requirements when enabling the transition purpose around each of the descriptions.
2. Position the different affectors and fields in the red and blue zones of the central wheel based on your collective initial judgment of their negative (red) or positive (blue) influence.
3. Review the selected contexts and reflect on the choices you have made. Ask whether they frame the health ecosystem in a way that helps you discover valid and novel paths to realise the transition purpose.

1.0 Choose and frame the focal lived experience with health context and set transition purpose

Decide the focal lived experience with health context of interest and then frame the focal experience ecosystem environment in a collaborative process using the provided framing elements and contexts: affectees, places-spaces, health and social affectors, health and social fields, ill-health and desired (valued) assemblage outlines and duration to realise transition purpose.

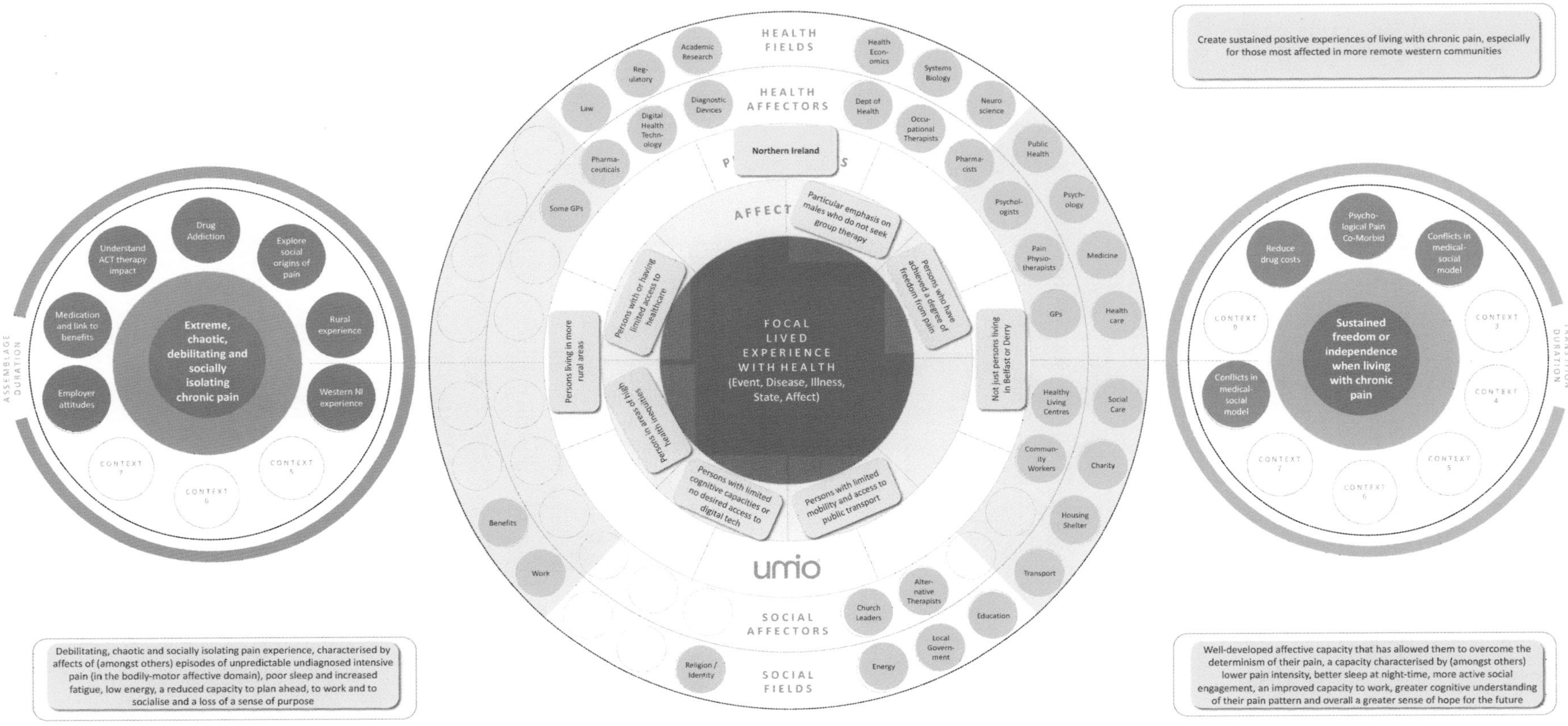

ASSEMBLAGE DURATION

Extreme, chaotic, debilitating and socially isolating chronic pain

Drug Addiction · Explore social origins of pain · Rural experience · Western NI experience · CONTEXT 5 · CONTEXT 6 · CONTEXT 7 · Employer attitudes · Medication and link to benefits · Understand ACT therapy impact

Debilitating, chaotic and socially isolating pain experience, characterised by affects of (amongst others) episodes of unpredictable undiagnosed intensive pain (in the bodily-motor affective domain), poor sleep and increased fatigue, low energy, a reduced capacity to plan ahead, to work and to socialise and a loss of a sense of purpose

HEALTH FIELDS

Academic Research · Reg-ulatory · Law · Health Econ-omics · Systems Biology · Neuro science · Public Health · Psych-ology · Medicine · Health care

HEALTH AFFECTORS

Diagnostic Devices · Digital Health Techn-ology · Pharma-ceuticals · Some GPs · Dept of Health · Occu-pational Therapists · Pharma-cists · Psychol-ogists · Pain Physio-therapists · GPs

Northern Ireland

AFFECT

Particular emphasis on males who do not seek group therapy

Persons who have achieved a degree of freedom from pain

Not just persons living in Belfast or Derry

Persons with limited mobility and access to public transport

Persons with limited cognitive capacities or no desired access to digital tech

Persons in areas of high health inequities

Persons living in more rural areas

Persons with or having limited access to healthcare

FOCAL LIVED EXPERIENCE WITH HEALTH (Event, Disease, Illness, State, Affect)

umio

SOCIAL AFFECTORS

Healthy Living Centres · Commun-ity Workers · Alter-native Therapists · Church Leaders

SOCIAL FIELDS

Social Care · Charity · Housing Shelter · Transport · Education · Local Govern-ment · Energy · Religion / Identity · Work · Benefits

Create sustained positive experiences of living with chronic pain, especially for those most affected in more remote western communities

TRANSITION DURATION

Sustained freedom or independence when living with chronic pain

Reduce drug costs · Psycho-logical Pain Co-Morbid · Conflicts in medical-social model · CONTEXT 3 · CONTEXT 4 · CONTEXT 5 · CONTEXT 6 · CONTEXT 7 · Conflicts in medical-social model · CONTEXT 9

Well-developed affective capacity that has allowed them to overcome the determinism of their pain, a capacity characterised by (amongst others) lower pain intensity, better sleep at night-time, more active social engagement, an improved capacity to work, greater cognitive understanding of their pain pattern and overall a greater sense of hope for the future

SUMMARY INSTRUCTIONS

1. Discuss, determine and add the eleven ecosystem framing contexts into the template: (1) primary health experience context (2) ill-health experience and related contexts (3) desired (valued) health experience and contexts of the desired transition purpose, (4) affectee(s), (5) place(s)/space(s) of interaction, (6) health affector(s), (7) health fields (8) social affector(s), (9) social fields (10) transition duration and (11) the transition purpose.
2. Describe the desired (valued) health experience and the ill-health experience in the two smaller blue and red circles respectively. Add contexts that are important in enabling the transition purpose around each.
2. Position the different affectors and fields in the red and blue zones of the central wheel based on your collective initial judgment of their negative (red) or positive (blue) influence.
3. Review the selected contexts and reflect on the choices you have made. Ask whether they frame the health ecosystem in a way that helps you discover valid and novel paths to realise the transition purpose.

Health Ecosystem Value Design® Framework 2.0
Created and designed by Chris Lawer 2021

umio

Template 1.0 version 2.0 Jan 2021

2.0 Identify the affects forming the ill-health and desired (valued) experiences for the focal context

Description

From your research with affectees, map the individual affects and affective capacities in four affective domains forming the whole unified interactional view of actual lived experience. Map those forming desired (valued) affects of experience and those forming the negative ill-health experience to visualize the extremes of lived experience within the focal experience ecosystem.

Purpose of Template 2.0

- To capture the range of affects and affective capacities present in the positive desired (valued) health experience pole and the negative ill-health experience pole for the focal context
- To reflect on the wider nature of lived experience with health / disease, beyond bodily originated sensations or symptoms
- To see the widest "beyond the body" context of affects and capacities forming and differentiating lived experiences with health, disease and illness
- To identify how affects and which particular ones are generated from interactions in interactional flows (or how experience is embodied)
- To reflect on the nature of community, group and place affects and affective capacities forming different, experiences and their reproduction
- To ask questions of how the objectification of health experience through data, language and other symbols can serve to abstract, reduce and distance our understanding of real (lived) experience

Template 2.0 summary instructions

1. Identify the individual affects and affective capacities that form the ill-health experience pole for the focal context. Place these closest to the centre of the left-hand circle (indicating negative ill-health affects) in each affective domain.
2. Identify the individual affects and affective capacities that form the desired valued experience pole for the focal context. Place these in the perimeter of the right-hand circle (indicating positive desired affects and affective capacities) in each affective domain.
3. Consider which affects and affective capacities are limiting the potential for affectees to realise desired value experience. Ask why do affectees have different capacities and how these arise and persist?
4. Consider how and if the affects and capacities are currently identified, measured and evaluated in existing methods to understand the focal lived experience with health context
5. What improvements can be made to how we sense, identify, review and value affects and capacities in current perceptions and approaches to health creation?
6. Consider how affects mediate between social determinants and other assumed-to-be outside, distal forces of disease and unwanted or poor outcomes. Do social determinants fully explain real health experience?

Practical tips

A. Research with affectees and affectors is necessary to complete the template. There is no prescribed research method. Umio can undertake this research on your behalf.

2.0 Identify the affects forming the ill-health and desired (valued) experiences for the focal context

From your research with affectees, map the individual affects and affective capacities in four affective domains forming a whole unified interactional model of actual lived experience. Map those forming desired (valued) affects of experience and those forming the negative ill-health experience to visualize the extremes of lived experience within the focal experience ecosystem.

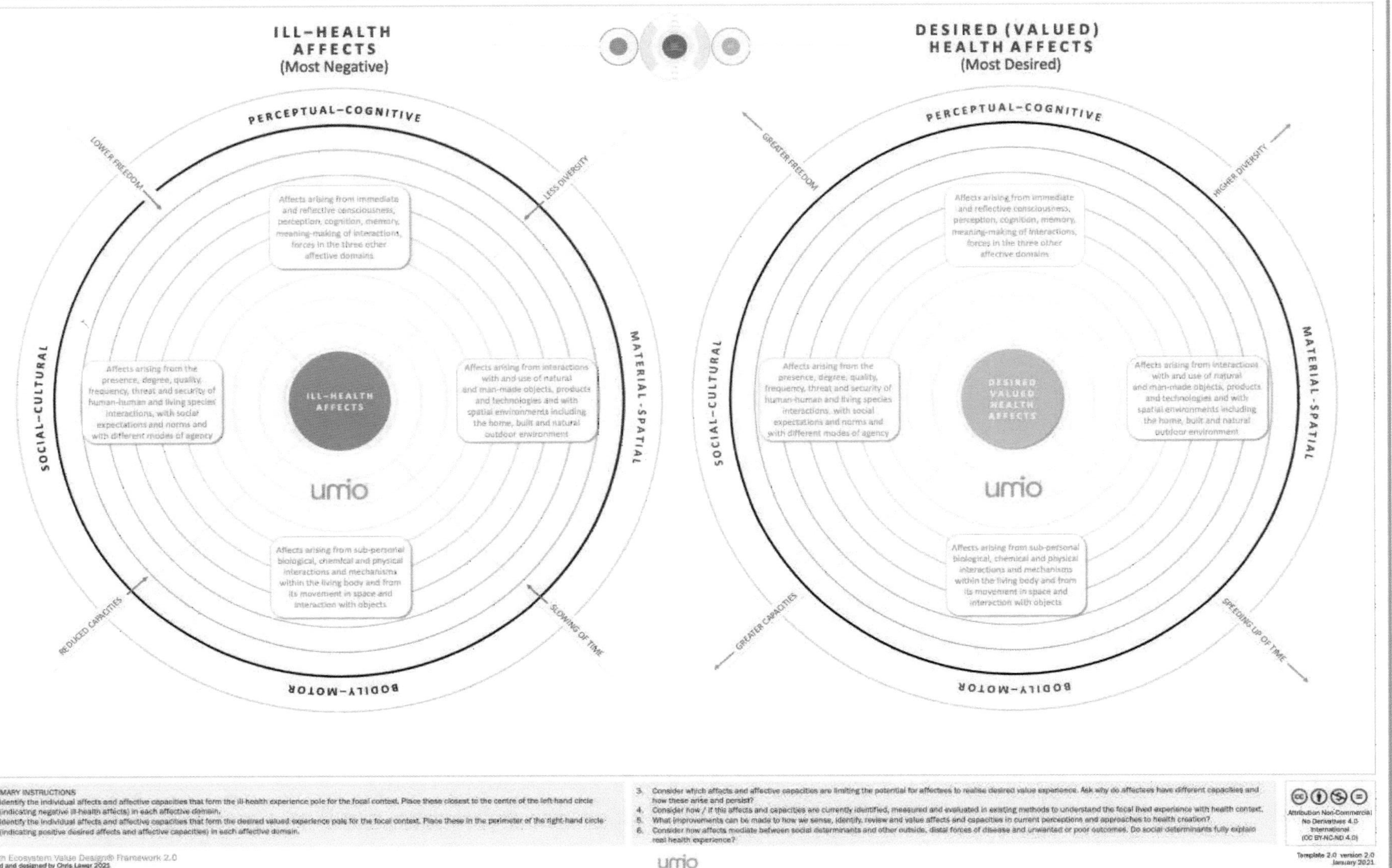

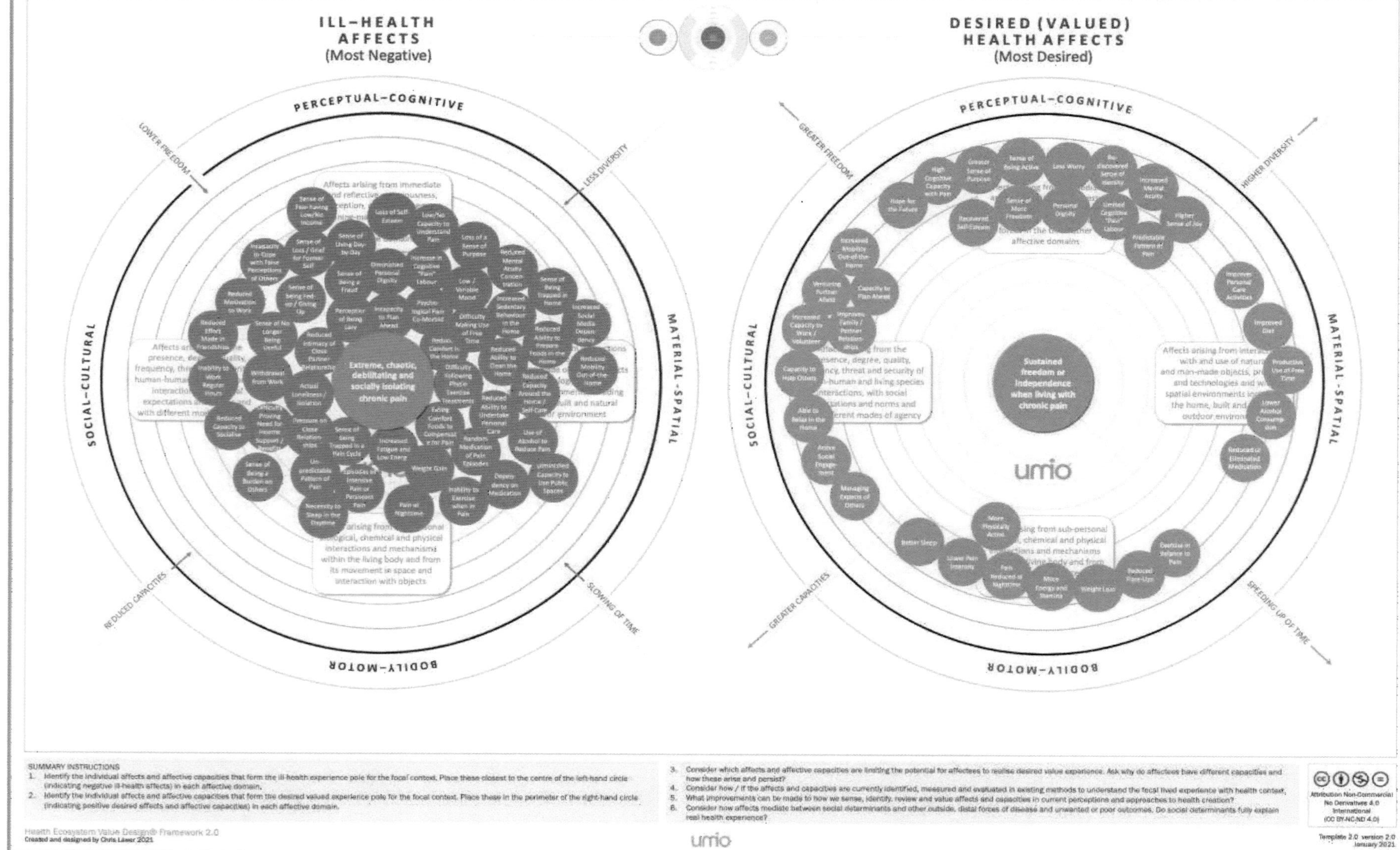
2.0 Identify the affects forming the ill-health and desired (valued) experiences for the focal context
From your research with affectees, map the individual affects and affective capacities in four affective domains forming a whole unified interactional model of actual lived experience. Map those forming desired (valued) affects of experience and those forming the negative ill-health experience to visualize the extremes of lived experience within the focal experience ecosystem.
ILL–HEALTH AFFECTS
(Most Negative)
DESIRED (VALUED) HEALTH AFFECTS
(Most Desired)
PERCEPTUAL–COGNITIVE
MATERIAL-SPATIAL
SOCIAL-CULTURAL
BODILY–MOTOR
LOWER FREEDOM
LESS DIVERSITY
REDUCED CAPACITIES
SLOWING OF TIME
Extreme, chaotic, debilitating and socially isolating chronic pain
GREATER FREEDOM
HIGHER DIVERSITY
GREATER CAPACITIES
SPEEDING UP OF TIME
Sustained freedom or independence when living with chronic pain
urrio
SUMMARY INSTRUCTIONS
1. Identify the individual affects and affective capacities that form the ill-health experience pole for the focal context. Place these closest to the centre of the left-hand circle (indicating negative ill-health affects) in each affective domain.
2. Identify the individual affects and affective capacities that form the desired valued experience pole for the focal context. Place these in the perimeter of the right-hand circle (indicating positive desired affects and affective capacities) in each affective domain.
3. Consider which affects and affective capacities are limiting the potential for affectees to realise desired value experience. Ask why do affectees have different capacities and how these arise and persist?
4. Consider how / if the affects and capacities are currently identified, measured and evaluated in existing methods to understand the focal lived experience with health context.
5. What improvements can be made to how we sense, identify, review and value affects and capacities in current perceptions and approaches to health creation?
6. Consider how affects mediate between social determinants and other outside, distal forces of disease and unwanted or poor outcomes. Do social determinants fully explain real health experience?
Health Ecosystem Value Design® Framework 2.0
Created and designed by Chris Lawer 2021
urrio
Attribution Non-Commercial No Derivatives 4.0 International (CC BY-NC-ND 4.0)
Template 2.0 version 2.0
January 2021

3.0 Map affector with affectee interactions in the health and social sub-ecosystems

Description

With inputs and an idea of differences in lived experience for the focal context captured from affectees, identify and map the human and non-human affectors with whom and with which the affectees with the extremes of positive and negative experience interact. Do so in the two ecosystem sub-domains, the health and the social.

Purpose of Template 3.0

- To identify the human and non-human affectors with whom and with which affectees interact in the focal experience ecosystem environment and which influence positively or negatively the origination, differenciation and stabilization of the focal lived experience with health context
- To see the widest scope of human and non-human interactions, interactional flows and tendential forces that are immanent in the creation, differenciation and recurrence of affects and affective capacities in the focal lived experience with health context
- To develop an interactional view of the mechanisms of creation and persistence of the focal lived experience with health context
- To consider the influence of interactional flows that are not usually included in an evaluation of the focal lived experience with health context and how it might be understood, prevented, recovered or eliminated

Template 3.0 summary instructions

1. The template depicts two sub-ecosystems or domains of the creation, differenciation and recurrence of the focal lived experience with health context. On the left is the social-cultural-spatial-economic-political domain, on the right is the formal health and social care (prescribed professional agency or service) domain.
2. Identify which types and categories of affectees, relations of affectees (e.g., a family, an extended family), peers or social groups and communities experience the focal lived experience with health context. Place these in the central "hourglass" segments of the template.
3. Referring to the focal lived experience with health context, identify the human and non-human affectors who directly or indirectly interact with the different affectees. Place these in the relevant segment of interaction in the large ovals on the template depending on which domain they belong to (social-spatial-economic-political or health and social care domain).
4. For each affectee and affector added to the template, identify whether they have a mostly positive, mostly negative, mixed or unknown affect or influence on the focal lived experience with health context. If you wish, you may just focus on the negative affectors.

Practical tips

A. To fully complete this exercise, prior research is needed

B. Add the affectees first then add the human affectors with whom they interact. Use a second sheet for non-human affectors if needed. Use different colours to distinguish affectors' positive, mixed, unknown or negative influence

C. You can use this template to assign different affectors to one of the nine interactional flows using different colored sticky-notes

3.0 Map affector with affectee interactions in the health and social sub-ecosystems

With inputs and an idea of differences in lived experience for the focal context captured from affectees, identify and map the human and non-human affectors with whom and with which the affectees with the extremes of positive and negative experience interact. Do so in the two ecosystem sub-domains, the health and the social.

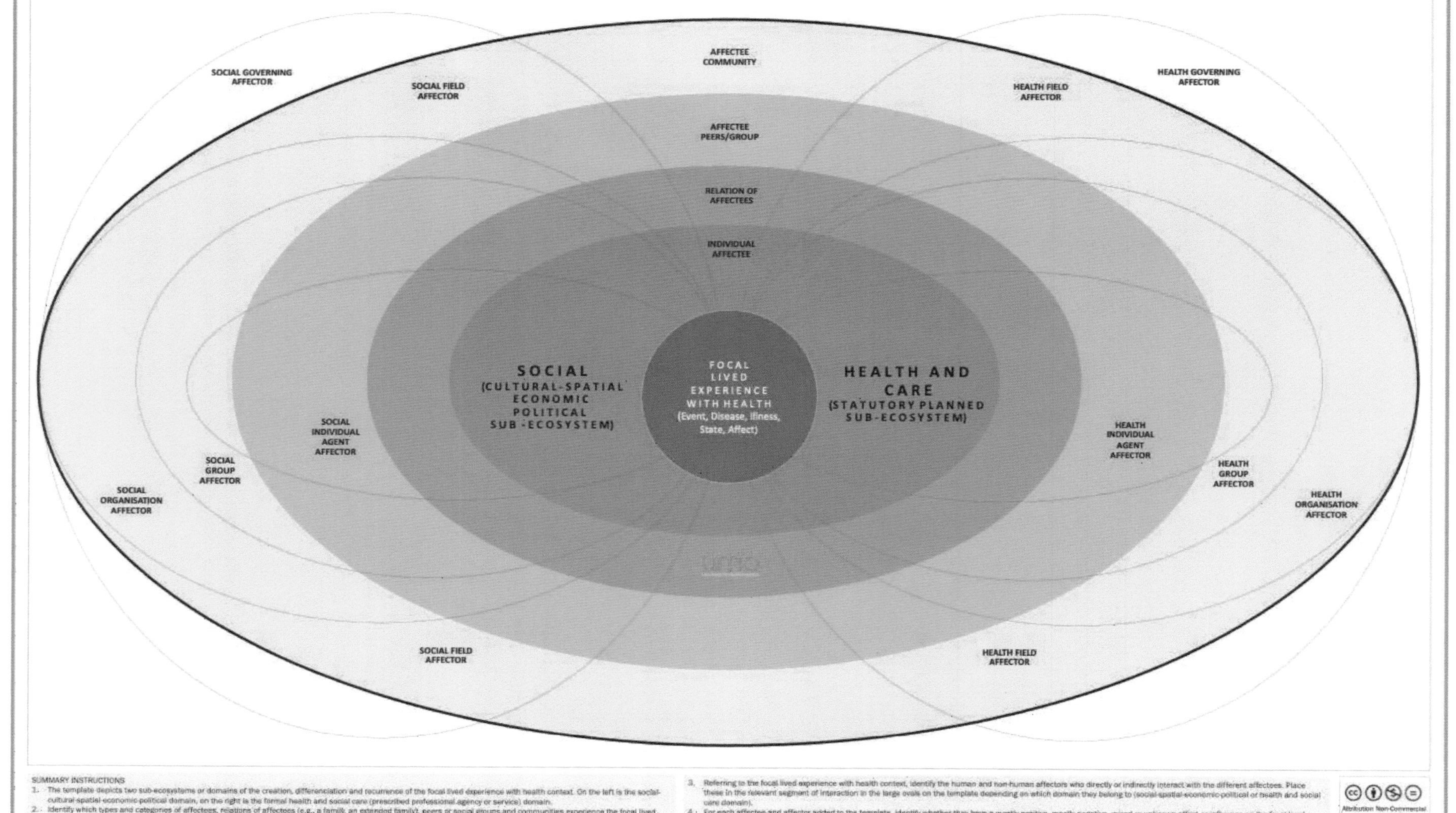

SUMMARY INSTRUCTIONS

1. The template depicts two sub-ecosystems or domains of the creation, differenciation and recurrence of the focal lived experience with health context. On the left is the social-cultural-spatial-economic-political domain, on the right is the formal health and social care (prescribed professional agency or service) domain.
2. Identify which types and categories of affectees, relations of affectees (e.g., a family, an extended family), peers or social groups and communities experience the focal lived experience with health context. Place these in the central "hourglass" segments of the template.
3. Referring to the focal lived experience with health context, identify the human and non-human affectors who directly or indirectly interact with the different affectees. Place these in the relevant segment of interaction in the large ovals on the template depending on which domain they belong to (social-spatial-economic-political or health and social care domain).
4. For each affectee and affector added to the template, identify whether they have a mostly positive, mostly negative, mixed or unknown affect or influence on the focal lived experience with health context.

Health Ecosystem Value Design® Framework 2.0
Created and designed by Chris Lawer 2021

umio

Template 3.0 version 2.0 Jan 2021

3.0 Map affector with affectee interactions in the health and social sub-ecosystems

With inputs and an idea of differences in lived experience for the focal context captured from affectees, identify and map the human and non-human affectors with whom and with which the affectees with the extremes of positive and negative experience interact. Do so in the two ecosystem sub-domains, the health and the social.

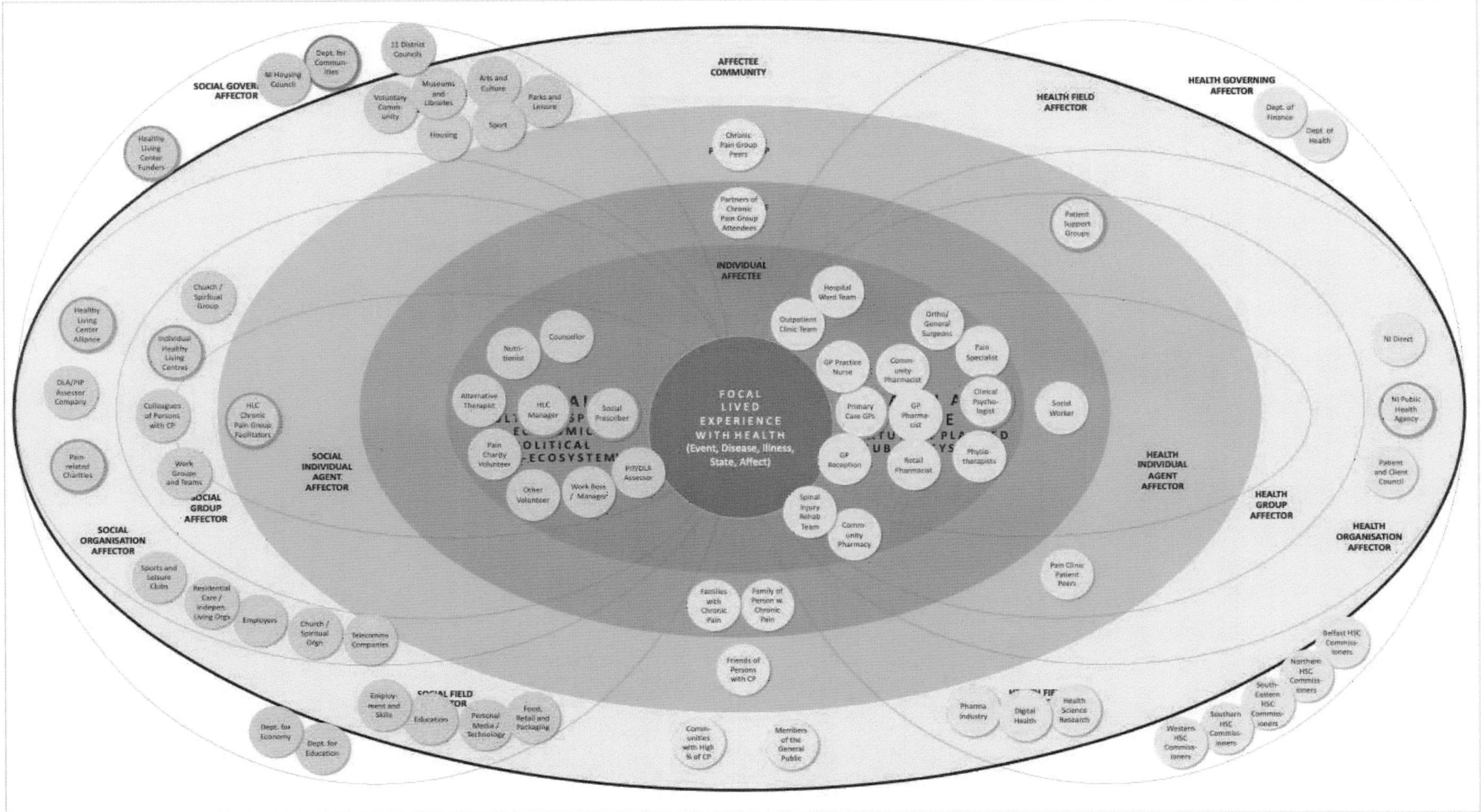

SOCIAL GOVERN. AFFECTOR
NI Housing Council
Dept. for Communities
11 District Councils
Voluntary Community
Museums and Libraries
Arts and Culture
Parks and Leisure
Housing
Sport
Healthy Living Center Funders
AFFECTEE COMMUNITY
Chronic Pain Group Peers
Partners of Chronic Pain Group Attendees
HEALTH FIELD AFFECTOR
Patient Support Groups
HEALTH GOVERNING AFFECTOR
Dept. of Finance
Dept. of Health
INDIVIDUAL AFFECTEE
Hospital Ward Team
Outpatient Clinic Team
Ortho/ General Surgeons
Pain Specialist
GP Practice Nurse
Community Pharmacist
Clinical Psychologist
Primary Care GPs
GP Pharmacist
Social Worker
GP Reception
Retail Pharmacist
Physiotherapists
Spinal Injury Rehab Team
Community Pharmacy
FOCAL LIVED EXPERIENCE WITH HEALTH (Event, Disease, Illness, State, Affect)
Church / Spiritual Group
Healthy Living Center Alliance
Individual Healthy Living Centres
Counsellor
Nutritionist
DLA/PIP Assessor Company
Colleagues of Persons with CP
HLC Chronic Pain Group Facilitators
Alternative Therapist
HLC Manager
Social Prescriber
Pain Charity Volunteer
Pain related Charities
Work Groups and Teams
SOCIAL INDIVIDUAL AGENT AFFECTOR
Other Volunteer
Work Boss / Manager
PIP/DLA Assessor
SOCIAL GROUP AFFECTOR
SOCIAL ORGANISATION AFFECTOR
Sports and Leisure Clubs
Residential Care / Independent Living Orgs.
Employers
Church / Spiritual Orgn
Telecomms Companies
Families with Chronic Pain
Family of Person w. Chronic Pain
Friends of Persons with CP
Employment and Skills
SOCIAL FIELD AFFECTOR
Education
Personal Media / Technology
Food, Retail and Packaging
Dept. for Economy
Dept. for Education
Communities with High % of CP
Members of the General Public
HEALTH INDIVIDUAL AGENT AFFECTOR
Pain Clinic Patient Peers
HEALTH GROUP AFFECTOR
HEALTH ORGANISATION AFFECTOR
NI Direct
NI Public Health Agency
Patient and Client Council
Belfast HSC Commissioners
Northern HSC Commissioners
South-Eastern HSC Commissioners
Southern HSC Commissioners
Western HSC Commissioners
Pharma Industry
Digital Health
Health Science Research

SUMMARY INSTRUCTIONS

1. The template depicts two sub-ecosystems or domains of the creation, differenciation and recurrence of the focal lived experience with health context. On the left is the social-cultural-spatial-economic-political domain, on the right is the formal health and social care (prescribed professional agency or service) domain.
2. Identify which types and categories of affectees, relations of affectees (e.g., a family, an extended family), peers or social groups and communities experience the focal lived experience with health context. Place these in the central "hourglass" segments of the template.
3. Referring to the focal lived experience with health context, identify the human and non-human affectors who directly or indirectly interact with the different affectees. Place these in the relevant segment of interaction in the large ovals on the template depending on which domain they belong to (social-spatial-economic-political or health and social care domain).
4. For each affectee and affector added to the template, identify whether they have a mostly positive, mostly negative, mixed or unknown affect or influence on the focal lived experience with health context.

Health Ecosystem Value Design® Framework 2.0
Created and designed by Chris Lawer 2021

umio

Template 3.0 version 2.0
Jan 2021

Reading template 3.0

In the template are three primary oval shapes. These are:

1. The base affectee layer, shown in shades of red/pink consisting of a "flat" hierarchy of five affectee types. These are with descriptions:
    - The focal lived experience with health context in the focus of your study
    - An individual person / human affectee
    - A relation of affectees such as a family including extended families and close friends
    - A group or peer group of affectees such as a self-help group, a community action group or an online patient or activist group or movement
    - A community of affectees that is less networked than a peer group but shares common lived experiences with health, disease or illness
1. The statutory planned health and social care sub-ecosystem overlaid onto the base red/pink affectee layer on the right-hand side of the template
2. The social sub-ecosystem overlaid onto the base red/pink affectee layer on the left-hand side of the template

Overlaid onto each of the health and social sub-ecosystems are two hierarchies of five interacting types of affectors. These are:

1. Individual affector agents that may be human (e.g., a GP) or non-human such as technologies or drugs
2. A group or team of affectors such as a GP practice, a functional team in a hospital, or a work team
3. An organization of affectors such as a pharmaceutical company, a digital health company, a hospital trust
4. A field of affectors that is a selection of types of interactional flows of interest in the study
5. Governing or overseer actors such as medical regulators, state and federal governments.

Seeing the spaces of affector-affectee interaction in the template

In the template, adjusting your perception to identify the segments of the bigger ovals, you can see several different segments or spaces where the two health and social domain ovals overlap with the base affectee layer. Altogether there are 50 different interaction spaces of various permutations of affectee-affector interactions.

4.0 Explore tendential forces in interactional flows for the focal lived experience context

Description

Uncover the tendencies present in tendential forces that influence the ideologies, powers, priorities and practices of human affectors and affectees in their interactions in interactional flows. Map the forces to the six categories of tendential forces in the outer ring and describe their effects in the inner rings to produce a relational model of forces of tendency present in the focal lived experience with health context.

Purpose of Template 4.0

- To surface deeper insights into the ontological, epistemological, innovation, capital with labour, biopolitical and regulatory tendential forces that modulate interactional flows of affectees and affectors in the focal experience ecosystem environment
- To understand how tendencies shape affector and affectee ideas, powers, priorities and practices of interaction for the focal lived experience with health context, and how these might contribute to the origination, differenciation and persistence of negative ill-health lived experiences

Template 4.0 summary instructions

1. For each of the two focal health and social experience sub-ecosystems shown on the template, discuss the influence of tendential forces in each category located in the outer rim of each circle
2. Consider how certain tendencies create and sustain an ideology (or ideologies), powers, priorities and practices of affectors and affectees in the focal lived experience with health context. Ask what are the dominant tendencies that influence differences in the focal context.
3. Add notes to describe the particular character and quality of the tendencies in each tendential force category in the outer circle
4. Add further notes to describe their particular relation to and production of forces of ideology, power, priorities and practices in the inner mollusk-like segments
5. What do the populated forces of tendency tell you about how you might realise or might be prevented from realising the transition purpose? How are affectees able to resist the tendencies to realise their desired valued (lived) experience with health?

Practical tips

A. Spend a few hours with this exercise as it is key linking step and learning activity in the Health Ecosystem Value Design® process

B. Use more than one copy of the template if needed

4.0 Explore tendential forces in interactional flows for the focal lived experience context

Uncover the tendencies present in tendential forces that influence the ideologies, powers, priorities and practices of human affectors and affectees in their interactions in interactional flows. Map the forces to the six types of tendential forces in the outer ring and describe their effects in the inner rings to produce a relational model of forces of tendency present in the focal lived experience with health context.

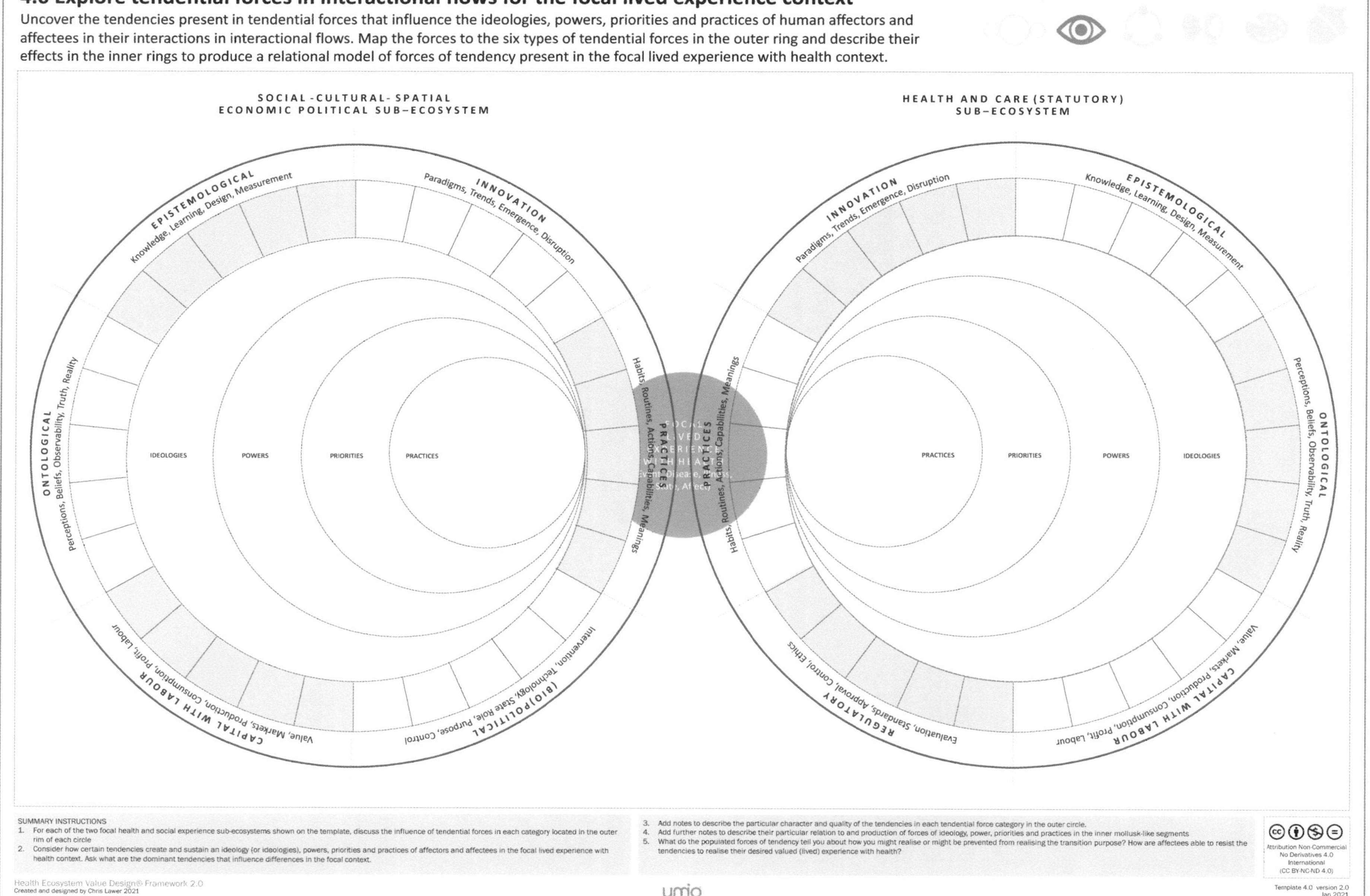

SUMMARY INSTRUCTIONS

1. For each of the two focal health and social experience sub-ecosystems shown on the template, discuss the influence of tendential forces in each category located in the outer rim of each circle
2. Consider how certain tendencies create and sustain an ideology (or ideologies), powers, priorities and practices of affectors and affectees in the focal lived experience with health context. Ask what are the dominant tendencies that influence differences in the focal context.
3. Add notes to describe the particular character and quality of the tendencies in each tendential force category in the outer circle.
4. Add further notes to describe their particular relation to and production of forces of ideology, power, priorities and practices in the inner mollusk-like segments
5. What do the populated forces of tendency tell you about how you might realise or might be prevented from realising the transition purpose? How are affectees able to resist the tendencies to realise their desired valued (lived) experience with health?

4.0 Explore tendential forces in interactional flows for the focal lived experience context

Uncover the tendencies present in tendential forces that influence the ideologies, powers, priorities and practices of human affectors and affectees in their interactions in interactional flows. Map the forces to the six types of tendential forces in the outer ring and describe their effects in the inner rings to produce a relational model of forces of tendency present in the focal lived experience with health context.

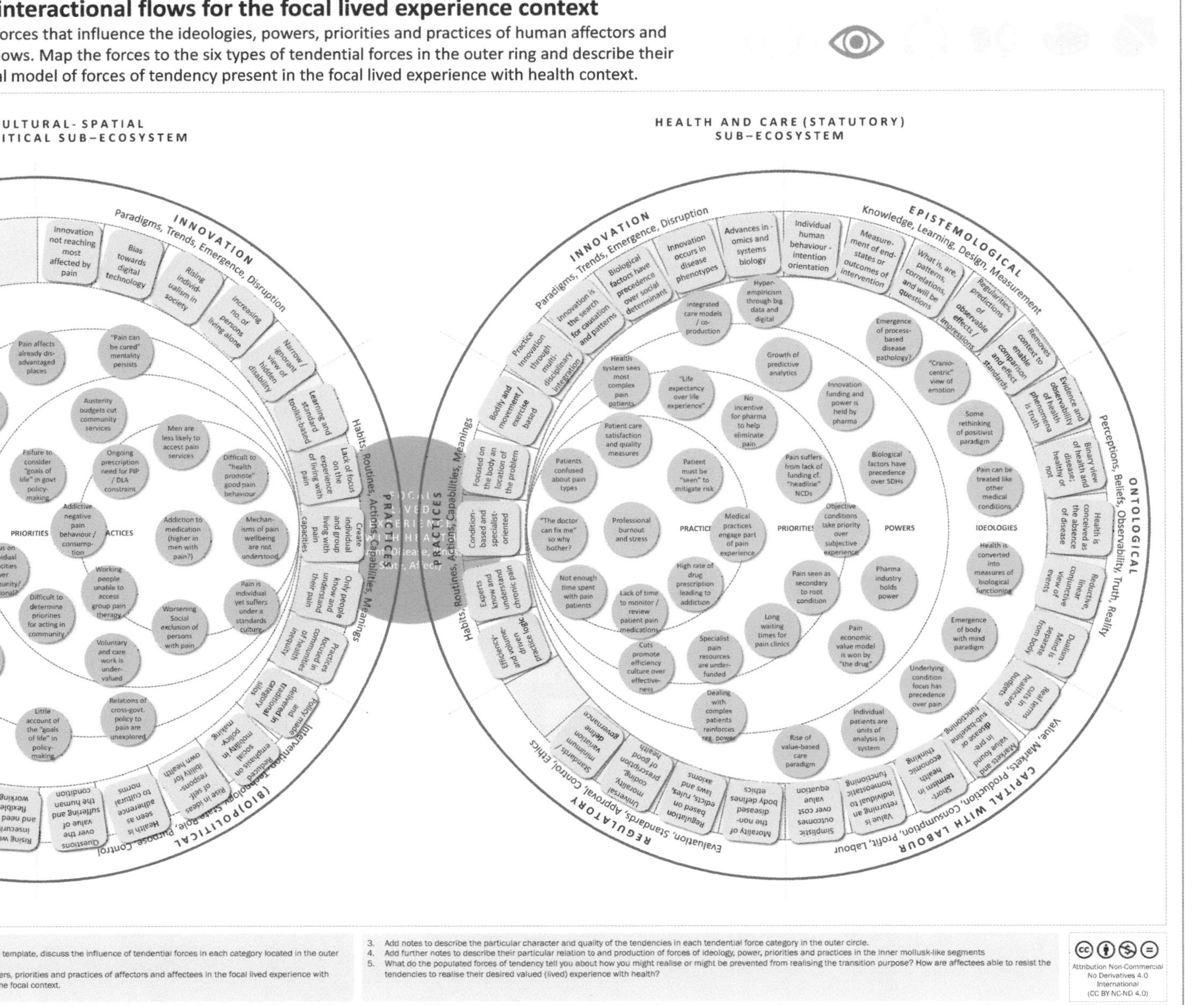

SUMMARY INSTRUCTIONS

1. For each of the two focal health and social experience sub-ecosystems shown on the template, discuss the influence of tendential forces in each category located in the outer rim of each circle
2. Consider how certain tendencies create and sustain an ideology (or ideologies), powers, priorities and practices of affectors and affectees in the focal lived experience with health context. Ask what are the dominant tendencies that influence differences in the focal context.
3. Add notes to describe the particular character and quality of the tendencies in each tendential force category in the outer circle.
4. Add further notes to describe their particular relation to and production of forces of ideology, power, priorities and practices in the inner mollusk-like segments
5. What do the populated forces of tendency tell you about how you might realise or might be prevented from realising the transition purpose? How are affectees able to resist the tendencies to realise their desired valued (lived) experience with health?

Health Ecosystem Value Design® Framework 2.0
Created and designed by Chris Lawer 2021

umio

Template 4.0 version 2.0
Jan 2021

5.0 Distinguish assemblages in the focal experience ecosystem environment

Description

Build the model of contingent assemblages of states, capacities and qualities of lived experience on the line of deterioration to ill-health, the line of recovery to desired valued health and points of stability in assemblages between the two poles. Develop a view of the nature and diversity of affective capacities, flows and tendencies of creation and interaction in assemblages within the focal experience ecosystem environment.

Purpose of Template 5.0

- To develop a novel perspective of contingent agencial assemblages interacting with interactional flows and tendential forces in the focal experience ecosystem environment
- To determine the different presence and nature of affects and affective capacities in the different assemblages and the types of interactional flows and tendencies that affectees in the assemblages interact with that shape their lived experience for the focal context
- To reveal the temporal and dynamic nature of the formation and ongoing transition of assemblages for the focal lived experience with health context
- To identify which assemblages are currently under-represented and/or - resourced (or even not known and addressed) in existing practices and to question the allocation of existing priorities and resources of affectors for the focal experience with health context

Template 5.0 summary instructions

1. Using research from templates 2.0, 3.0 and 4.0, distinguish different assemblages of affectee states, qualities, intensities and stabilities of lived experience for the focal lived experience with health context
2. For each assemblage, discuss and record the distinguishing perceptual-cognitive, bodily-motor, social-cultural and material-spatial affects and affective capacities, affectors, tendencies and interactional flows. Make a simple representation of the affects and affective capacities for each assemblage using the mini affect circles. Choose and add your own names of the identified assemblages in the larger segments around the "assemblage wheel".
3. Determine the distribution, proportion and types of affectees present in each of the newly discerned assemblages
4. Identify the predominant transitions or movements of affectees within and between the assemblages
5. Ask what your model tells you about prevailing ideas of lived experience for the focal context in question. Do current perspectives and interventions see and act on these differences in experience, and upon the transitions between assemblages? How might this view of assemblages and their different affective capacity be used to effectuate the transition purpose and create impact in the focal experience ecosystem environment?

Practical tips

A. This exercise relies on further research with diverse affectees as well as a degree of precision intuition

B. It may be populated with more detailed quantitative analysis using surveys

C. Two versions of the template are also provided, one for the line of deterioration assemblages (5.1), the other for the line of recovery assemblages (5.2)

5.0 Distinguish assemblages in the focal experience ecosystem environment

Build the model of contingent agencial assemblages of states, capacities and qualities of lived experience on the line of deterioration to ill-health, the line of recovery to desired valued health and points of stability in assemblages between the two poles. Develop the view of the diversity of affective capacities and the forces of creation and interaction present within assemblages within the focal experience ecosystem environment.

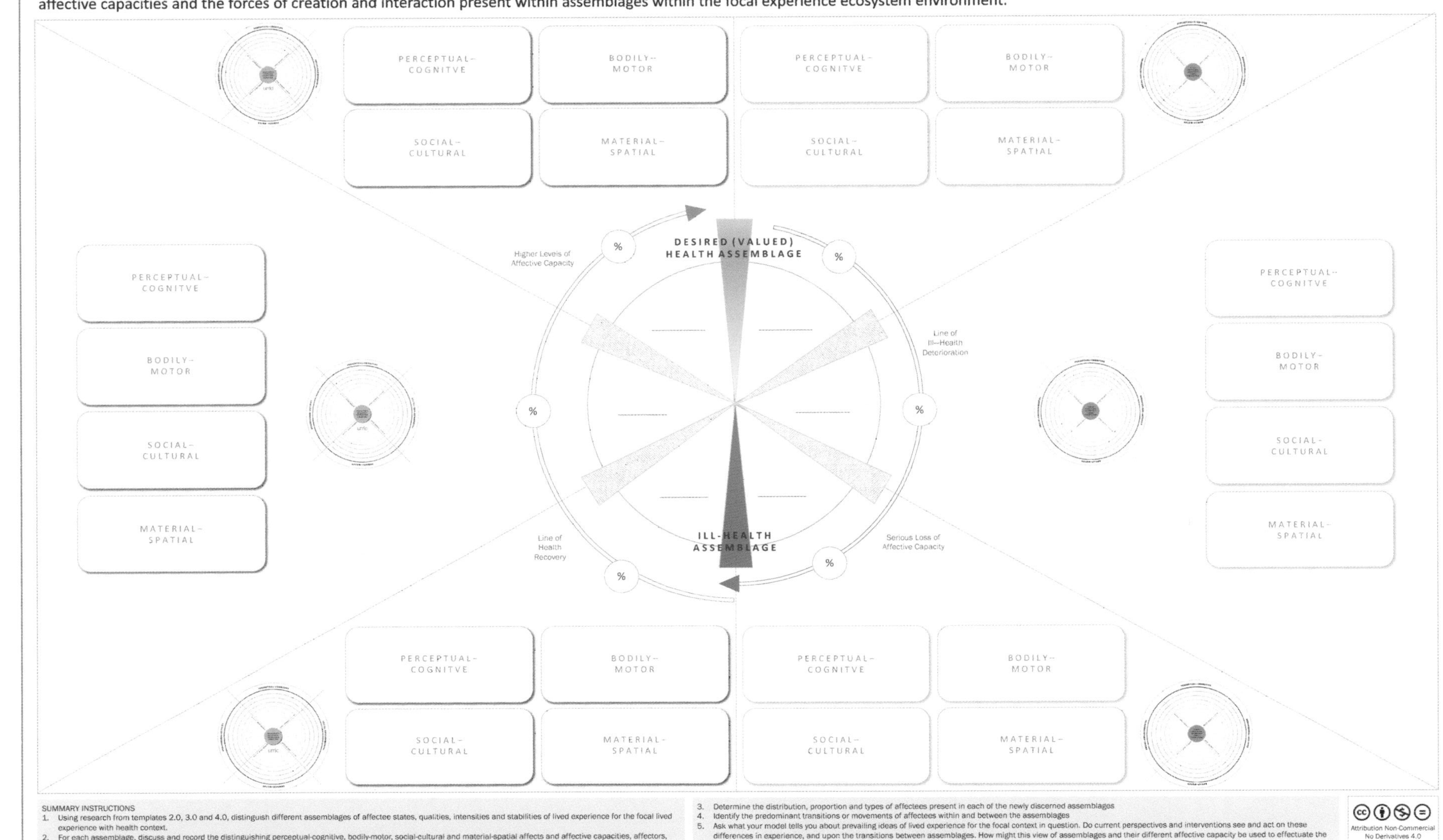

SUMMARY INSTRUCTIONS

1. Using research from templates 2.0, 3.0 and 4.0, distinguish different assemblages of affectee states, qualities, intensities and stabilities of lived experience for the focal lived experience with health context.
2. For each assemblage, discuss and record the distinguishing perceptual-cognitive, bodily-motor, social-cultural and material-spatial affects and affective capacities, affectors, tendencies and interactional flows. Make a simple representation of the affects and affective capacities for each assemblage using the mini affect circles. Choose and add your own names of the identified assemblages in the larger segments around the "assemblage wheel".
3. Determine the distribution, proportion and types of affectees present in each of the newly discerned assemblages
4. Identify the predominant transitions or movements of affectees within and between the assemblages
5. Ask what your model tells you about prevailing ideas of lived experience for the focal context in question. Do current perspectives and interventions see and act on these differences in experience, and upon the transitions between assemblages. How might this view of assemblages and their different affective capacity be used to effectuate the transition purpose and create impact in the focal experience ecosystem environment?

Health Ecosystem Value Design® Framework 2.0
Created and designed by Chris Lawer 2021

umio

Template 5.0 version 2.0
January 2021

5.1 Distinguish assemblages in the line of deterioration to ill-health

Build the model of contingent agencial assemblages of states, capacities and qualities of lived experience on the line of deterioration to ill-health between the two poles. Develop a view of the nature and diversity of affective capacities, flows and tendencies of creation and interaction in assemblages within the focal experience ecosystem environment.

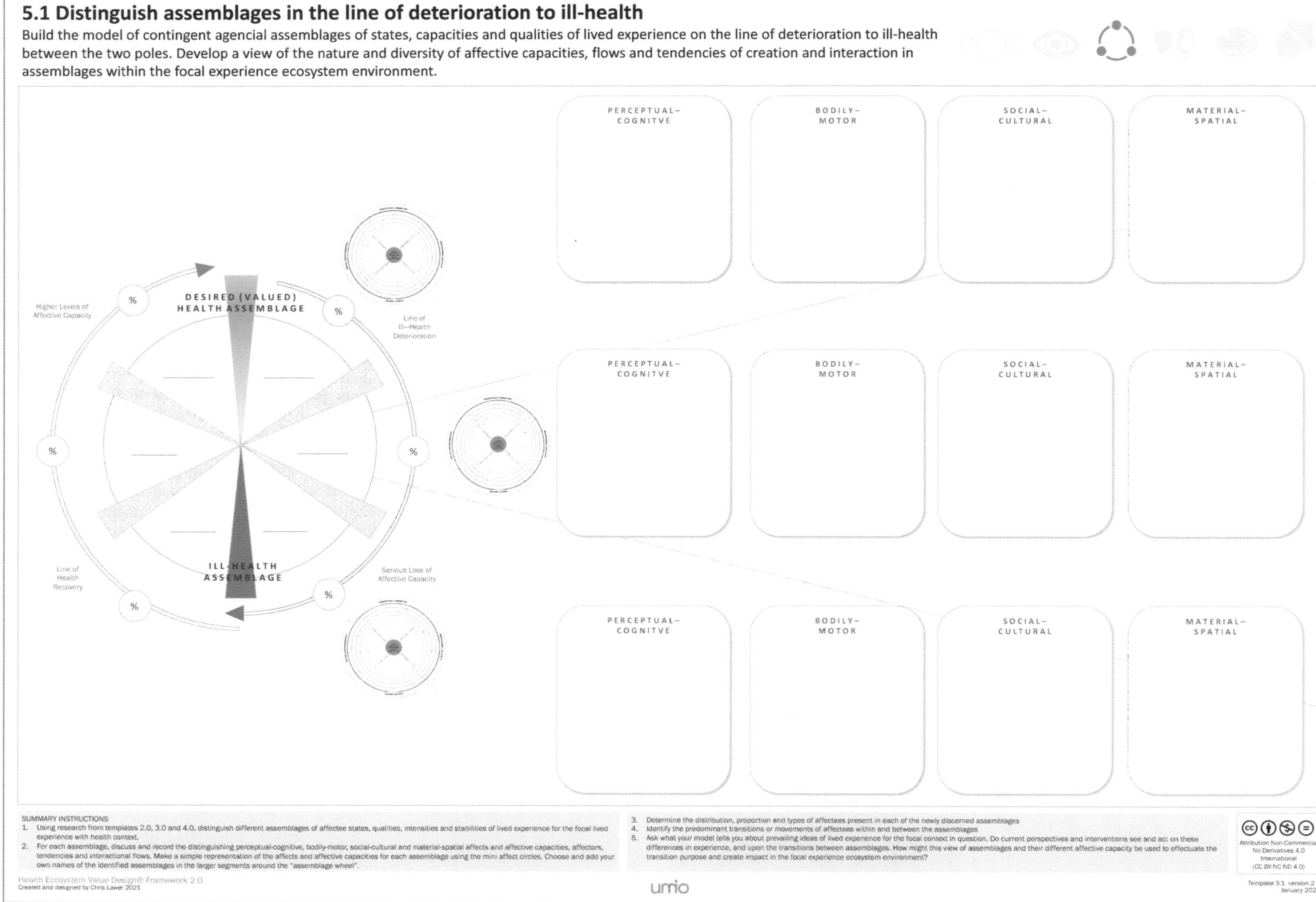

SUMMARY INSTRUCTIONS

1. Using research from templates 2.0, 3.0 and 4.0, distinguish different assemblages of affectee states, qualities, intensities and stabilities of lived experience for the focal lived experience with health context.
2. For each assemblage, discuss and record the distinguishing perceptual-cognitive, bodily-motor, social-cultural and material-spatial affects and affective capacities, affectors, tendencies and interactional flows. Make a simple representation of the affects and affective capacities for each assemblage using the mini affect circles. Choose and add your own names of the identified assemblages in the larger segments around the "assemblage wheel".
3. Determine the distribution, proportion and types of affectees present in each of the newly discerned assemblages
4. Identify the predominant transitions or movements of affectees within and between the assemblages
5. Ask what your model tells you about prevailing ideas of lived experience for the focal context in question. Do current perspectives and interventions see and act on these differences in experience, and upon the transitions between assemblages. How might this view of assemblages and their different affective capacity be used to effectuate the transition purpose and create impact in the focal experience ecosystem environment?

5.1 Distinguish assemblages in the line of deterioration to ill-health

Build the model of contingent agencial assemblages of states, capacities and qualities of lived experience on the line of deterioration to ill-health between the two poles. Develop a view of the nature and diversity of affective capacities, flows and tendencies of creation and interaction in assemblages within the focal experience ecosystem environment.

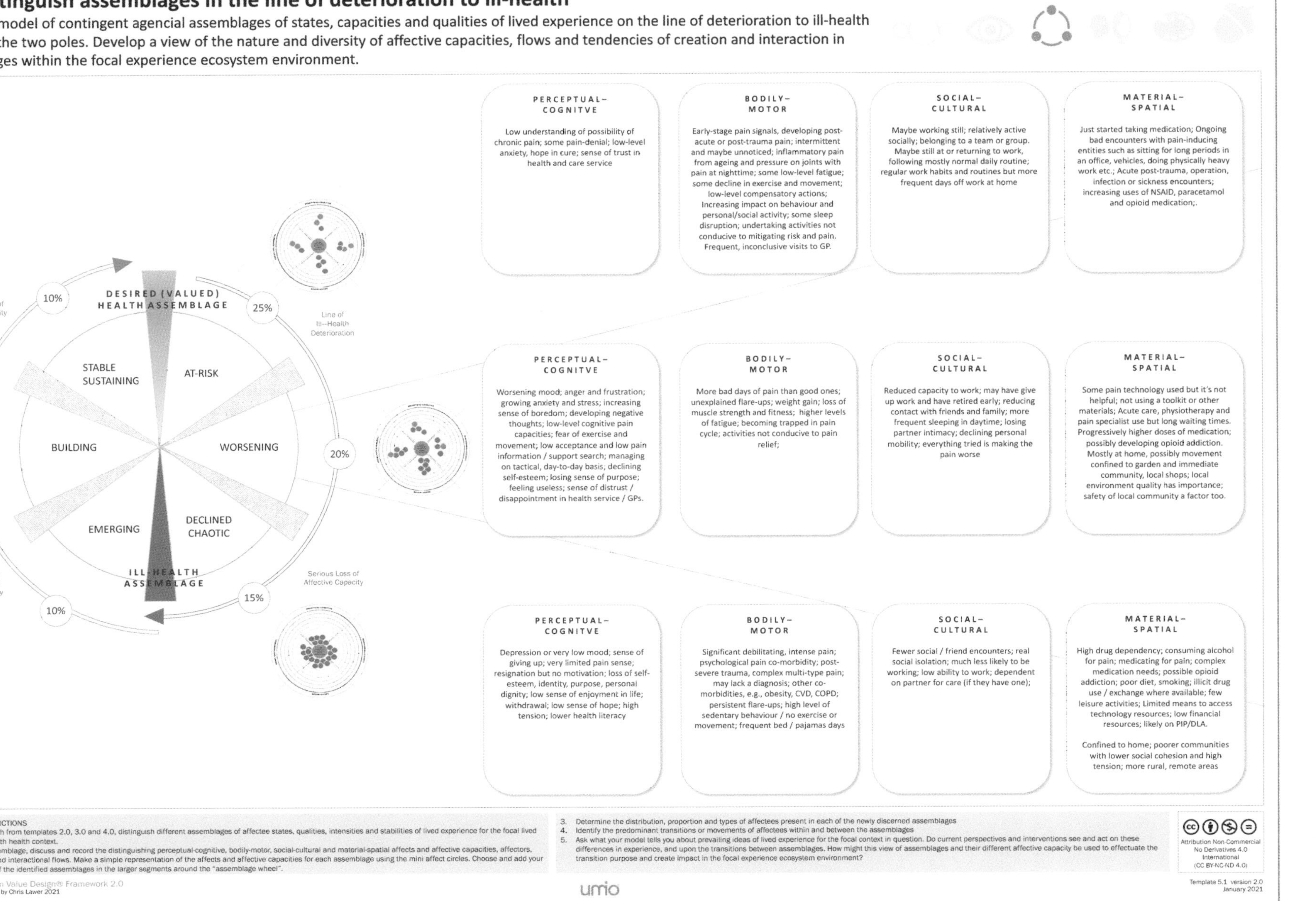

SUMMARY INSTRUCTIONS

1. Using research from templates 2.0, 3.0 and 4.0, distinguish different assemblages of affectee states, qualities, intensities and stabilities of lived experience for the focal lived experience with health context.
2. For each assemblage, discuss and record the distinguishing perceptual-cognitive, bodily-motor, social-cultural and material-spatial affects and affective capacities, affectors, tendencies and interactional flows. Make a simple representation of the affects and affective capacities for each assemblage using the mini affect circles. Choose and add your own names of the identified assemblages in the larger segments around the "assemblage wheel".
3. Determine the distribution, proportion and types of affectees present in each of the newly discerned assemblages
4. Identify the predominant transitions or movements of affectees within and between the assemblages
5. Ask what your model tells you about prevailing ideas of lived experience for the focal context in question. Do current perspectives and interventions see and act on these differences in experience, and upon the transitions between assemblages. How might this view of assemblages and their different affective capacity be used to effectuate the transition purpose and create impact in the focal experience ecosystem environment?

Health Ecosystem Value Design® Framework 2.0
Created and designed by Chris Lawer 2021

umio

Template 5.1 version 2.0
January 2021

5.2 Distinguish assemblages in the line of recovery to health

Build the model of contingent agencial assemblages of states, capacities and qualities of lived experience on the line of recovery to desired valued health. Develop a view of the nature and diversity of affective capacities, flows and tendencies of creation and interaction in assemblages within the focal experience ecosystem environment.

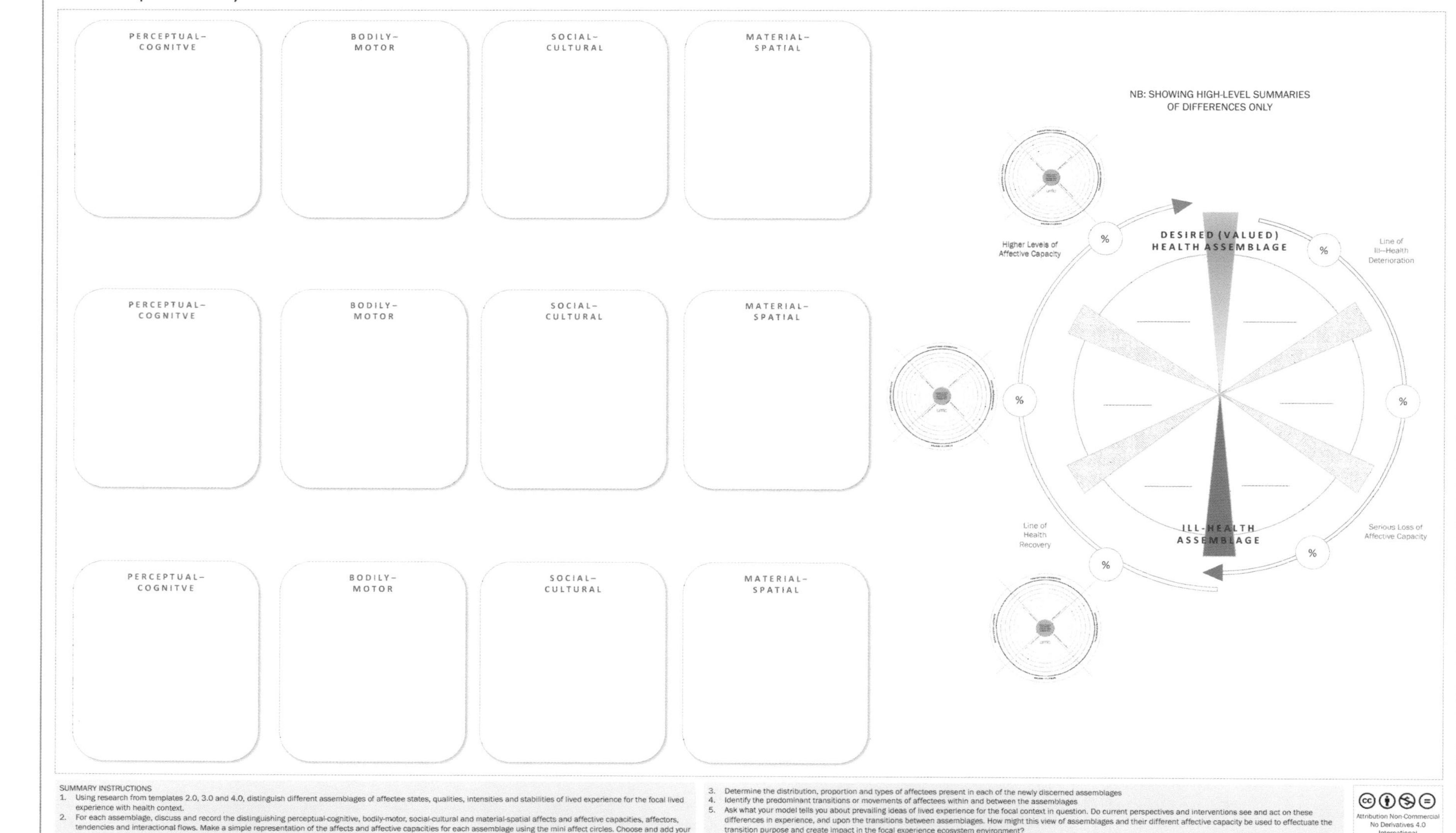

SUMMARY INSTRUCTIONS

1. Using research from templates 2.0, 3.0 and 4.0, distinguish different assemblages of affectee states, qualities, intensities and stabilities of lived experience for the focal lived experience with health context.
2. For each assemblage, discuss and record the distinguishing perceptual-cognitive, bodily-motor, social-cultural and material-spatial affects and affective capacities, affectors, tendencies and interactional flows. Make a simple representation of the affects and affective capacities for each assemblage using the mini affect circles. Choose and add your own names of the identified assemblages in the larger segments around the "assemblage wheel".
3. Determine the distribution, proportion and types of affectees present in each of the newly discerned assemblages
4. Identify the predominant transitions or movements of affectees within and between the assemblages
5. Ask what your model tells you about prevailing ideas of lived experience for the focal context in question. Do current perspectives and interventions see and act on these differences in experience, and upon the transitions between assemblages. How might this view of assemblages and their different affective capacity be used to effectuate the transition purpose and create impact in the focal experience ecosystem environment?

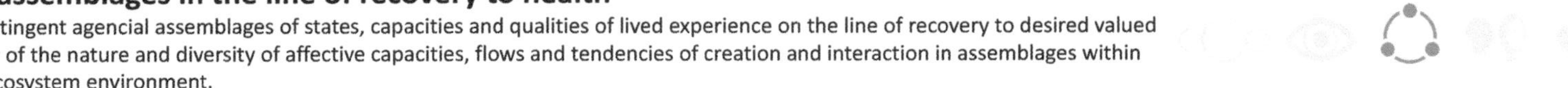

5.2 Distinguish assemblages in the line of recovery to health

Build the model of contingent agencial assemblages of states, capacities and qualities of lived experience on the line of recovery to desired valued health. Develop a view of the nature and diversity of affective capacities, flows and tendencies of creation and interaction in assemblages within the focal experience ecosystem environment.

PERCEPTUAL–COGNITVE	BODILY–MOTOR	SOCIAL–CULTURAL	MATERIAL–SPATIAL
Power to affect is greater than affects of pain leading to sense of real purpose and responsibility recovered; sense of personal achievement and possibility, growth; strong acceptance to drive powers of acting in mental space beyond the pain; sense of near control of pain; balanced body with mind understanding; predictive, cognitive capacities that can link activities with pain response; sense of joy and frequent laughter; less worry about making pain worse; more sense of free time. Clear understanding of capacities in context.	Pain persists but takes up less "mind space"; more energy; better stamina to cope with pain; fewer aches and pains; Successful pacing of personal and social activities; doing more fun and pleasurable activities; using physical activity to release endorphins	Maybe offering help to others; managing expectations of others such as family, friends and colleagues; finding new friends; having fun with a wider social circle	Reducing or eliminating medication use altogether; encounters with more spaces. Places of negative affect are fewer; exploring new places; wider travel horizons;
Reducing stress, tension and anxiety; achieving regular states of calm; building sense of control over pain; reducing mental attention on pain; improving mood; reduced anxiety; developing effective cognitive pain capacities; reducing fear of exercise and movement; developed acceptance and understanding of pain; forming personal strategy; improving self-esteem; greater sense of purpose; sense of possibility of living with pain; some ongoing frustration with slow pace; feeling more useful	Pain flare-ups may still occur randomly; pain persists yet seems to occupy mind and time less; Doing more enjoyable personal and social activities within cautious limits; Increasing use of exercise and social activities in balance to pain intensity becoming appropriately confident; not overdoing light activities leading to flares; sleep quality improving	Increasing level of social engagement; building peer-network and relations with other pain persons; improving social relations with family and friends; possible return to work but volunteering in the meantime.	Optimising use of medications and slowly reducing dose; using toolkits and technologies as reminders; engaging with objects to take mind off pain, e.g., hobbying. Widening places and spaces of activities; using own transport to get ahead; walking longer distances in public
Realising that things can be done to address the pain; Emerging from low mood and possible depression; developing acceptance and understanding of personal pain experience; building a strategy of baseline activity and flare warning signals; developing early-stage commitment to living with pain; building up personal tolerance levels	Set-backs and flares less frequent; having higher number of good than bad days; still a tendency to be overconfident and overdo activities leading to flares; or doing too little for fear of increasing the pain; experimenting with light exercise and relaxation	Getting value from new peer connections of from pain clinic; reducing dependency on informal carer, family; finding it difficult to communicate improvements	Changing with a view to optimising medications; experimenting alternative group and human therapies; may use a pain management digital technology or manual toolkit Becoming more confident, leaving the home and venturing out-and-about in local places and spaces

NB: SHOWING HIGH-LEVEL SUMMARIES OF DIFFERENCES ONLY

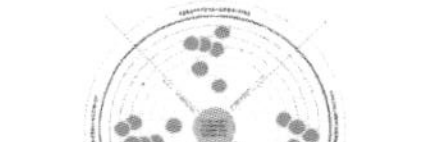
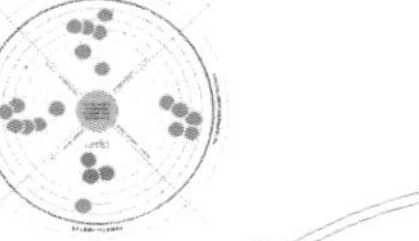
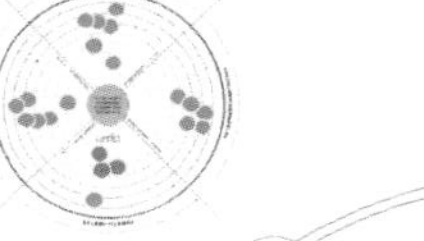
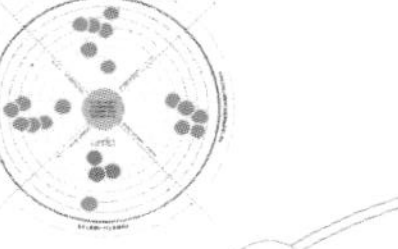
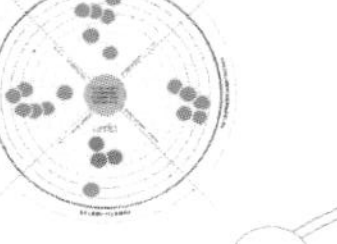
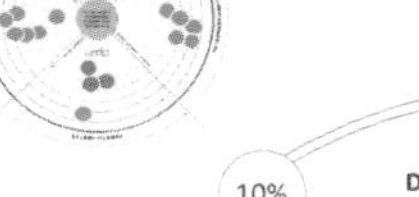
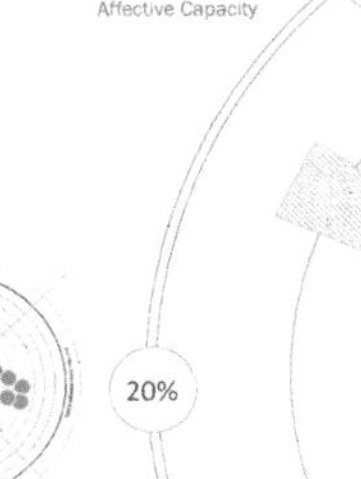
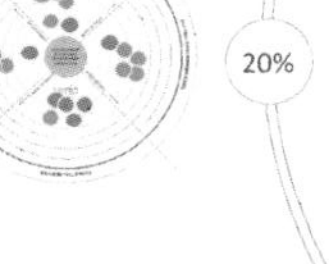
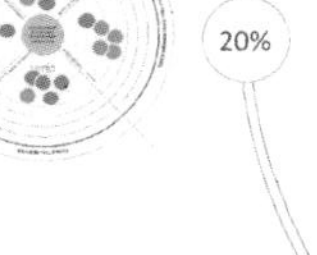
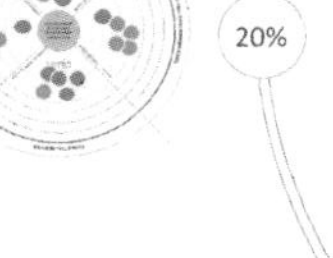
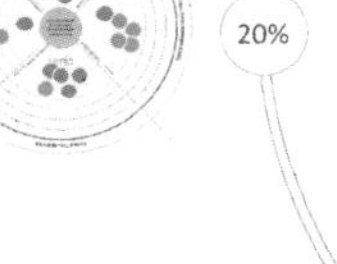
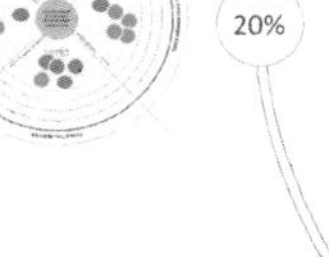
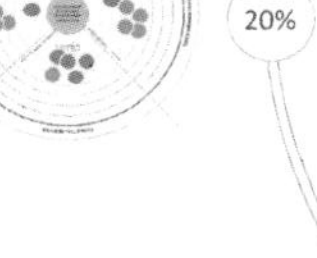
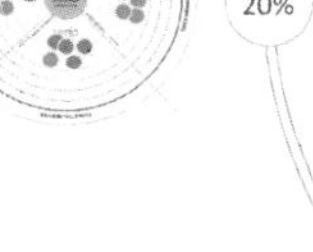
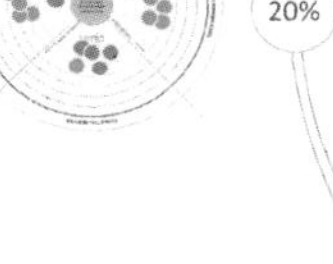
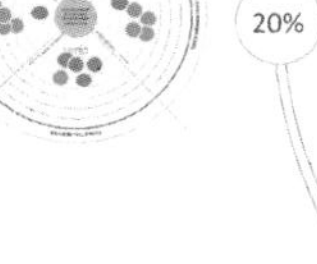
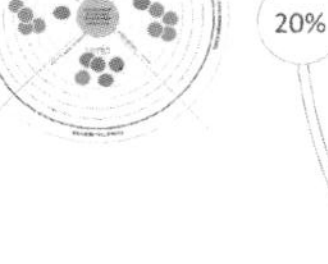
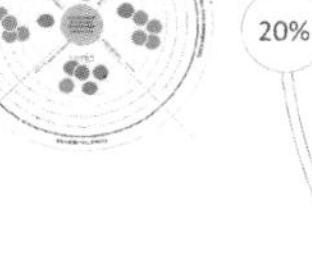
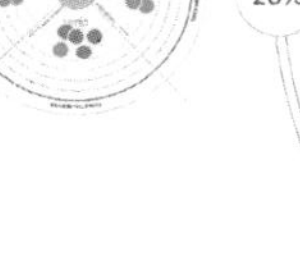
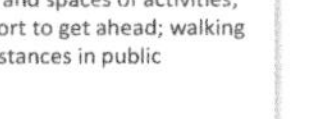
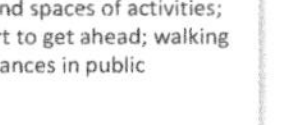
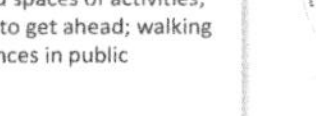
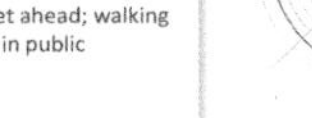
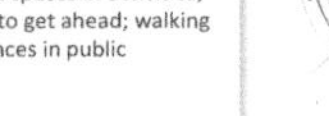

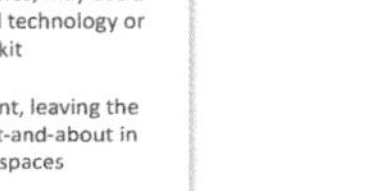
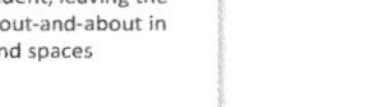
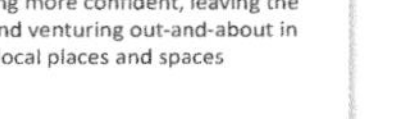
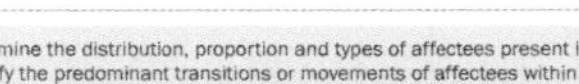
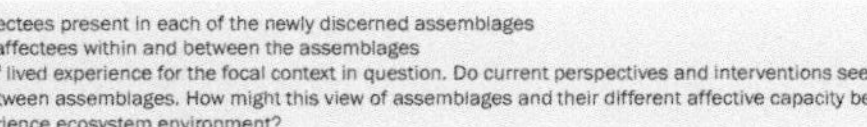

SUMMARY INSTRUCTIONS

1. Using research from templates 2.0, 3.0 and 4.0, distinguish different assemblages of affectee states, qualities, intensities and stabilities of lived experience for the focal lived experience with health context.
2. For each assemblage, discuss and record the distinguishing perceptual-cognitive, bodily-motor, social-cultural and material-spatial affects and affective capacities, affectors, tendencies and interactional flows. Make a simple representation of the affects and affective capacities for each assemblage using the mini affect circles. Choose and add your own names of the identified assemblages in the larger segments around the "assemblage wheel".
3. Determine the distribution, proportion and types of affectees present in each of the newly discerned assemblages
4. Identify the predominant transitions or movements of affectees within and between the assemblages
5. Ask what your model tells you about prevailing ideas of lived experience for the focal context in question. Do current perspectives and interventions see and act on these differences in experience, and upon the transitions between assemblages. How might this view of assemblages and their different affective capacity be used to effectuate the transition purpose and create impact in the focal experience ecosystem environment?

umio

Template 5.2 version 2.0
January 2021

6.0 Determine target desired transitions in lived experiences with health of affectees

Description

Identify the targeted desired transitions in affective capacities of affectee lived experiences with health. Decide the target affectees and map the target movements and transitions in all four affective domains to maintain a whole unified view of potential social desire.

Purpose of Template 6.0

- To identify the particular affectee types, affects and capacities in focus within the focal lived experience with health context
- To decide which transitions and movements of affects and affective capacities (in the four affective domains) of affectee lived experiences are to be the focus of design and interactional creation
- To identify relations between affects and affective capacity transitions across and within the four domains, and to discover which might be in conflict, related and/or could be grouped as design challenges
- To facilitate discussion of the target agencial assemblage(s) transitions in the experience ecosystem in the accompanying template 6.5

Template 6.0 summary instructions

1. Using the learning from templates 2.0-5.0, decide which affects and affective capacities must be transitioned to create greater powers of acting and creation of the focal lived experience with health context for the affectee type
2. For each of the four affective domains, decide which transitions, their nature and the degree they need to be created
3. Consider which of the nine interactional flows are the primary originating source(s) of the desired affects and affective capacities enabling the targeted transitions towards health (as social desire affective capacity)
4. Use the transition contexts developed in step / template 1.0 (when initially deciding the transition purpose and framing) to determine any available or potential capacities and resources for enacting the transitions. Ask what other capacities and resources can be used.
5. Annotate the transitions in the whole unified lived experience model and describe the desired capacity transitions in the boxes provided

Practical tips

A. Use the Umio definition of health to use a wide-angle view of lived experience framed by the ideal of social desire to define and mark targeted desired transitions in affective capacities

B. When marking the transitions in the lived experience model, show the directions of movement and where possible relate the individual transitions to one another

C. Ask if any transitions conflict with one another, which are the most difficult to enact and sustain, and why? Consider the influences of the tendential forces from your analysis in step / template 4.0

D. Discuss which of the four affective domains receive less (or sometimes no) attention in efforts to create and improve desired valued lived experiences with health for the focal context, and discuss why?

6.0 Determine target desired transitions in lived experiences with health of affectees

Identify the targeted desired transitions in affective capacities of affectee lived experiences with health. Decide the target affectees and map the target movements and transitions in all four affective domains to maintain a whole unified view of potential social desire.

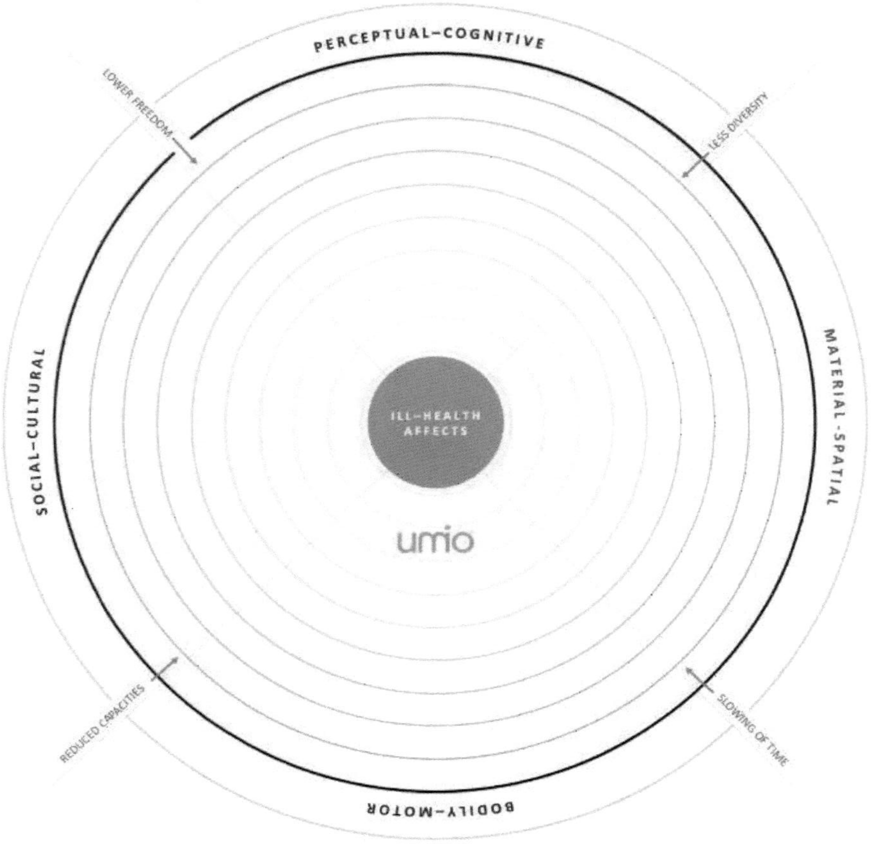

DEGREE OF PERCEPTUAL COGNITIVE TRANSITION	A B C D E F G H
DEGREE OF BODILY MOTOR TRANSITION	A B C D E F G H
DEGREE OF SOCIAL CULTURAL TRANSITION	A B C D E F G H
DEGREE OF MATERIAL SPATIAL TRANSITION	A B C D E F G H

AFFECTEE TYPE SUMMARY

SUMMARY INSTRUCTIONS

1. Using the learning from Templates 2.0-5.0, decide which affects and affective capacities are most critical to support creation of improved focal lived experience with health context
2. Decide which transitions in the whole lived experience with health context are to be the focus
3. Do so for each of the four affective domains that are higher-level combinations of the nine interactional flows.
3. Consider which of the four affective domains (of the nine interactional flows) could be the primary originating source of the desired affects and affective capacities enabling the targeted transitions
4. Use the transition contexts developed in Step 1.0 when initially deciding the transition purpose and framing to determine any available or potential capacities and resources for enacting the transition as this may influence what's possible
5. For one or more of the four affective domains, annotate the transitions in the whole unified lived experience model and describe the desired transition in the boxes provided along with enabling affectors and target affectee types

Health Ecosystem Value Design® Framework 2.0
Created and designed by Chris Lawer 2021

umio

Template 6.0 version 2.0
January 2021

6.0 Determine target desired transitions in lived experiences with health of affectees

Identify the targeted desired transitions in affective capacities of affectee lived experiences with health. Decide the target affectees and map the target movements and transitions in all four affective domains to maintain a whole unified view of potential social desire.

SUBSTANTIALLY CREATE PERCEPTUAL-COGNITIVE affective capacities in cognitive interactional flows ...	A.... to develop a useful "pain memory" B.... to recall personal physical/motor factors forming an experience of pain C.... to understand how personal outlook / mindset affects pain experience D.... to take good care of mental health E.... to understand reasons for variations in pain experience F.... to have renewed purpose and self-belief in living well with pain
MODERATELY CREATE bodily-MOTOR affective capacities in motor interactional flows...	A.... to undertake basic self personal care B.... to avoid random disorderly use of pain medications C.... to adapt / optimise use of pain medications D....to reduce risk of co-morbid "lifestyle" disease arising from bodily-motor changes E.... to avoid weight gain and increased pain F.... to stay active / less sedentary in the home
SUBSTANTIALLY IMPROVE SOCIAL affective capacities in social interactional flows ...	A.... to socialize with others with pain and develop new friendships B.... to be able to communicate pain experience and affects to family/friends C.... to correct/overcome the false perceptions of others D.... to share and learn from the experience of other persons who live well with pain E.... to ask the right questions of GPs for advice
IMPROVE MATERIAL and SPATIAL affective capacities ...	A.... to adapt the home to live comfortably with pain B.... to move freely and safely in the local built environment C.... to avoid ease of access to off-prescription "behind the wall" pain medications D.... to access and use digital pain self-management tools

DECLINED / CHAOTIC LIVED EXPERIENCFE WITH PAIN

15% or approx. 60,000 persons characterised by depression or very low mood; sense of giving up; very limited pain sense; resignation and loss of motivation; loss of self-esteem, identity, purpose, personal dignity; low sense of enjoyment in life; withdrawal; low sense of hope; high tension; lower health literacy); High drug dependency; consuming alcohol for pain; medicating for pain; persistent flare-ups; high level of sedentary behaviour / no exercise or movement; frequent bed / pajamas days; complex medication needs; possible opioid addiction; poor diet, smoking; illicit drug use / exchange where available; few leisure activities; Fewer social / friend encounters; real social isolation; much less likely to be working; low ability to work; dependent on partner for care (if they have one); Significant debilitating, intense pain; psychological pain co-morbidity; post-severe trauma, complex multi-type pain; may lack a diagnosis, other co-morbidities, e.g., obesity, CVD, COPD; Confined to home; poorer communities with lower social cohesion and high tension; more rural, remote areas; Limited means to access technology resources; low financial resources; likely on PIP/DLA

SUMMARY INSTRUCTIONS

1. Using the learning from Templates 2.0-5.0, decide which affects and affective capacities are most critical to support creation of improved focal lived experience with health context
2. Decide which transitions in the whole lived experience with health context are to be the focus
3. Do so for each of the four affective domains that are higher-level combinations of the nine interactional flows.
3. Consider which of the four affective domains (of the nine interactional flows) could be the primary originating source of the desired affects and affective capacities enabling the targeted transitions
4. Use the transition contexts developed in Step 1.0 when initially deciding the transition purpose and framing to determine any available or potential capacities and resources for enacting the transition as this may influence what's possible
5. For one or more of the four affective domains, annotate the transitions in the whole unified lived experience model and describe the desired transition in the boxes provided along with enabling affectors and target affectee types

Health Ecosystem Value Design® Framework 2.0
Created and designed by Chris Lawer 2021

umio

Template 6.0 version 2.0
January 2021

6.5 Determine target desired transitions in assemblages in the focal experience ecosystem

Description

Identify the desired targeted transitions in affective capacities of health in assemblages within the body of agencial assemblages in the focal experience ecosystem environment. Restate the focus, explore the developmental impact and refine the high-level transition purpose to inform the design challenge.

Purpose of Template 6.5

- To decide which individual agencial assemblage or assemblages having distinct states, qualities and capacities of lived experience for the focal context are to be the focus of design and interactional creation within the focal experience ecosystem environment, and to determine which target transitions in the body of assemblages to make
- To identify the affectors and types of affectors that can help enact, support or influence directly or indirectly the desired transition(s) in the assemblage and in affectee lived experience
- To assess the potential ecosystem-level developmental impact that may be realized from enacting the targeted transition in assemblage affective capacity in the focal experience ecosystem
- To facilitate discussion and agreement about where to focus and how the design challenge might be organized, by whom and with which affector and affectee types for different developmental impacts

Template 6.5 summary instructions

1. Using the learning from templates 2.0-5.0 and the transition decisions made in template 6.0, decide which transitions in which agencial assemblages in the body of assemblages in the focal experience ecosystem environment are to be targeted. Decide which are the priority transitions and label them with numbers.
2. Consider the current developmental impact of the different assemblages in the focal experience ecosystem environment and use this to inform your selections and prioritizations
3. Select the target assemblage(s), write in the assemblage names in the assemblage model, then annotate and describe the desired assemblage transitions in the large boxes in priority order
4. Add existing and revised percentage distribution and numbers of affectees in the different assemblages for each transition in the boxes to the right of the assemblage descriptions
5. Provide a summary of the developmental impacts of your selected assemblage transitions in the box provided and the transition duration over which you intend to realise the desired impact

Practical tips

A. When marking the transitions in the assemblage model, show the directions of movement and where possible relate the transitions to one another

B. Transitions are not always required or may be the focus of a creation effort. Focus may be on sustaining the existing agencial creational capacity of an assemblage

C. Ask if any transitions conflict with one another, which are the most difficult to enact and sustain, and why?

D. Consider the influences of the tendential forces from your analysis in step / template 4.0.

6.5 Determine target desired transitions in assemblages in the focal experience ecosystem

Identify the desired targeted transitions in affective capacities of health in assemblages within the body of agencial assemblages in the focal experience ecosystem environment. Restate the focus, explore the developmental impact and refine the high-level transition purpose to inform the design challenge.

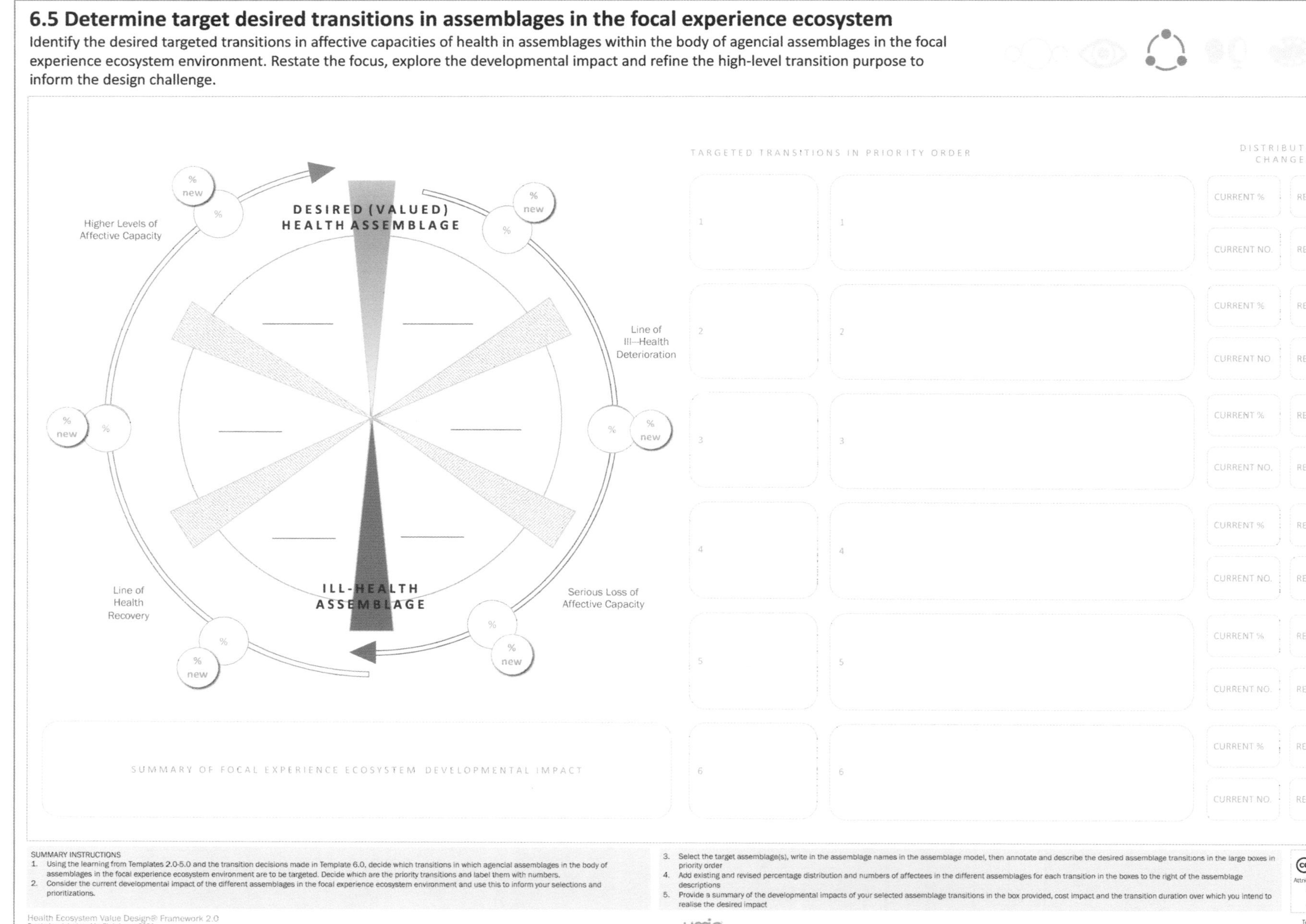

SUMMARY INSTRUCTIONS

1. Using the learning from Templates 2.0-5.0 and the transition decisions made in Template 6.0, decide which transitions in which agencial assemblages in the body of assemblages in the focal experience ecosystem environment are to be targeted. Decide which are the priority transitions and label them with numbers.
2. Consider the current developmental impact of the different assemblages in the focal experience ecosystem environment and use this to inform your selections and prioritizations.
3. Select the target assemblage(s), write in the assemblage names in the assemblage model, then annotate and describe the desired assemblage transitions in the large boxes in priority order
4. Add existing and revised percentage distribution and numbers of affectees in the different assemblages for each transition in the boxes to the right of the assemblage descriptions
5. Provide a summary of the developmental impacts of your selected assemblage transitions in the box provided, cost impact and the transition duration over which you intend to realise the desired impact

6.5 Determine target desired transitions in assemblages in the focal experience ecosystem

Identify the desired targeted transitions in affective capacities of health in assemblages within the body of agencial assemblages in the focal experience ecosystem environment. Restate the focus, explore the developmental impact and refine the high-level transition purpose to inform the design challenge.

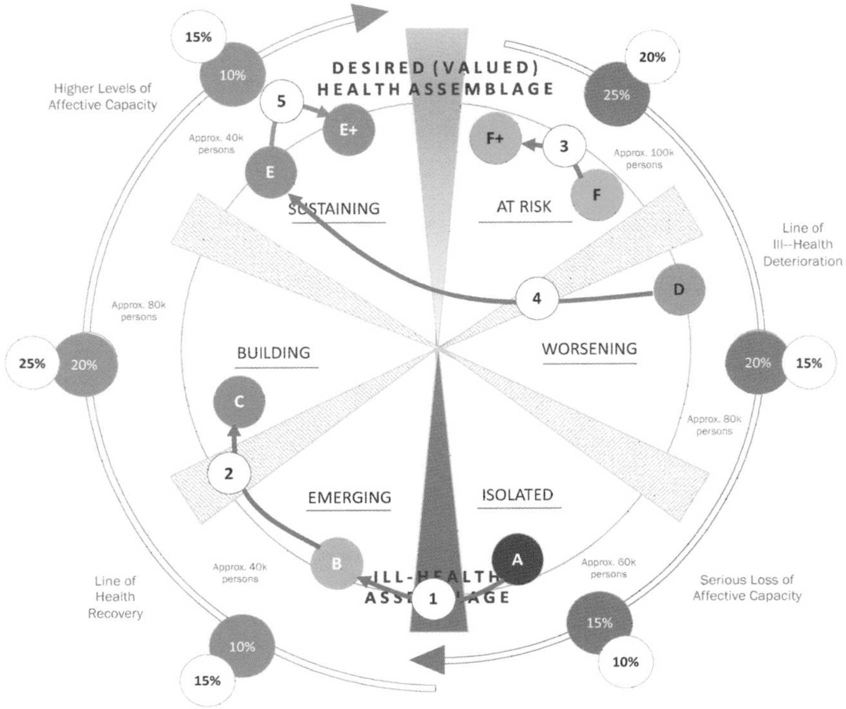

DESIRED (VALUED) HEALTH ASSEMBLAGE

ILL-HEALTH ASSEMBLAGE

Higher Levels of Affective Capacity

Line of Ill–Health Deterioration

Serious Loss of Affective Capacity

Line of Health Recovery

SUSTAINING — AT RISK — WORSENING — ISOLATED — EMERGING — BUILDING

15% / 10% — Approx. 40k persons

20% / 25% — Approx. 100k persons

20% / 15% — Approx. 80k persons

15% / 10% — Approx. 60k persons

10% / 15% — Approx. 40k persons

25% / 20% — Approx. 80k persons

TARGETED TRANSITIONS IN PRIORITY ORDER

Transition	Description	Current % / No.	Revised % / No.
1. A TO B MOST ISOLATED TO EMERGING	Develop whole pain lived experience affective capacities of those most isolated, withdrawn and debilitated affectees with chronic pain, majority of whom are living in more rural western areas, remote from pain centres as well as poorer neighborhoods in towns and cities. Focus on interactional social and material flow capacities of affect capacity creation. Target reduction of 33% in this group (15% to 10%)	15 % / 60k	10 % / 40k
2. B TO C EMERGING TO BUILDING	Sustain emergence of whole health affective capacities of those formerly isolated and debilitated with their chronic pain by ensuring continuity of support and avoiding relapse and withdrawal back to an isolated state	10 % / 40k	15 % / 60k
3. F TO F+ AT RISK TO LESS AT RISK	Prevent early deterioration of those with intermittent signs of chronic pain to avoid decline into worsening and later assemblages	25 % / 100k	20 % / 80k
4. D TO E WORSENING TO SUSTAINING	Prevent further worsening of those with early-stage chronic pain by developing whole health lived experience affective capacity beyond body-motor pain understanding with the potential to transition them to the sustaining assemblage	20 % / 80k	15 % / 60k
5. E TO E+ SUSTAINING TO MORE SUSTAINING	Improve further affective capacities of those living well with chronic pain through ongoing support when needed and engagement, and where possible increasing work and leisure-related interactional and creational capacities, thereby preventing decline into at risk or worsening assemblages	10 % / 40k	15 % / 60k
6	6	CURRENT % / CURRENT NO.	REVISED % / REVISED NO.

- Wider community awareness and understanding of chronic pain
- Widening of the pain ecosystem to incorporate non-healthcare actors (employers, local government, planners, pain peers, pain helpers, etc.)

- Create employer awareness and more tolerance of those with pain at work
- Improved affectees' practical knowledge and capability for self-management of whole lived experience and interactional nature of pain

- Reduced dependency (systemic and patient) on pain drug treatments (including opioids) and reduced costs of medication
- Reduce unnecessary and costly pain specialist visits including referrals from GPs

- Diversified nature of interactions from bodily-motor to whole health lived experiences
- Improve GP/clinician knowledge of pain affectee's whole lived experiences
- Reduce total cost of chronic pain by 15% (£700m) over 5 years

SUMMARY INSTRUCTIONS

1. Using the learning from Templates 2.0-5.0 and the transition decisions made in Template 6.0, decide which transitions in which agencial assemblages in the body of assemblages in the focal experience ecosystem environment are to be targeted
2. Use the transition contexts developed in Step 1.0 when initially deciding the transition purpose as these might influence your decisions. Consider the relative current developmental impact of the different assemblages in the focal experience ecosystem environment.
3. Select the target assemblage(s), write in the assemblage names in the assemblage model and percentage distribution of affectees in the experience ecosystem, then annotate and describe the desired assemblage transitions in the large boxes
4. Provide a summary of the developmental impact of your selected assemblage transitions in the impact box provided
5. Copy over the summary of the affectee type(s) from Template 6.0 that will be included in the transition and add the enabling, supporting and influencing affector types in the boxes provided also

Health Ecosystem Value Design® Framework 2.0
Created and designed by Chris Lawer 2021

umio

Template 6.0 version 2.0 January 2021

7.0 Capture and reflect on the learning so far in relation to the transition purpose

Description

With the target transitions decided, reflect on the learning to date for the focal lived experience with health context. Determine the key tendencies that are preventing, limiting or have the potential to enable the targeted movement(s) in the experience ecosystem towards the transition purpose. Set up challenge questions to guide subsequent design and ideation of concepts, propositions and offerings in the next steps.

Purpose of Template 7.0

- To reflect on learnings to date through the lens of social desire (the reverse parabola has reached its furthest point back in the virtual domain), whole unified lived experience with health, agencial assemblages of different experience states, qualities and capacities, and tendencies in interactional flows in the virtual social with natural body of an experience ecosystem
- To deepen understanding of how current and prevailing tendencies are preventing, limiting or could enable realization of the transition purpose in the focal lived experience with context in the two health and social sub-ecosystems
- To create, organize and define a series of challenges in different tendency categories to inform the design of affectee, affector and focal experience ecosystem offerings, value propositions and enablers using templates 8.0, 8.5 and 9.0

Template 7.0 summary instructions

1. Using the insights and findings from all the previous templates, and especially the tendential forces analysis in template 4.0 and the assemblages modelling in template 5.0, capture the tendencies and learning to date in relation to targeted movements and the transition purpose (which may at this point be refined). State these as "how might we?" questions in the individual boxes for the different tendency categories in the top row of the matrix.
2. Do so for both the health and social sub-ecosystems and where possible, link the tendencies and learning using the corresponding numbers system in each sub-ecosystem. Doing so helps to develop a relational model of tendencies and learning and a complete view of the limits and potential to realise the transition purpose for the focal lived experience with health context spanning the two sub-ecosystems.
3. Ask which tendencies stated as design challenges act as the biggest constraints and which are the most likely enablers? Why do these persist? In which interactional flows do they arise?
4. What is the relation between the constraining and enabling tendencies and sources of power in the focal experience ecosystem? Which affectors (both human and non-human) hold this power? Ask how this power is changing, where and why?

Practical tips

A. Consider which tendencies and design challenges in the seven categories is the hardest to address and why they persist

B. Examine the different design challenges in the health and social sub-ecosystems, reflect on what that have in common and what are their differences

C. Determine what it will take to bring affectors together from the health and social sub-ecosystems in order to pursue interactional creation

7.0 Capture and reflect on the learning so far in relation to the transition purpose

With the target transitions decided, ask a series of questions to support group reflection of the present situation in the focal lived experience with health context. Determine the key tendencies that if overcome or modified can support movement towards the transition purpose. Set up a series of challenge questions to guide subsequent design and ideation of concepts, propositions and offerings.

TENDENCY CATEGORIES →	SEEING-DESCRIBING Health, Affects, Assemblages, Problems, Opportunities, Ecosystem		KNOWING-LEARNING Types of Knowledge, Methods, Review, Sharing, Reflecting		PRACTICING-ACTING Motives, Routines, Bias, Habits, Technologies, Guidelines		ASSESSING-VALUING Value Model, Measurement, Monitoring, Timescales, Bias		RESOURCING-DECIDING Resource Types, Availability, Social, Economic, Cultural Capital		CONNECTING-FLOWING Organisation, Collaboration, Intra-/ Inter-functional, Peer-Peer, Silos		ADAPTING-TRANSITIONING Purpose, Design, Innovation, Capacity, Capability	
HEALTH AND CARE DOMAIN	1	2	1	2	1	2	1	2	1	2	1	2	1	2
	3	4	3	4	3	4	3	4	3	4	3	4	3	4
	5	6	5	6	5	6	5	6	5	6	5	6	5	6
	7	8	7	8	7	8	7	8	7	8	7	8	7	8
SOCIAL-CULTURAL-SPATIAL-POLITICAL-ECONOMIC DOMAIN	1	2	1	2	1	2	1	2	1	2	1	2	1	2
	3	4	3	4	3	4	3	4	3	4	3	4	3	4
	5	6	5	6	5	6	5	6	5	6	5	6	5	6
	7	8	7	8	7	8	7	8	7	8	7	8	7	8

SUMMARY INSTRUCTIONS

1. Using the insights and findings from all the previous templates, and especially the tendential forces analysis in Template 4.0 and the assemblages modelling in Template 5.0, capture the tendencies limiting the means and potential to realise the transition purpose. State these as "how might we" questions in the individual boxes and for the different tendency categories in the top row of the matrix.
2. Do so for both the health and social sub-ecosystems and where possible, link the tendencies using the number system in each sub-ecosystem. Doing so helps to develop a relational model of tendencies inhibiting potential to realise the transition purpose for the focal lived experience with health context.
3. Ask, which tendencies act as the biggest constraints? Why do these persist? In which interactional flows do they arise?
4. What is the relation between dominant tendencies and the sources of power in the focal experience ecosystem? Which affectors (both human and non-human) hold this power? Ask how this power is changing, where and why?
5. Finally, "flip" the constraints, conflicts and challenges by asking which could act as key enablers of the transition purpose if modified or overcome

Health Ecosystem Value Design® Framework 2.0
Created and designed by Chris Lawer 2021

umio

Template 6.0 version 2.0
January 2021

7.0 Capture and reflect on the learning so far in relation to the transition purpose

With the target transitions decided, reflect on the learning to date for the focal lived experience with health context. Determine the key tendencies that are preventing, limiting or have the potential to enable the targeted movement(s) in the experience ecosystem towards the transition purpose. Set up challenge questions to guide subsequent design and ideation of concepts, propositions and offerings in the next steps.

	SEEING-DESCRIBING Health, Affects, Assemblages, Problems, Opportunities, Ecosystem		KNOWING-LEARNING Types of Knowledge, Methods, Review, Sharing, Reflecting		PRACTICING-ACTING Motives, Routines, Bias, Habits, Technologies, Guidelines		ASSESSING-VALUING Value Model, Measurement, Monitoring, Timescales, Bias		RESOURCING-DECIDING Resource Types, Availability, Social, Economic, Cultural Capital		CONNECTING-FLOWING Organisation, Collaboration, Intra-/ Inter-functional, Peer-Peer, Silos		ADAPTING-TRANSITIONING Purpose, Design, Innovation, Capacity, Capability	
HEALTH AND SOCIAL CARE DOMAIN	How to change bodily- and condition-centric pain clinician mindsets?	How to raise DoH awareness of the impact of pain?	How to augment pain objectification with qualitative experience?	How to detect emerging addictive behaviour?	How to incorporate varied lived experience into a clinical standards culture?	How to introduce drug optimisation programme?	How to shift froman outcomes-cost model to experience value?	What does an ecosystem pain value model look like?	How to get round limited GP time?	How to help chronic pain services to receive more funding from DofH?	How to bring person-with-pain insights into the health system?	How to bring professional health and community actors in pain ecosystem	How to reduce the power of the bodily metaphor?	Where do we start?
	How to see & differentiate people with pain based on their capacities?	How to create wider sense of pain experience in health practice?	How to understand people's different pain capacities?	What does a model of pain cognition look like?	How to influence the new NICE pain guidelines in draft development?	How to influence the new NICE pain guidelines in draft development?	How to change the perception of pain (to get more funding)?		How to evidence the consequences of pharma's power in pain ecosystem?	What is needed to boosted specialist pain centre capacity?			How do we balance techno-science innovation with social?	How to overcome constraints on home-delivered services?
	What does a model of pain experience look like?		How to link "omic" advances with insight into real pain experience?	How to improve pain person comms skills with specialists?	How to develop common GP sensitivity towards pain?	How to emerge a process-based pathology in diagnostic practice?			How do we get specialist pain services into the community?	How to reduce long wait times for pain clinics?			How to / can we adapt pain care / service model towards capacities?	
SOCIAL-CULTURAL-SPATIAL-POLITICAL-ECONOMIC DOMAIN	How to better understand the social contexts of pain?	How to see increasing social exclusion of persons with pain?	How to determine impact of austerity on increase on pain?	How to distinguish people's experiences?	How to determine community pain assets / capital?	How to break over-the-wall drug practices?	How to include pain wellbeing in Stormont and County policy-making?	How to prove the value of HLC community, social, group ACT models?	How to determine community pain assets / capital?		How to reach working people in an at-risk state earlier?	How to better connect people with pain with community services?	How to build community capacities for supporting people with pain?	How do we bring about preventive action in pain?
	How to better understand social determinants of pain?	How to see and track the impact of pain on poorer communities?	How to educate policymakers about pain?	The language of pain is too vague?	How to break the link between benefits and drug prescriptions?	Do we need to change incentives of outsourced assessors?	What does a societal pain value model look like?	How to demonstrate value of social prescribing on pain outcomes	How to scale social / group ACT model?		How to better connect people with pain to others, and match capacities?	How to develop a pain-adapted social care policy?		
	How to change employer's mindset and increase their pain empathy?	How to improve society's view of pain, esp. the "fraud, lazy" view?			How to change assumption that digital pain apps are the only solution?		How to change value perception of community volunteer work?		How to prove need for social prescribers as link workers?		How to link cross-departmental decisions to improve pain experience?			
	How to change perception of community volunteer work?	How to change a negative perception of value of social workers?												

SUMMARY INSTRUCTIONS

1. Using the insights and findings from all the previous templates, and especially the tendential forces analysis in Template 4.0 and the assemblages modelling in Template 5.0, capture the tendencies limiting the means and potential to realise the transition purpose. State these as "how might we" questions in the individual boxes and for the different tendency categories in the top row of the matrix.
2. Do so for both the health and social sub-ecosystems and where possible, link the tendencies using the number system in each sub-ecosystem. Doing so helps to develop a relational model of tendencies inhibiting potential to realise the transition purpose for the focal lived experience with health context.
3. Ask, which tendencies act as the biggest constraints? Why do these persist? In which interactional flows do they arise?
4. What is the relation between dominant tendencies and the sources of power in the focal experience ecosystem? Which affectors (both human and non-human) hold this power? Ask how this power is changing, where and why?

Health Ecosystem Value Design® Framework 2.0
Created and designed by Chris Lawer 2021

umio

Template 6.0 version 2.0 January 2021

8.0 Co-design affectee value propositions to build desired valued lived experiences

Description

Co-design value propositions that build the affective capacities of affectees for the targeted transitions in their lived experiences, enabling affectees with the potential to create desired valued (lived) experiences with health for the focal lived experience with health context.

Purpose of Template 8.0

- To facilitate ideation and design of affectee value propositions that address the design challenges identified in template 7.0 and for the assemblage and lived experience transitions selected and prioritized in templates 6.0 and 6.5
- To organise ideation and co-design in a frame of whole unified lived experience consisting of four affective domains of interactional flows for the focal contexts and also within the three see, enable and emerge dynamic capabilities for creating interactional, creational and valuational affective capacities.

Template 8.0 summary instructions

1. In conjunction with templates 6.0. 6.5 and 7.0, co-design offerings, ideas and concepts (collectively propositions) to support and enable affectees to acquire and enjoy more health as social desire
2. Do so in each of the four affective interactional flow domains forming whole lived experiences with health and for your targeted affectee and targeted movements in lived experience defined in template 6.0.
3. When completed, look at the distribution of designed propositions in the model and ask,
    - Which affective domains in the lived experience model has the most designed propositions? Why is that? How does this reflect your existing assumptions about the role of each domain in creating and differentiating lived experience?
    - How might the propositions in one affective domain influence another affective domain? Draw circles and link those related.
    - Do the propositions cover all four affective domains of affectee lived experience?
    - What do the populated affective domains tell you about the primary paths for achieving the transition purpose?
    - How do your design collaborators differ, where and why? Record these insights on a separate sheet.

Practical tips

A. Complete this template and its sister affector design template 9.0 in separate concurrent groups, then swap and repeat the process

B. Challenge your assumptions, reflect and ask why throughout

C. Repeat the exercise for the different affectee types and the targeted transitions identified in template 6.0

8.0 Co-design affectee value propositions to build desired valued lived experiences

Co-design value propositions that build the affective capacities of affectees for the targeted transitions in their lived experiences, enabling affectees the potential to create desired valued (lived) experiences with health for the focal lived experience with health context.

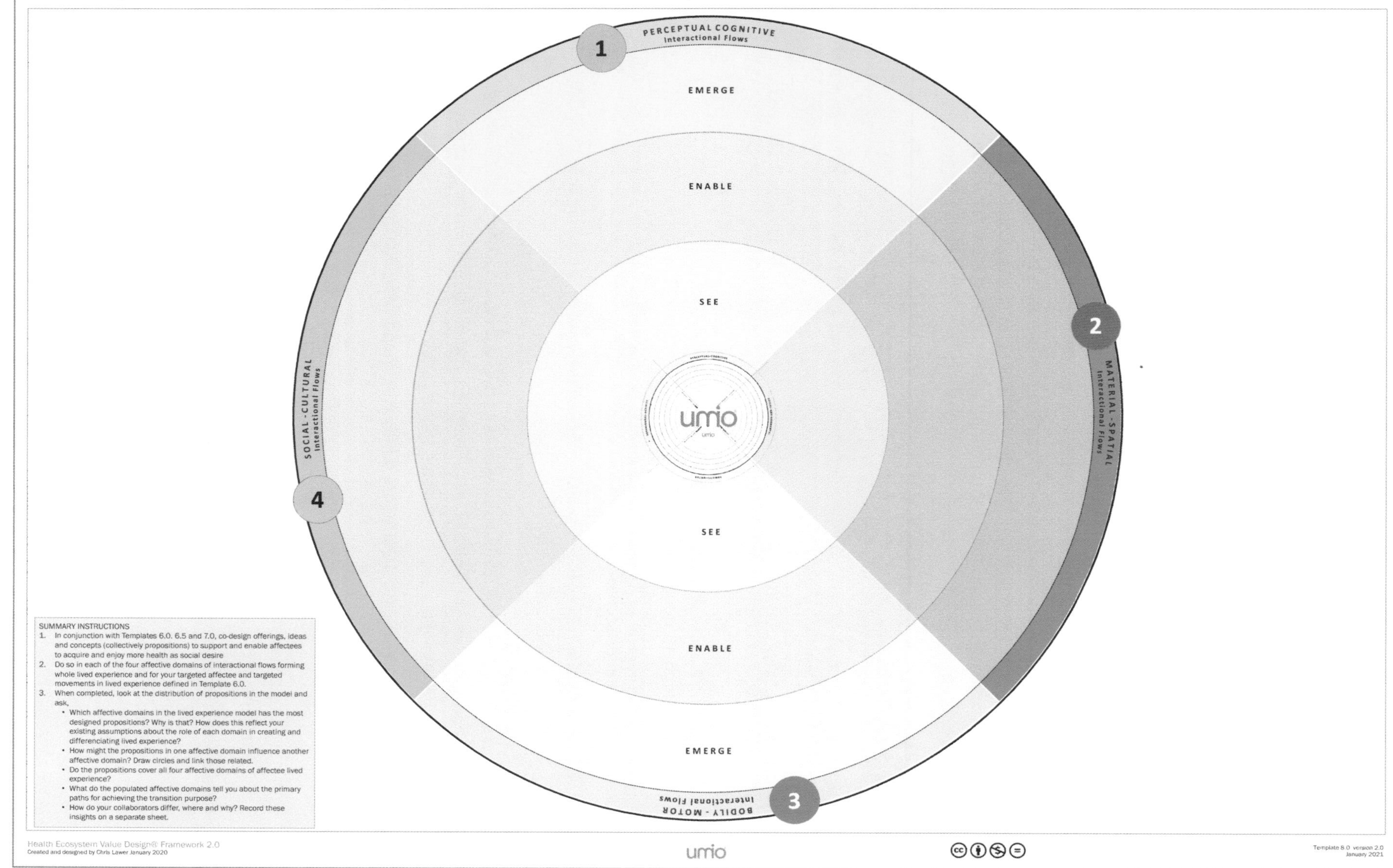

SUMMARY INSTRUCTIONS

1. In conjunction with Templates 6.0, 6.5 and 7.0, co-design offerings, ideas and concepts (collectively propositions) to support and enable affectees to acquire and enjoy more health as social desire
2. Do so in each of the four affective domains of interactional flows forming whole lived experience and for your targeted affectee and targeted movements in lived experience defined in Template 6.0.
3. When completed, look at the distribution of propositions in the model and ask,
   - Which affective domains in the lived experience model has the most designed propositions? Why is that? How does this reflect your existing assumptions about the role of each domain in creating and differenciating lived experience?
   - How might the propositions in one affective domain influence another affective domain? Draw circles and link those related.
   - Do the propositions cover all four affective domains of affectee lived experience?
   - What do the populated affective domains tell you about the primary paths for achieving the transition purpose?
   - How do your collaborators differ, where and why? Record these insights on a separate sheet.

8.0 Co-design affectee value propositions to build desired valued lived experiences

Co-design value propositions that build the affective capacities of affectees for the targeted transitions in their lived experiences, enabling affectees the potential to create desired valued (lived) experiences with health for the focal lived experience with health context.

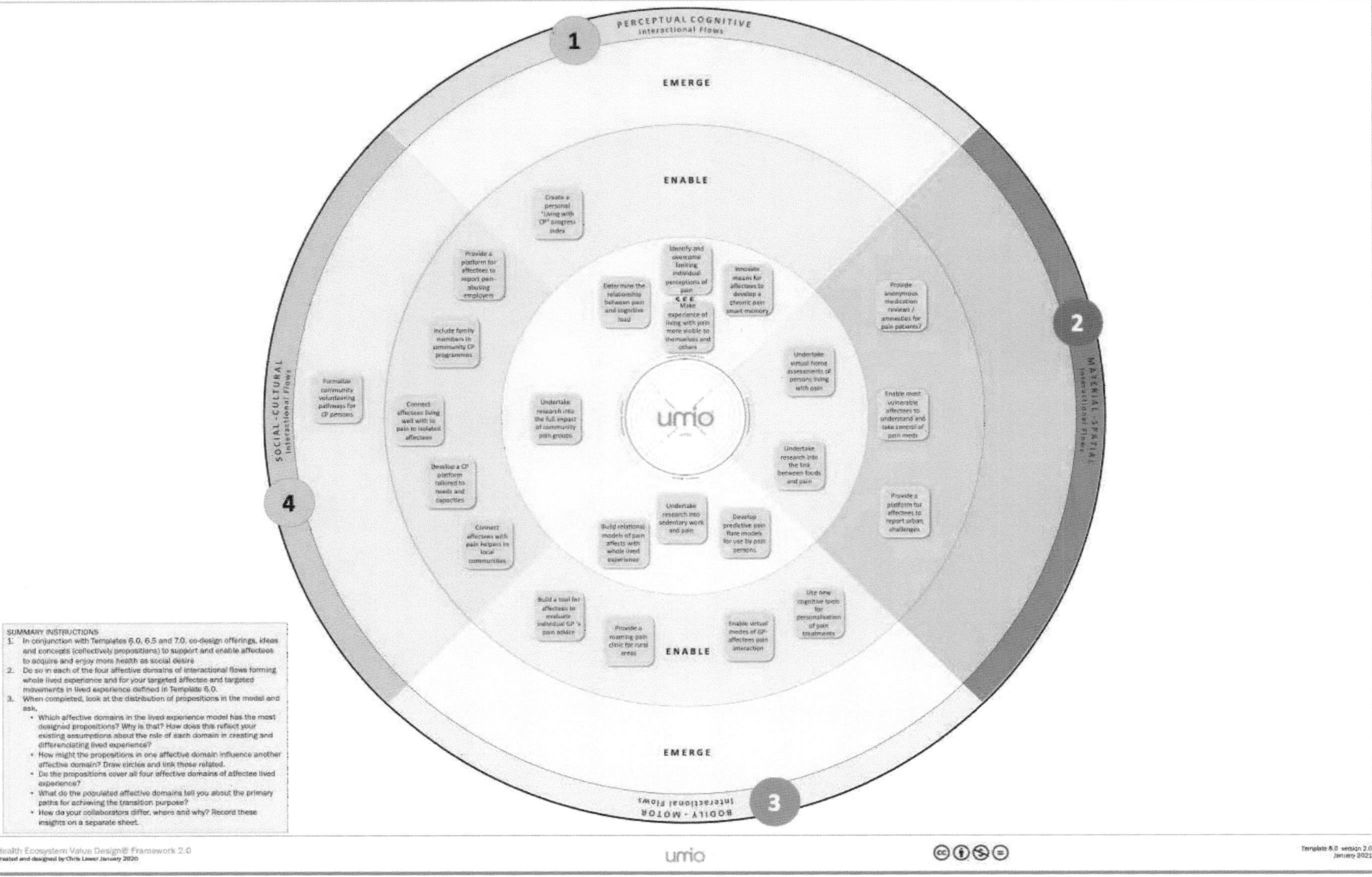

9.0 Co-design **affector** value propositions to build ecosystem affective capacity

Description

Co-design value propositions to generate and distribute affective capacity in the focal experience ecosystem, and that unlock and mobilise agencial assemblages to create desired valued (lived) experiences with health for the focal lived experience with health context.

Purpose of Template 9.0

- To facilitate ideation and design of experience ecosystem-level value propositions that address the design challenges identified in template 7.0 and for the assemblage and lived experience transitions selected and prioritised in templates 6.0 and 6.5, and for the affectee designs in template 8.0
- To organise ideation and co-design in five value frames, each of which supports enactment of transitions in tendential forces, potential capacities and desired movements in the lived experiences of targeted affectees (stated in template 8.0). Each value frame entails the design of propositions that create capacities for affectors to:
    1. Sense, see and frame the focal ecosystem, assemblages, capacities and difference
    2. Innovate and enable new or modified human and technological practices to enact and sustain developmental impact in the focal lived experience with health context
    3. Connect, interact and create value with different affectors and with affectees across interactional flows of lived experiences
    4. Assess, value and learn about interactional flows, tendencies, experiences, events and impacts
    5. Undo and adapt tendencies in habits and routines and embrace and emerge positive ones

Template 9.0 summary instructions

1. In conjunction with templates 6.0. 6.5 and 7.0, co-design offerings, ideas and concepts (collectively propositions) to unlock and mobilise the targeted assemblage transitions, and also the affectee designs added into the four affective domains of interactional flows in the lived experience model in template 8.0
2. Do so for each of five value frames across six hierarchical levels of agent affectors ranging from individual agent affectors through teams and groups to organizations, to fields and to the regulatory / governance level
3. When completed, look at the distribution of propositions in the model and ask,
    - Which value frames have the most designed propositions? Why is that? How does this reflect your existing assumptions? How might the propositions in one value frame influence another value frame?
    - Do the propositions cover all four affective domains of affectee lived experience and the designs in template 8.0? What do the populated value frames tell you about the primary paths, affectors and types of affectors for achieving the transition purpose?
    - How do your co-designers differ, where and why? Record these insights on a separate sheet.

Practical tips

A. Complete this template and its sister 8.0 in separate concurrent groups, then swap and repeat the process

B. Challenge your assumptions, reflect and ask why throughout

9.0 Co-design affector value propositions to build ecosystem affective capacity

Co-design value propositions to generate and distribute affective capacity in the focal experience ecosystem, and that unlock and mobilise agencial assemblages to create desired valued (lived) experiences with health for the focal lived experience with health context.

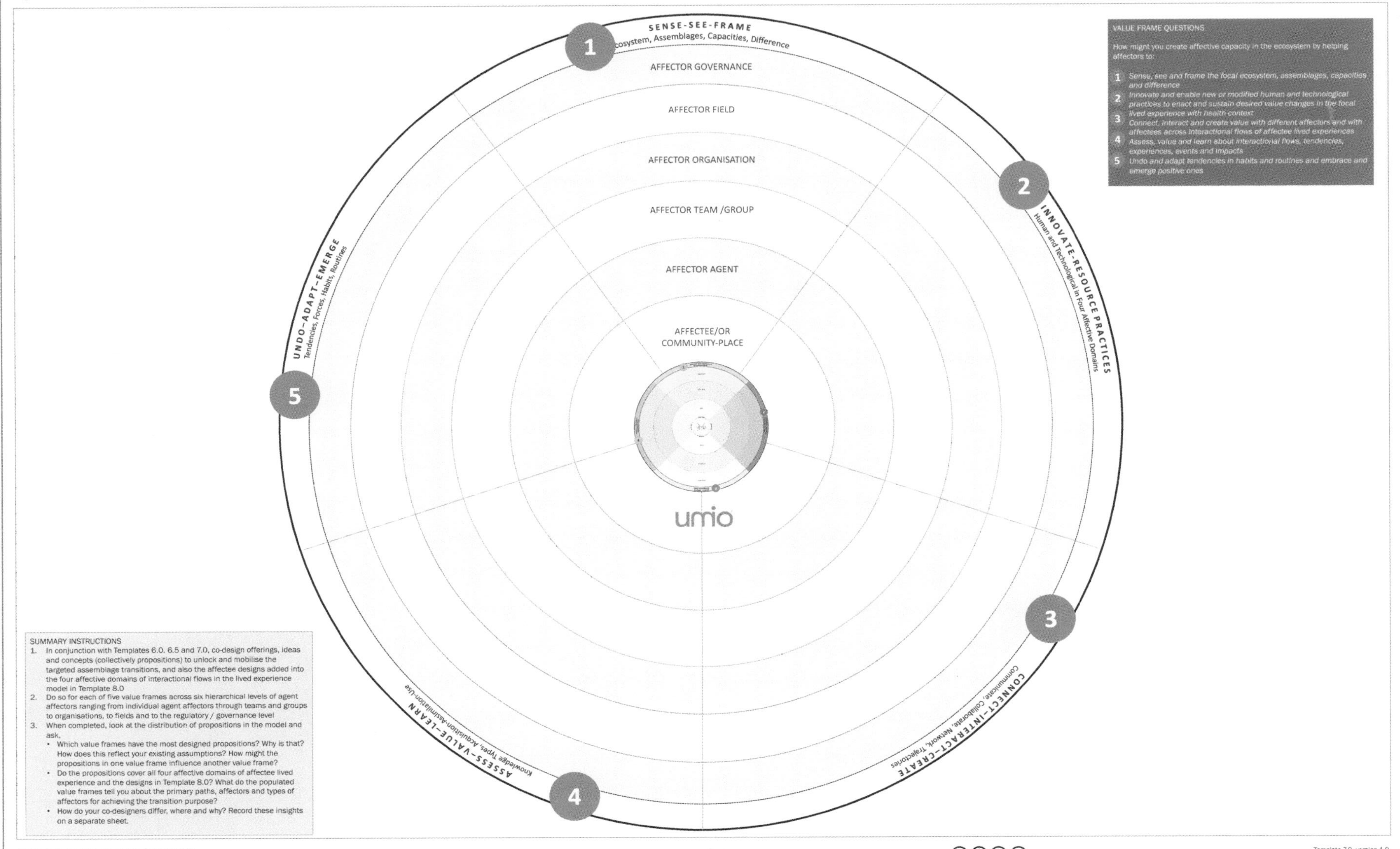

VALUE FRAME QUESTIONS

How might you create affective capacity in the ecosystem by helping affectors to:

1. Sense, see and frame the focal ecosystem, assemblages, capacities and difference
2. Innovate and enable new or modified human and technological practices to enact and sustain desired value changes in the focal lived experience with health context
3. Connect, interact and create value with different affectors and with affectees across interactional flows of affectee lived experiences
4. Assess, value and learn about interactional flows, tendencies, experiences, events and impacts
5. Undo and adapt tendencies in habits and routines and embrace and emerge positive ones

SUMMARY INSTRUCTIONS

1. In conjunction with Templates 6.0, 6.5 and 7.0, co-design offerings, ideas and concepts (collectively propositions) to unlock and mobilise the targeted assemblage transitions, and also the affectee designs added into the four affective domains of interactional flows in the lived experience model in Template 8.0
2. Do so for each of five value frames across six hierarchical levels of agent affectors ranging from individual agent affectors through teams and groups to organisations, to fields and to the regulatory / governance level
3. When completed, look at the distribution of propositions in the model and ask,
   - Which value frames have the most designed propositions? Why is that? How does this reflect your existing assumptions? How might the propositions in one value frame influence another value frame?
   - Do the propositions cover all four affective domains of affectee lived experience and the designs in Template 8.0? What do the populated value frames tell you about the primary paths, affectors and types of affectors for achieving the transition purpose?
   - How do your co-designers differ, where and why? Record these insights on a separate sheet.

Health Ecosystem Value Design® Toolkit 2.0
Created and designed by Chris Lawer January 2020

umio

Template 7.0 version 1.0
May 2020

9.0 Co-design affector value propositions to build ecosystem affective capacity

Co-design value propositions to generate and distribute affective capacity in the focal experience ecosystem, and that unlock and mobilise agencial assemblages to create desired valued (lived) experiences with health for the focal lived experience with health context.

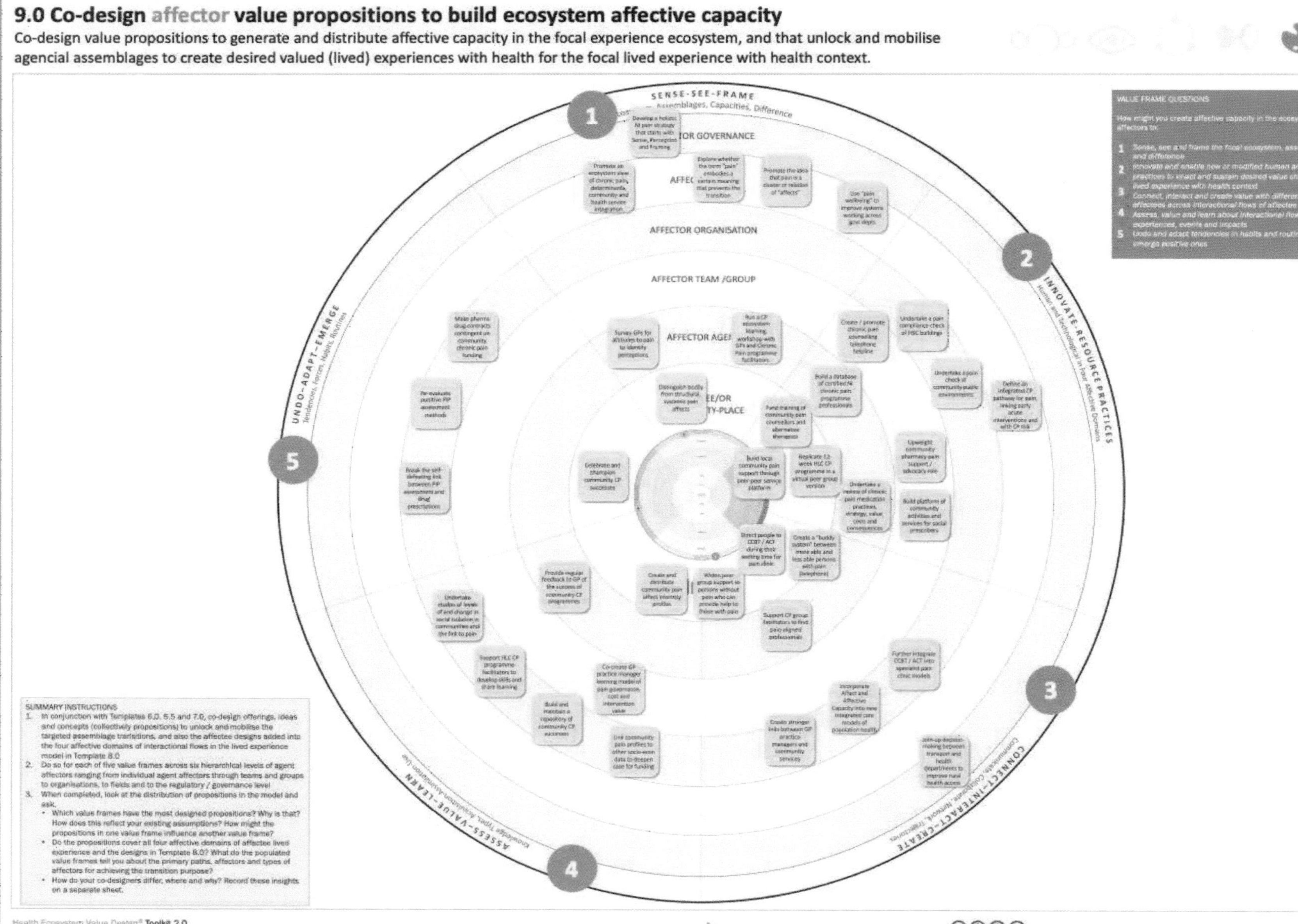

VALUE FRAME QUESTIONS

How might you create affective capacity in the ecosystem by helping affectors to:

1. Sense, see and frame the focal ecosystem, assemblages, capacities and difference
2. Innovate and enable new or modified human and technological practices to enact and sustain desired value changes in the focal lived experience with health context
3. Connect, interact and create value with different affectors and with affectees across interactional flows of affectee lived experiences
4. Assess, value and learn about interactional flows, tendencies, experiences, events and impacts
5. Undo and adapt tendencies in habits and routines and embrace and emerge positive ones

SUMMARY INSTRUCTIONS

1. In conjunction with Templates 6.0, 6.5 and 7.0, co-design offerings, ideas and concepts (collectively propositions) to unlock and mobilise the targeted assemblage transitions, and also the affectee designs added into the four affective domains of interactional flows in the lived experience model in Template 8.0
2. Do so for each of five value frames across six hierarchical levels of agent affectors ranging from individual agent affectors through teams and groups to organisations, to fields and to the regulatory / governance level
3. When completed, look at the distribution of propositions in the model and ask,
   - Which value frames have the most designed propositions? Why is that? How does this reflect your existing assumptions? How might the propositions in one value frame influence another value frame?
   - Do the propositions cover all four affective domains of affectee lived experience and the designs in Template 8.0? What do the populated value frames tell you about the primary paths, affectors and types of affectors for achieving the transition purpose?
   - How do your co-designers differ, where and why? Record these insights on a separate sheet.

10.0: Develop a value-in-interactional creation impact model for the focal experience ecosystem

Description

Build up a value-in-interactional creation impact model by assessing and relating the individual and cumulative potential of the co-designed value propositions to create developmental impact in six inter-relating domains of affective capacity creation.

Purpose of Template 10.0

- To build up a relational view of value-in-interactional creation not a transactional one
- To see how building affective capacity flows into creation of potential improved lived experiences for all affectees and affectors in the focal experience ecosystem
- To support systemic thinking when modeling and seeking to co-create and enact value-in-interactional creation in an experience ecosystem
- To identify where resistance is likely to be met from within certain fields and types of affectors, and to develop ideas and strategies to overcome these in the next step / template
- To help put together a robust experience ecosystem value case for investors, funders and other identified decision-makers

Template 10.0 summary instructions

1. Build up the health ecosystem value model by assessing the individual and cumulative potential of your template 8.0 and 9.0 propositions to impact six inter-relating domains of affective capacity creation (which together build ecosystem affective capacity)
2. For each of the six value domains, identify and state the key individual positive indicators of developmental impact in that domain
3. Start with the affectee experience changes on the left and work through the value model horizontally through the other domains
4. Where possible, provide a measure of the relative difference or impact on the individual dimension of value created in each value domain
5. Work out an approximate cost, return and duration for the lived experience and assemblage transitions to be realised for the focal lived experience with health context
6. Ask, which are the critical value domains and indicators in the value model? Which new value connections does the model reveal that were hitherto hidden? How can you communicate these new connections to affectors, funders and decision-makers outside your group?

Practical tips

A. Think relationally again. What effect does an improvement in one affective capacity domain and/or indicator have on other elements and domains?

B. Use the assemblage model in template 6.5 to explore where most impact can be made or where there is greatest potential for transition and revisit your assumptions

10.0 Develop a value-in-interactional creation impact model for the focal experience ecosystem

Build up a value-in-interactional creation value model by assessing and relating the individual and cumulative potential of the co-designed value propositions to create developmental impact in six inter-relating domains of affective capacity creation.

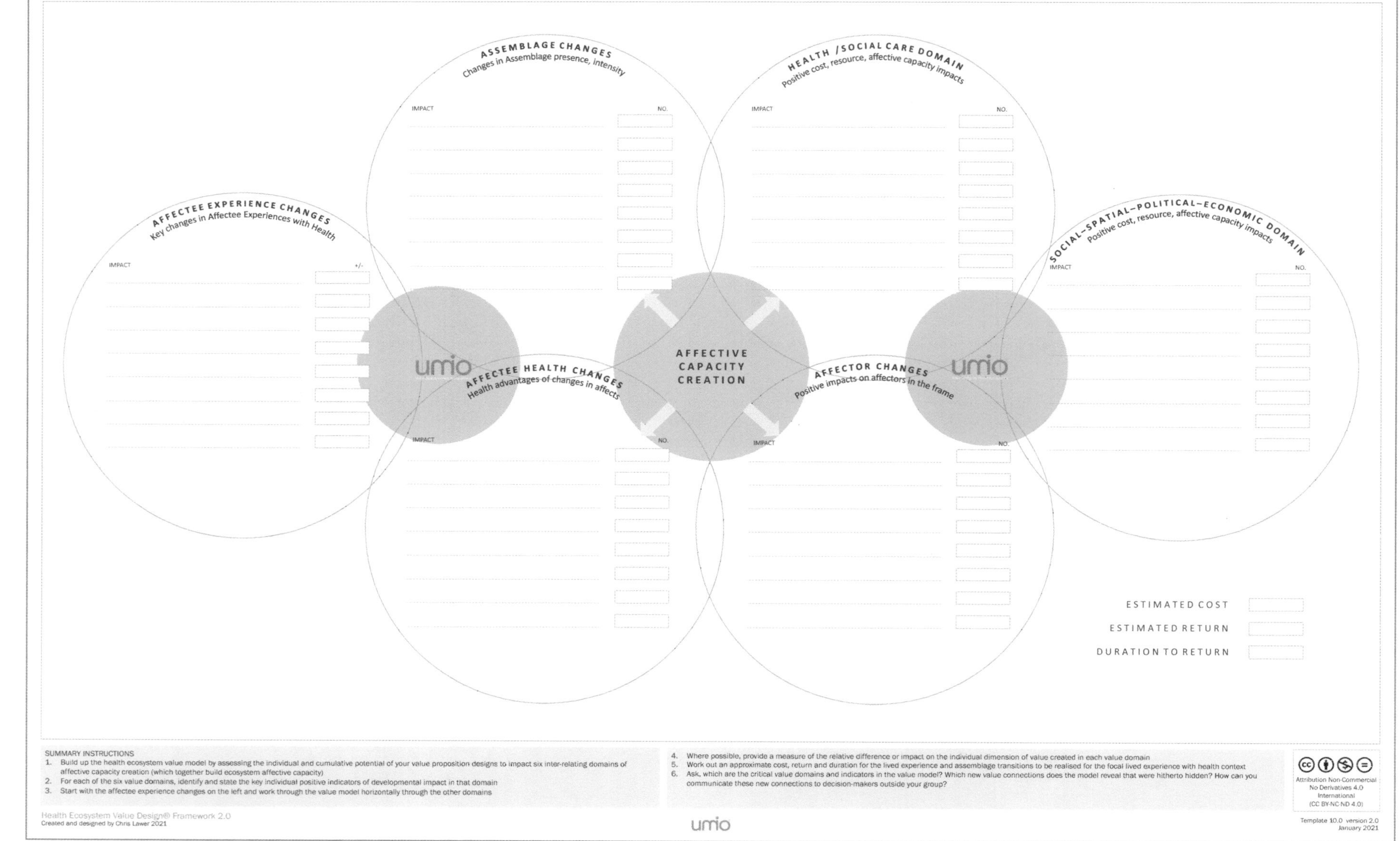

SUMMARY INSTRUCTIONS

1. Build up the health ecosystem value model by assessing the individual and cumulative potential of your value proposition designs to impact six inter-relating domains of affective capacity creation (which together build ecosystem affective capacity)
2. For each of the six value domains, identify and state the key individual positive indicators of developmental impact in that domain
3. Start with the affectee experience changes on the left and work through the value model horizontally through the other domains
4. Where possible, provide a measure of the relative difference or impact on the individual dimension of value created in each value domain
5. Work out an approximate cost, return and duration for the lived experience and assemblage transitions to be realised for the focal lived experience with health context
6. Ask, which are the critical value domains and indicators in the value model? Which new value connections does the model reveal that were hitherto hidden? How can you communicate these new connections to decision-makers outside your group?

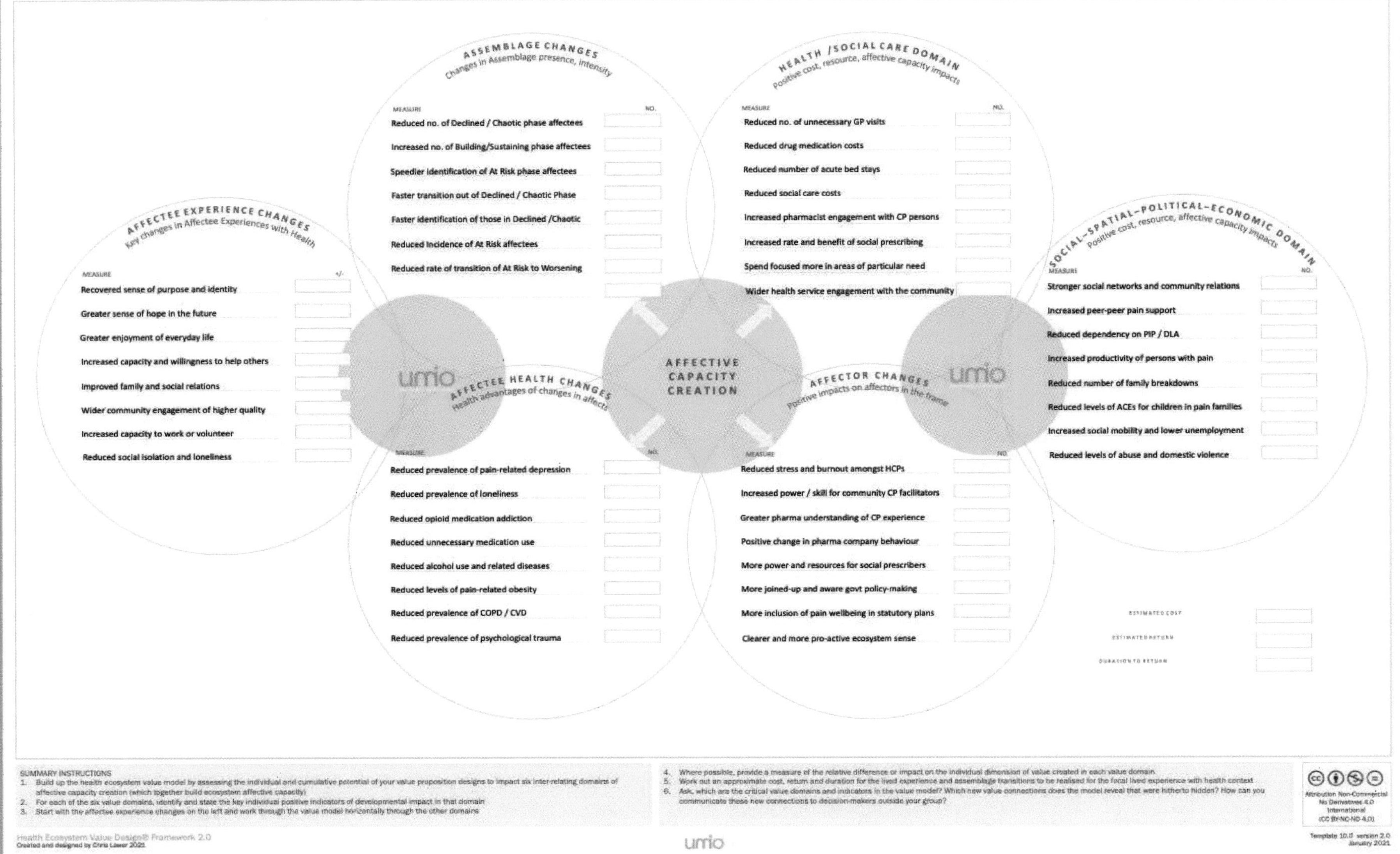
10.0 Develop a value-in-interactional creation impact model for the focal experience ecosystem
Build up a value-in-interactional creation value model by assessing and relating the individual and cumulative potential of the co-designed value propositions to create developmental impact in six inter-relating domains of affective capacity creation.
AFFECTEE EXPERIENCE CHANGES
Key changes in Affectee Experiences with Health
MEASURE
+/-
Recovered sense of purpose and identity
Greater sense of hope in the future
Greater enjoyment of everyday life
Increased capacity and willingness to help others
Improved family and social relations
Wider community engagement of higher quality
Increased capacity to work or volunteer
Reduced social isolation and loneliness
ASSEMBLAGE CHANGES
Changes in Assemblage presence, intensity
MEASURE
NO.
Reduced no. of Declined / Chaotic phase affectees
Increased no. of Building/Sustaining phase affectees
Speedier identification of At Risk phase affectees
Faster transition out of Declined / Chaotic Phase
Faster identification of those in Declined /Chaotic
Reduced incidence of At Risk affectees
Reduced rate of transition of At Risk to Worsening
HEALTH /SOCIAL CARE DOMAIN
Positive cost, resource, affective capacity impacts
MEASURE
NO.
Reduced no. of unnecessary GP visits
Reduced drug medication costs
Reduced number of acute bed stays
Reduced social care costs
Increased pharmacist engagement with CP persons
Increased rate and benefit of social prescribing
Spend focused more in areas of particular need
Wider health service engagement with the community
SOCIAL-SPATIAL-POLITICAL-ECONOMIC DOMAIN
Positive cost, resource, affective capacity impacts
MEASURE
NO.
Stronger social networks and community relations
Increased peer-peer pain support
Reduced dependency on PIP / DLA
Increased productivity of persons with pain
Reduced number of family breakdowns
Reduced levels of ACEs for children in pain families
Increased social mobility and lower unemployment
Reduced levels of abuse and domestic violence
umio
AFFECTIVE CAPACITY CREATION
umio
AFFECTEE HEALTH CHANGES
Health advantages of changes in affects
MEASURE
NO.
Reduced prevalence of pain-related depression
Reduced prevalence of loneliness
Reduced opioid medication addiction
Reduced unnecessary medication use
Reduced alcohol use and related diseases
Reduced levels of pain-related obesity
Reduced prevalence of COPD / CVD
Reduced prevalence of psychological trauma
AFFECTOR CHANGES
Positive impacts on affectors in the frame
MEASURE
NO.
Reduced stress and burnout amongst HCPs
Increased power / skill for community CP facilitators
Greater pharma understanding of CP experience
Positive change in pharma company behaviour
More power and resources for social prescribers
More joined-up and aware govt policy-making
More inclusion of pain wellbeing in statutory plans
Clearer and more pro-active ecosystem sense
ESTIMATED COST
ESTIMATED RETURN
DURATION TO RETURN
SUMMARY INSTRUCTIONS
1. Build up the health ecosystem value model by assessing the individual and cumulative potential of your value proposition designs to impact six inter-relating domains of affective capacity creation (which together build ecosystem affective capacity)
2. For each of the six value domains, identify and state the key individual positive indicators of developmental impact in that domain
3. Start with the affectee experience changes on the left and work through the value model horizontally through the other domains
4. Where possible, provide a measure of the relative difference or impact on the individual dimension of value created in each value domain.
5. Work out an approximate cost, return and duration for the lived experience and assemblage transitions to be realised for the focal lived experience with health context
6. Ask, which are the critical value domains and indicators in the value model? Which new value connections does the model reveal that were hitherto hidden? How can you communicate these new connections to decision-makers outside your group?
Health Ecosystem Value Design® Framework 2.0
Created and designed by Chris Lawer 2021
umio
Attribution Non-Commercial No Derivatives 4.0 International (CC BY-NC-ND 4.0)
Template 10.0 version 2.0
January 2021

11.0 Design the emergence of affective capacity in the focal experience ecosystem

Description

Identify and sequence the main actions and activities to see, enable and emerge the transition purpose and realise the developmental impacts in the focal experience ecosystem environment.

Purpose of Template 11.0

- To make an emergent design strategy for transitioning the focal lived experience with health context in the focal experience ecosystem context
- To see how emergence of developmental impact demands an appropriate combination of see, enable and emerge capabilities and activities in context to the transitions being pursued
- To identify the critical starting actions and levers for enabling the turn and flow of your emergent design
- To reflect on what needs to be *undone* to move forward (this is why the template incorporates a Fibonacci Spiral that flows backwards as well as forwards)

Template 11.0 summary instructions

1. Using the affectee and affector propositions developed in templates 8.0 and 9.0 and the developmental impacts identified in template 10, determine the sequence of activities and actions to begin and develop the ecosystem transition purpose
2. The Umio emergence model consists of three broad inter-related and dynamic action frames – See, Enable and Emerge. Each action can be undertaken together in different emphasis, intensity and content. In HEVD, after the initial learning undertaken in the reverse parabolic flow, there is no linear, prescriptive method for generation of affective capacity
3. Ask which propositions would best kick-start the transition purpose in the SEE phase, which can be deployed quickly in the ENABLE phase and which existing activities can be intensified and further supported in the EMERGE phase
4. Discuss in your groups different combinations of SEE, ENABLE and EMERGE activities and model these against the value-in-interactional creation model developed in template 10.0 to identify the best mix

Practical tips

A. There may be a need for some iteration between this activity and the value-in-interactional creation impact model created in template 10.0

B. Refer to the capabilities model in template 12.0 and the capabilities in each of the SEE, ENABLE, EMERGE dynamic capabilities for guidance.

11.0 Design the emergence of affective capacity in the focal experience ecosystem

Identify and sequence the main actions, priorities and activities needed to see, enable and emerge the transition purpose to realise the developmental impacts from the design of creational and interactional movements in the focal experience ecosystem.

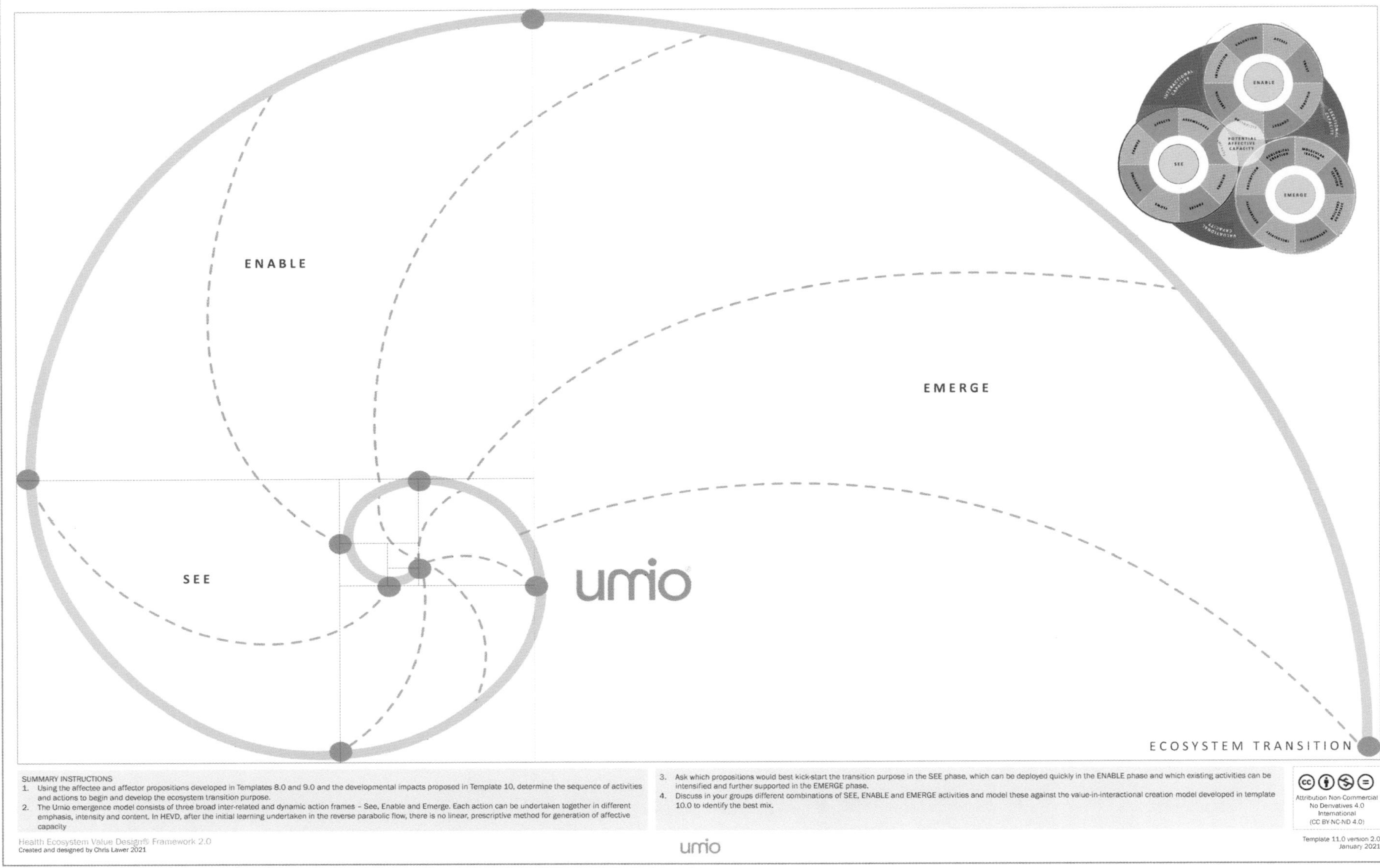

SUMMARY INSTRUCTIONS

1. Using the affectee and affector propositions developed in Templates 8.0 and 9.0 and the developmental impacts proposed in Template 10, determine the sequence of activities and actions to begin and develop the ecosystem transition purpose.
2. The Umio emergence model consists of three broad inter-related and dynamic action frames – See, Enable and Emerge. Each action can be undertaken together in different emphasis, intensity and content. In HEVD, after the initial learning undertaken in the reverse parabolic flow, there is no linear, prescriptive method for generation of affective capacity
3. Ask which propositions would best kick-start the transition purpose in the SEE phase, which can be deployed quickly in the ENABLE phase and which existing activities can be intensified and further supported in the EMERGE phase.
4. Discuss in your groups different combinations of SEE, ENABLE and EMERGE activities and model these against the value-in-interactional creation model developed in template 10.0 to identify the best mix.

Health Ecosystem Value Design® Framework 2.0
Created and designed by Chris Lawer 2021

umio

Template 11.0 version 2.0
January 2021

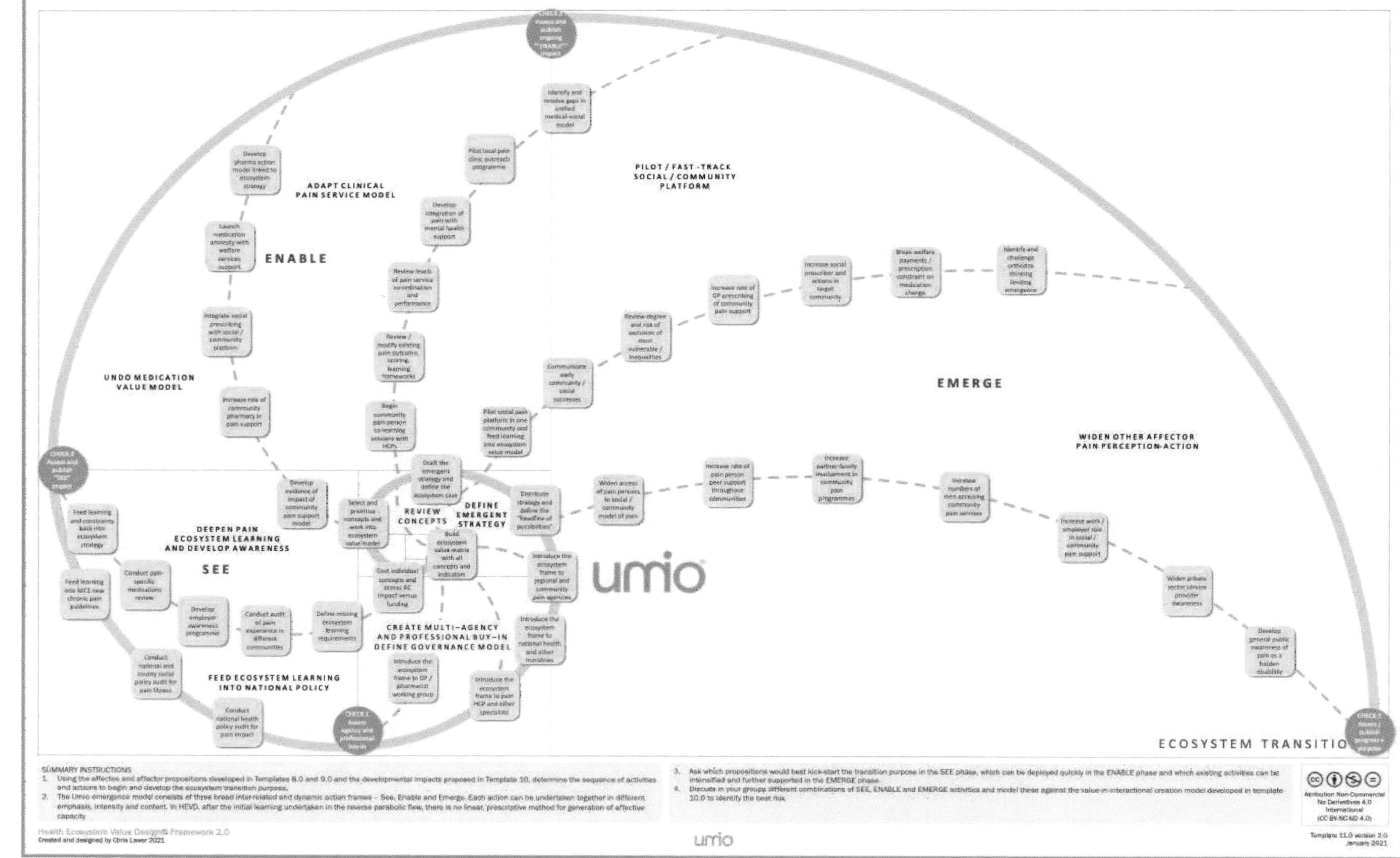
11.0 Design the emergence of affective capacity in the focal experience ecosystem
Identify and sequence the main actions, priorities and activities needed to see, enable and emerge the transition purpose to realise the developmental impacts from the design of creational and interactional movements in the focal experience ecosystem.
ENABLE
ADAPT CLINICAL PAIN SERVICE MODEL
PILOT / FAST-TRACK SOCIAL / COMMUNITY PLATFORM
UNDO MEDICATION VALUE MODEL
EMERGE
WIDEN OTHER AFFECTOR PAIN PERCEPTION-ACTION
DEEPEN PAIN ECOSYSTEM LEARNING AND DEVELOP AWARENESS
SEE
REVIEW CONCEPTS
DEFINE EMERGENT STRATEGY
CREATE MULTI-AGENCY AND PROFESSIONAL BUY-IN DEFINE GOVERNANCE MODEL
FEED ECOSYSTEM LEARNING INTO NATIONAL POLICY
umio
ECOSYSTEM TRANSITIO
SUMMARY INSTRUCTIONS
1. Using the affectee and affector propositions developed in Templates 8.0 and 9.0 and the developmental impacts proposed in Template 10, determine the sequence of activities and actions to begin and develop the ecosystem transition purpose.
2. The Umio emergence model consists of three broad inter-related and dynamic action frames – See, Enable and Emerge. Each action can be undertaken together in different emphasis, intensity and content. In HEVD, after the initial learning undertaken in the reverse parabolic flow, there is no linear, prescriptive method for generation of affective capacity
3. Ask which propositions would best kick-start the transition purpose in the SEE phase, which can be deployed quickly in the ENABLE phase and which existing activities can be intensified and further supported in the EMERGE phase.
4. Discuss in your groups different combinations of SEE, ENABLE and EMERGE activities and model these against the value-in-interactional creation model developed in template 10.0 to identify the best mix.
Attribution Non-Commercial No Derivatives 4.0 International (CC BY-NC-ND 4.0)
Health Ecosystem Value Design® Framework 2.0
Created and designed by Chris Lawer 2021
umio
Template 11.0 version 2.0 January 2021

12.0 Assess your Health Ecosystem Value Design capabilities for ongoing interactional creation

Description

Assess and diagnose gaps and discover potential opportunities in your group's capabilities and fitness for ongoing interactional creation of value in a focal experience ecosystem environment.

Purpose of Template 12.0

- To help affectors, organizations and teams make an initial assessment of their Health Ecosystem Value Design® fitness
- To reflect on what capabilities and resources are needed to not only undertake an HEVD programme but to sustain the programme over time

Template 12.0 summary instructions

1. Rather than a linear, analytical research-idea-act/solve end-to-end process, HEVD functions via three interrelating cycles of ongoing affective capacity (AC) co-creation
2. Each of the three – a dynamic ecosystem value design capability – is formed of eight capabilities
3. In a group, rate your fitness for each of the 24 capabilities in the three circles
4. Rate also the three underlying drivers of affective capacity.
5. All have a simple three-scale rating, either 1) Starting, 2) Developing or 3) Advanced capability.
6. The purpose of this exercise is not necessarily to get an accurate rating of your fitness but to enable exploration and discussion of the capabilities needed to drive value-in-interactional creation in an experience ecosystem environment, and to learn how they are related dynamically to achieve developmental impact on an ongoing basis

Practical tips

A. Ask what are the constraints preventing development and advancement of the capabilities and what can be done about them?

12.0 Assess your Health Ecosystem Value Design capabilities for ongoing interactional creation

Assess and diagnose gaps and discover potential opportunities in your group's capabilities and fitness for ongoing interactional creation of value in a focal experience ecosystem environment.

UNDERLYING AFFECTIVE CAPACITY MECHANISMS	
INTERACTIONAL CAPACITY	The potential capacity of assemblages to democratize, de-centre and distribute engagement and interactions with and between affectees and affectors within interactional flows in an experience ecosystem environment
CREATIONAL CAPACITY	The potential capacity to invent, pursue and realise one or more transitions supporting growth, development and novelty in experience ecosystem environments
VALUATIONAL CAPACITY	The potential capacity to identify, review and reflect upon the conditions and possibilities of actual lived experience of affectees produced from interactions in interactional flows and tendential forces in the experience ecosystem environment.

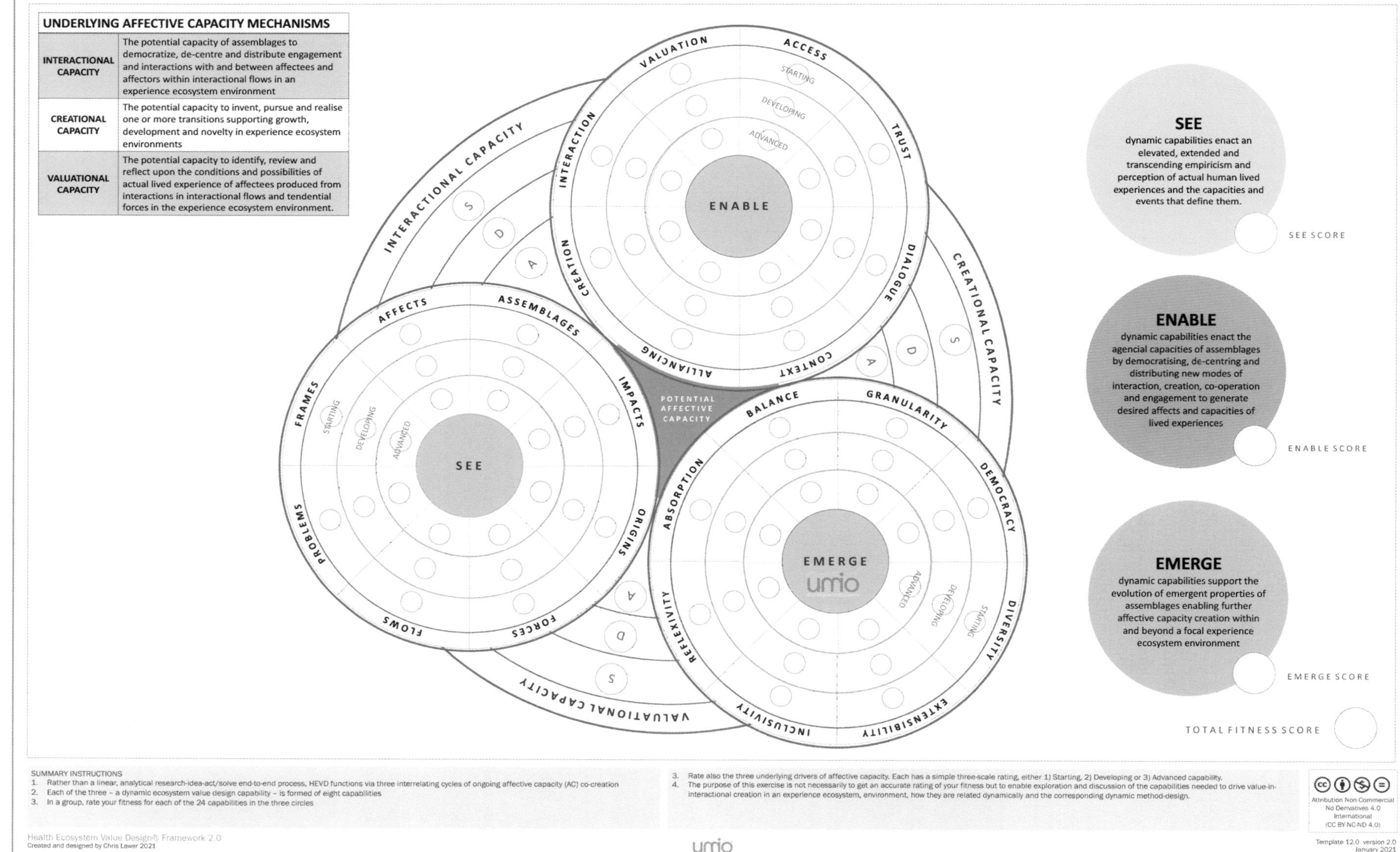

SEE

dynamic capabilities enact an elevated, extended and transcending empiricism and perception of actual human lived experiences and the capacities and events that define them.

SEE SCORE

ENABLE

dynamic capabilities enact the agencial capacities of assemblages by democratising, de-centring and distributing new modes of interaction, creation, co-operation and engagement to generate desired affects and capacities of lived experiences

ENABLE SCORE

EMERGE

dynamic capabilities support the evolution of emergent properties of assemblages enabling further affective capacity creation within and beyond a focal experience ecosystem environment

EMERGE SCORE

TOTAL FITNESS SCORE

SUMMARY INSTRUCTIONS

1. Rather than a linear, analytical research-idea-act/solve end-to-end process, HEVD functions via three interrelating cycles of ongoing affective capacity (AC) co-creation
2. Each of the three – a dynamic ecosystem value design capability – is formed of eight capabilities
3. In a group, rate your fitness for each of the 24 capabilities in the three circles
3. Rate also the three underlying drivers of affective capacity. Each has a simple three-scale rating, either 1) Starting, 2) Developing or 3) Advanced capability.
4. The purpose of this exercise is not necessarily to get an accurate rating of your fitness but to enable exploration and discussion of the capabilities needed to drive value-in-interactional creation in an experience ecosystem, environment, how they are related dynamically and the corresponding dynamic method-design.

Summary: Finalise the Health Ecosystem Value Design® Canvas

Description

Provide a one-page summary view of all elements of your health experience ecosystem transition and its design

Canvas summary instructions

1. Capture the key and distinctive elements of your Health Ecosystem Value Design® programme.
2. Take the opportunity to review your templates to summarize all insights, models, concepts and actions.
3. Think of your audience for the canvas and your purpose, especially who needs to know and "get" your framing and design, and what you need them to do for it to be executed.

Practical tips

A. The boxes contain numbers that relate to the number of the individual templates in the flow of Health Ecosystem Value Design®

B. You may need to produce a rolling canvas by keeping it updated with latest developments and progress. HEVD is never done!

Summary: Finalise the Health Ecosystem Value Design® canvas

Provide a one-page summary view of all elements of your health ecosystem transition and its design

PRIMARY EXPERIENCE CONTEXT, VALUE TRANSITION PURPOSE AND DURATION
1.0

ILL-HEALTH ASSEMBLAGE
1.0

HEALTH ASSEMBLAGE
1.0

PRIMARY AFFECTEE(S)
1.0

PLACE(S) / SPACE(S)
1.0

NEGATIVE AFFECTS
2.0

POSITIVE AFFECTS
2.0

NEGATIVE AFFECTORS
3.0

POSITIVE AFFECTORS
3.0

DESIRED AFFECTEE LIVED EXPERIENCE TRANSITIONS
6.0

DESIRED ASSEMBLAGE TRANSITIONS
6.5

SUMMARY DESIGN CHALLENGES (HEALTH)
7.0

SUMMARY DESIGN CHALLENGES (SOCIAL)
7.0

KEY AFFECTEE PROPOSITIONS SUMMARY
8.0

KEY AFFECTOR PROPOSITIONS SUMMARY
9.0

PRIMARY VALUE MEASURES
10.0

ECOSYSTEM COST SAVING
10.0

TRANSITION FUNDING OPTIONS
10.0

SEE ACTIONS
11.0

CAPABILITY FITNESS

ENABLE ACTIONS
11.0

CAPABILITY FITNESS

EMERGE ACTIONS
11.0

CAPABILITY FITNESS

SUMMARY INSTRUCTIONS
1. Capture the key and distinctive elements of your Health Ecosystem Value Design programme.
2. Take the opportunity to review your templates of all insights, models, concepts and actions.
3. Think of your audience for the Canvas and your purpose, especially who needs to know and "get" your framing and design, and what you need them to do for it to be executed.

COMPLETED BY: ____________

DATE: ____________

LOCATION: ____________

TIPS
A. The boxes contain numbers that relate to the number of the individual templates in the flow of Health Ecosystem Value Design®
B. You may need to produce a rolling canvas by keeping it updated with latest developments and progress. HEVD is never done!

Health Ecosystem Value Design® Framework 2.0
Created and designed by Chris Lawer 2021

umio

Template 5 version 2.0
January 2021

Selected Bibliography and Cited References

Selected bibliography and cited references

Ansell-Pearson, K. (2018) *Bergson: Thinking Beyond the Human Condition.* London. Bloomsbury

Bergson H. (2004) *Matter and Memory* [1896], trans. N. M. Paul and W. Scott Palmer. New York: Dover Publications.

Bergson, Henri (1944, 1911 [1907]) *Creative Evolution* (trans. Arthur Mitchell), London and New York: Macmillan. Bergson,

Callon, M. (2008). Economic markets and the rise of interactive agencements: From prosthetic agencies to habilitated agencies. In T. Pinch & R. Swedberg (Eds.), Living in a material world: Economic sociology meets science and technology studies (pp. 29-56). Cambridge: MIT Press.

DeLanda, M. (2002) *Intensive Science and Virtual Philosophy*. New York: Continuum

DeLanda, M. (2006). *A new philosophy of society: Assemblage theory and social complexity*. London, U.K.: Bloomsbury Academic

DeLanda, M. (2016) *Assemblage Theory*. Edinburgh, U.K.: Edinburgh University Pres

Deleuze, G. (1988) *Bergsonism*. New York: Zone Books

Deleuze, G. (1988) *Spinoza: Practical Philosophy*. San Francisco: City Lights

Deleuze, G. (1994) *Difference and Repetition*. New York: Columbia University Press

Deleuze, G., & Guattari, F. (1987) *A Thousand Plateaus: Capitalism and Schizophrenia*. Minneapolis: University of Minnesota Press

Di Paolo, E., Buhrmann, T. and Barandiaran, X.E. (2017). *Sensorimotor Life: An Enactive Proposal*: Oxford. Oxford University Press

Duff, C. (2014) *Assemblages of Health: Deleuze's Empiricism and the Ethology of Life*. New York: Springer

Foucault, M. (1973) *The Birth of the Clinic* [1963] New York: Pantheon

Foucault, M. (1994) *The Order of Things. An Archaeology of Human Sciences*. New York: Vintage Books

Gallagher, S. (2017) *Enactivist Interventions: Rethinking the Mind.* Oxford: Oxford University Press

Guerlac, S. (2006) *Thinking in Time: An Introduction to Henri Bergson*: Cornell University Press

Lemke, T. (2011) *Biopolitics: An Advanced Introduction:* New York: NYU Press

Mangabeira-Unger, R. (2007) *The Self-Awakened: Pragmatism Unbound*. Harvard

Massumi, B. (2018) *99 Theses on the Revaluation of Value*: Minneapolis: University of Minnesota

Merleau-Ponty, Maurice (1962) *Phenomenology of Perception* (trans. C. Smith), London and Henley: Routledge and Kegan Paul

Minkowski E. (1979) *Lived Time: Phenomenological and Psychopathological Studies*, Evanston: Northwestern University Press

Nussbaum, M. (2000) *Creating Capabilities: The Human Capability Development Approach*. Belknap Harvard University Press

Popper, K. (1945). *The Open Society and its Enemies*

Prahalad, C. K., and Ramaswamy, V. (2004). *The Future of Competition: Co-Creating Unique Value with Customers*. Boston: Harvard Business School Press

Ramaswamy, V., and Ozcan, K. (2014). *The Co-Creation Paradigm*. Stanford, CA: Stanford University Press

Ramaswamy, V., and Ozcan, K. (2018). What is co-creation? An interactional creation framework and its implications for value creation. Journal of Business Research, 84(March), 196-205

Schumpeter, J. (1908) On the Concept of Social Value. Quarterly Journal of Economics, vol. 23, pp.213-232

Schumpeter (1954) *History of Economic Analysis*: London: Allen and Unwin

Thrift, N. J. (2008). *Non-representational Theory: Space, Politics, Affect*. London: Routledge.

Vargo, S. L., and Lusch, R. F. (2016). Institutions and axioms: an extension and update of service-dominant logic. Journal of the Academy of Marketing Science, 44(1), 5-23

Weber, M. (1922). *Economy and Society: An Outline of Interpretive Sociology*

Accessing the templates and license

About the Author

Chris Lawer

Chris founded Umio in 2014 (previously ZinC and OMC Group from 2003), and since has developed and continually evolved the Health Ecosystem Value Design® framework.

Over the past 20 years, Chris has met with hundreds of people, patients, carers, health care practitioners, community leaders and other professionals in diverse settings and specialisms with real experience of different health problems. These multi-stakeholder engagements include studies into the real experience of anxiety, chronic pain, diabetic obesity, T2D diabetes and insulin dosing, nursing home incontinence, disability and bowel incontinence, surgical stress, workplace burnout, living with a stoma, depression therapy (CBT), self-injection, digital health technology use, and many others.

Using his perspective and methods, Chris has advised several start-ups and established enterprises on their problem framing, strategy, innovation approach and market plans. He has also created and shaped several winning propositions to help secure EU Horizon PCP funding (including RELIEF, NIGHTINGALE, and STARS) for multi-stakeholder consortia, along with other UK research and development grants (NI Chronic Pain SBRI, Anxiety UK).

Prior to Umio, Chris was MD of Strategyn UK, providing Outcome-Driven Innovation and Jobs-to-be-Done methods. He has conducted and mentored dozens of ODI and JTBD projects (and still does), drawing on his extensive experience in multiple industries and markets spanning automotive, chemicals, energy and materials (all B2B), healthcare, pharma and medtech, financial services and consumer goods.

During this time, Chris earned a pre-PhD research degree from Cranfield School of Management and published a handful of journal papers that explored novel perspectives in market orientation, customer knowledge co-creation and dynamic capabilities.

Chris is based near Oxford U.K. and works globally.

Contact Chris to discuss:

- Your organization's goals and plans
- Your identified challenges and opportunities
- How Umio Health Ecosystem Value Design® can help
- Speaking at your event
- Academic teaching and course development / input

He can be contacted at chris.lawer@umio.io.

Printed in Great Britain
by Amazon